Praise for
Ethics & Risk Management for Christian Coaches

"At long last, an integration of our Christian worldview and morality with the standards and code of ethics of the International Coach Federation. Dr. Marx has blessed the Christian coaching community with a much-needed resource to elevate our professional standards of practice."

—**Christopher McCluskey**, MSW, PCC, CMCC, president, Professional Christian Coaching Institute, and co-host of Professional Christian Coaching Today

"*Ethics and Risk Management for Christian Coaches* is a very practical guide filled with relatable case studies and probing questions for further reflection. While ethics can be dry reading, Michael's book aptly addresses the challenging issues in a comprehensive easy-to-read style. A must-read for every Christian coach."

—**Georgia Shaffer** MA, BCLC, author of *Coaching the Coach*

"If you seek a book that is easy to read, about a topic as thought-provoking as ethics and risk management, a book that invites you to sit in a virtual living room beside the author for a profound and sometimes humorous conversation, you have found it. As you read Dr. Marx's challenging questions and engaging stories, you may find yourself digging into your essence to answer them. You may come to recognize the alignment we can (and must) have between our professional and spiritual philosophies.

"Although the book is targeted at novice Christian coaches, it would be a good required text for seasoned coaches of any faith. The quality, depth and expansiveness about coaching ethics written by Dr. Marx shows that coaching has grown beyond a fad into a true profession."

—**Teri-E Belf**, MA, CAGS, MCC, author of *Coaching with Spirit*

"Michael Marx has written a valuable addition to the personal coaching industry and the Christian coaching segment in particular. As an author on ethics myself, I realize how necessary such resources are for reference and professional guidance. This book is a masterfully written and expertly organized, with useful information for those who are Christians first and coaches second. A much needed resource for the profession."

—**Dr. Patrick Williams**, MCC, BCC Coach, speaker, author, and trainer

"Michael Marx's *Ethics and Risk Management for Christian Coaches*, is a one-stop guide to real ethics and legal issues faced by coaches in any specialty of the coaching endeavor. The book is concise yet comprehensive, reinforcing the ethics of Christian coaching while firmly rooted in the fundamentals and core competencies of coaching, defined by the International Coach Federation. This is a thought-provoking, extremely useful desk-top guide to those tough, ethical situations one hopes to never face as a coach."

—**Phillip Janzen**, Phil Janzen Coaching, Inc.

"In his call to examine ethics and practice, Michael Marx has inspired the professional Christian coaching community to engage in essential discussion, take action, and act with integrity. This unique resource will enhance the library of every professional Christian coach, from brand new to mastery level. Thank you for doing this work, Michael!"

—**Linda C. Hedberg**, author of *The Complete Guide to Christian Coach Training*

"*Ethics and Risk Management for Christian Coaches* fills a gap that has been too long ignored. Finally, we have a guide that honors our profession while speaking in the language of our calling. I am using this now in my coach practice and soon in my coach training classes."

—**Joseph Umidi**, DMin, Executive Vice President Regent University, CEO Lifeforming Leadership Coaching

"*Ethics and Risk Management for Christian Coaches* is a practical, thought-provoking, and insightful text to resource coaches in a comprehensive easy-to-read style. The depth of application and the connection to scriptural principles invites integrity at the center of our coaching profession. It's a must for the coach's library."

—**Mary Verstraete**, PCC, President, Center for Coaching Excellence

"The International Coach Federation has identified the 'code of ethics' as the first core competency in coaching. This signifies the importance of this topic for the coaching profession. Dr. Marx does a masterful job in this book as he shares wisdom, practical tips, case studies, and thought-provoking questions at the end of each chapter. Whether you are new to the coaching profession, or a master coach, this book is a must read."

—**Janice LaVore-Fletcher**, PCC, CPCC, President, Christian Coach Institute

ETHICS & RISK MANAGEMENT FOR CHRISTIAN COACHES

Michael J. Marx, EdD

This book is available at special discounts when purchased in quantity for use as premiums, promotions, fundraisers, or for educational use. For inquiries and details, contact the publisher at info@mounttabormedia.com.

Published by Mount Tabor Media, Inc.
Edgar Springs, Missouri
MountTaborMedia.com

Editing and Design by My Writers' Connection
Cover photo and author photo courtesy of Steven A. Greer. Old Town Tower–San Juan, Puerto Rico, January 15, 2015

Library of Congress Control Number: 2016908281
Hardcover ISBN: 978-0-9707934-0-9
Ebook ISBN: 978-0-9707934-1-6
First Printing: May 2016

MOUNT TABOR MEDIA

CONTENTS

INTRODUCTION

All good Christian coaches want to get their professional relationships *right*—right with clients, right with other coaches, and right with the community. Ethical standards are essential to any coach's professionalism and success, but Christian coaches adhere to a higher standard than success. Yes, they want to help their clients, but more importantly, they want to stand before God's throne one day and hear, "Well done, good and faithful servant" (Matthew 25:21, NIV).

In today's society, very few voices are calling out to stand up for what is right. Even fewer voices clearly identify ethical boundaries and explain how to navigate them safely. This void exists, irrespective of the area of coaching, be it executive business coach or life coaching. *Ethics and Risk Management for Christian Coaches* offers you, the Christian professional, the information and ability to make right decisions. The questions presented in this book will open your eyes, ears, and heart to the realities of coaching with integrity. Whether you're just getting started or are a seasoned professional, you will find answers to the dilemmas you face in your practice every day.

Scenario 1

Tom hung up the phone, bewildered by the call from a client who was threatening him with a lawsuit to recover the money she had "wasted" on his coaching. Until that call, he believed his client was happy with her progress. Where did things go wrong, and how did Tom miss the warning signs?

Scenario 2

Mary hung up the phone, exhilarated and encouraged. Her client just shared with her that the coaching he was receiving was well worth the money invested. His intention was to tell at least three other people that week how great it was to work with her as a coach. He said, "I'll tell them Mary is fair and honest, and you can trust her."

This book is for people like Tom. No one wants to receive a call from a dissatisfied or angry coaching client. As coaches, we want to be like Mary. We want to earn our clients' respect and referrals. This book will help you see and avoid the pitfalls that lead to dissatisfaction, frustration, and ethical risks inherent to coaching. Additionally, this book seeks to specifically address the practical and logistical concerns a coach will have when working with clients and planning, developing, and implementing a coaching business. The instruction and guidance provided is based on biblical principles and is intended to meet the unique needs of the Christian coach.

How to Use This Book

While initially intended and utilized as a textbook, *Ethics and Risk Management for Christian Coaches* is a useful guide for all ethical matters pertaining to establishing and running a successful coaching business. While perusing a certain chapter might be useful for finding a quick solution to a specific dilemma, readers are encouraged to study the entire book.

Each chapter delivers a portion of the overall foundation for ethical coaching business practices and includes the following sections:

- *Common Challenges* addresses reoccurring issues that are present in all facets of ethics and risk management.

- *At the Heart of the Matter* endeavors to look past facts to examine feelings.

- *Factors That Muddle the Issue* speaks specifically to the gray areas inherent to most ethics discussions.

- *Which of My Values Is Relevant Here?* looks at the balance between expectations and principles.

- *What Are the Dangers?* points out typical pitfalls and problems.

- *What Are the Opportunities?* highlights the potential gains of ethical challenges.

- *Who Will Know?* speaks to the human tendency to hide the bad and exaggerate the good.

- *How Do I Do It Right?* attempts to provide clear solutions to challenging ethical dilemmas.

Each chapter also features questions intended to provoke thought and discussion. Additionally, case studies and scenarios based on real-life situations provide context for the principles discussed. (Of course, all names and identifying references have been altered to provide anonymity.)

! Important

The offerings in this book do not and should not supersede the laws within the venue practiced. Local, state, and federal rules must be followed as you establish and grow your coaching practice. It is important to seek the assistance of legal counsel and tax advisors.

CHAPTER 1

INTRODUCTION TO THE ETHICAL PRACTICE OF THE PROFESSION OF COACHING

"Relativity applies to physics, not ethics."

—Albert Einstein, (1879–1955)

The term *ethics* refers to a set of principles of right conduct based on moral duty and obligation. In this chapter, we will consider the ways and means to understand the ethics of coaching in terms of biblical purity and professional quality. The chapter will define and explain coaching, with particular regard to Christian coaching. From this basis, we will examine the three dominant approaches to ethics: outcome-based, code-based, and care-based.

The fundamental problems Christian coaches face concerning ethics relate to motives (beliefs about who you are), methods (how you behave as a result of those beliefs), and the consequences of those beliefs and behavior. Because our motives drive our methods, we will explore the following questions in this chapter: Who are you? Are you who you say you are? What are the dangers of not being who you say you are? Your answers depend on how you balance your ideals with your actions, your principles with your practices, and your values with your virtues.

After reading this chapter, you will be able to do the following:

- Find your operative ethical premise;
- Evaluate your ethical perspective;
- Establish your basis for ethical practice;
- Identify your ethical vulnerabilities.

Sally's Story

Sally has been a lay counselor in her church for many years. She recently attended a seminar that explained the benefits of coaching in a non-directive fashion rather than advising and prescribing. The seminar piqued her interests in exploring coaching as a career. She feels that understanding the hazards of coaching would help her become a good, ethical coach. She has met many "imposters" and desires to act only with integrity and honesty. Determined to be qualified and professional, Sally buys a book on coaching that promises to explain professional coaching standards. However, because the book focuses primarily on case studies, she finds it confusing. Ultimately, the book gives her the impression that there are no real answers or specific guidelines to follow.

Sally looks at several different codes of ethics and finds one or two that agree with her worldview. The problem with these codes is that they do not explain to her how to act ethically as a coach. She recognizes that she will need to learn the practical applications as she goes along. As she begins her ethical coaching journey, the exploration of values and principles upon which she will operate is most important.

Having recognized her desire to present herself as an ethical and professional coach, her next task is to discover the approach she will use and determine how to put it into practice. She is excited about formulating a personal ethical code that lives up to industry and biblical standards

Directive vs. Non-directive Coaching

Professional coaches around the world use a variety of approaches in their practices. Despite the difference in tactics, most coaches fall into one of two camps of professionals: *directive* and *non-directive*. Those in the directive camp see coaching as a new way to add value for the client by asking exploratory or discovery questions, in addition to the regular practice of giving advice. Directive coaches tend to be prescriptive, ready to share their knowledge and experience. In the other camp, non-directive coaches believe the client is fully capable of forming his or her own solutions and executing successful plans to implement positive change. Non-directive coaches are fully present but not prescriptive.

This book advocates non-directive coaching because it is an approach that allows coaches to minimize risk and liability. When the client is in charge of and fully owns the results, the coach simply helps facilitate the client's decision-making process and creates a no-judgment zone in which she can explore and experiment.

Common Challenges

Sally values integrity and believes she is a good listener, but she can't help but ask herself whether coaching is the right way to go. How can she know if coaching is the right career path?

You may have some of the same questions. What is the right way? What is the righteous way? How do you know that the methods you are using as a coach are indeed correct, honorable, and worthy of praise? These are good questions for a coach to reflect upon regularly. In fact, identifying one's reasons for beginning a coaching practice is the first and most important step to becoming an ethical coach.

Like Sally, a good coach wants to be acutely aware of what he or she should and should not do. Beyond the basic requirements, ethical coaching demands practicing at the highest standards. Thankfully, we do our work with the Holy Spirit beside us as a guide and comforter and with a host of fellow Christian coaches surrounding us.

Who Are You?

When asked introspectively, the question *Who are you?* points to our values. The answer, when evaluated honestly, points to our very essence—our core being. Since the days of the ancient Greeks, humans have been commissioned with the task to "know thyself."

When we know who we are in Jesus, we know what we can become through Him. This knowledge leads us down the straight and narrow path to ethical coaching. The best we can be is what God has made us to be.

The Way to Righteousness

The way to righteous coaching is a well-defined path. Proverbs 12:28 describes such righteousness as the "way to life." The opposite direction leads to death. If this way will keep us from stumbling and killing ourselves professionally, why not take it?

Would it not make sense for us to follow a set of guidelines with clearly mapped directions, tips, and hints? Just like the Bible, coaching codes for ethical behavior set boundaries, but they are not always prescriptive; they provide general rather than specific guidelines. Nevertheless, neither the Bible nor any codes can force you to behave ethically. It is up to you to make that choice each day.

At the Heart of the Matter

Sally's research of ethical standards reveals two ethics codes that go along with the type of non-directive coaching she has in mind. Both the International Coach Federation (ICF) and the Christian Coaches Network International (CCNI) clearly define non-directive coaching and offer standards and tips for respecting the client's space and doing what is best for the client. Sally also learns that there are three basic approaches to interpreting ethics: outcome-based, code-based, and care-based.

Coaching

The coaching process is often referred to as a dance in which clients use coaching to help them navigate through their lives. They need a forward-thinking partner who will help them discover and embrace new perspectives on who they are and what they can do.

ICF defines coaching as "partnering with clients in a thought-provoking and creative process that inspires them to maximize their personal and professional potential" ("Code of Ethics," n.d. para. 1). Likewise, the organization refers to coaching as a *professional-services business.* Coaching forms a trust relationship in which the client can learn, grow, and make decisions. From these decisions, clients act to develop, change, and create new experiences. Coaching, especially life coaching, centers on values, and at its very heart is discovery. Coaching can provide that mental cup of coffee—and the desperately needed wake-up call—a client needs to start fresh.

Business philosopher Peter F. Drucker writes, "Ethics requires that you ask yourself, 'What kind of person do I want to see in the mirror in the morning?'" (Drucker 2005, 105). Coaching calls us to reflect on the answer to Drucker's question. As you assist clients in finding the answer to that age-old "Who am I?" question, you help them discover new realizations of *what* to do and *how* to do it. Here is the formula:

Who = What + How

The client reveals *who* he is by *what* he does and *how* he does it. The coach's moral imperative and professional task is to help people discover the details of this equation for themselves.

Christian Coaching

The Christian Coaches Network International (CCNI) defines a Christian coach as follows:

A Christian coach employs the skills of professional coaching to enable clients, create new awareness, and move into action, while keeping in mind the bigger picture of humanity as taught by a biblical worldview. Since clientele vary in their walks of life and perspectives on faith, the coach chooses frameworks that best suit the client's agenda. The biblical perspective remains the lens from which the coach views the client, but the integration of that perspective is sensitively adapted to the individuality of the client ("CCNI Definition of Christian Coaching," n.d., para. 5).

God-powered coaching is effective coaching. In the words of Gary R. Collins, author of *Christian Coaching,* "The coaching that is most effective is coaching done by a person with coach training who seeks the power and guidance of the Spirit of God. That's Christian coaching" (Collins 2002, 350). As Christian coaches, we enter into a professional relationship that focuses on empowering a client to effect change, find new awareness, and move into action through abundant Christian living both personally and professionally. Additionally, a Christian coach must follow a strict ethical code and practice high moral standards.

Standards

The term *morals* comes from Latin and refers to the correct or proper way to behave. *Ethics* comes from the Greek and refers to one's character or proper way of life. The duty of the Christian coach is to be true to the ethical standards of the profession and the moral principles of the Bible.

Leadership expert and former pastor John Maxwell writes, "There are really only two important points when it comes to ethics. The first is a standard to follow. The second is the will to follow it" (Maxwell 2003, 23). Fortunately, organizations like ICF and CCNI provide clear standards upon which Christian coaches can rely. Yes, for coaches like Sally, there are codes and laws that establish clear boundaries and identify ethical practices.

Respect

Ultimately, ethics comes down to one central practice: respect. You respect the other person's rights. You respect the other person's property. You respect the other person's ability to make correct choices. (That last one is tough, isn't it?) Therefore, you respect the client's right to make decisions that you might not make for yourself. You respect the client's right to fail. You honor your agreement to not lead or direct the client. You ask questions that

have the client's best interests at heart with every business, marketing, and financial decision you make.

So here is an operative sentence that dictates the basis for ethical decision making related to coaching: *Do what is best for the client.*

What is best for the client might be hiring a different coach. What is best for the client might be seeing a therapist instead of a coach. What is best for the client might be experiencing inner healing with the aid of a trained spiritual counselor or pastor. This bears repeating: You might not be the right coach for the client—or potential client—sitting in front of you.

Way of Life Coaching Founder Cheryl Scanlan says she has learned she has to be willing to "risk possibly losing the coaching relationship in order for it to have the best chance of flourishing" (Scanlan 2013, 196). We will discuss this conflict in more detail in later chapters. Suffice it to say that a good match—the right coach for the right client—allows for the greatest possibility of long-term client success. Problems in the coaching relationship are often the result of a poorly matched pairing of coach and client. The nitty-gritty of problems brought before coaching internal review boards (IRBs) frequently come down to one simple conclusion: this particular coach and this particular client should not have been in a coaching relationship to begin with. When considering taking on a client, you must always carefully consider whether you are the right coach for that individual.

When in Doubt, Refer

If a client needs a professional service other than coaching, there is no need to abandon him. Every good coach should have a list of trusted pastors, counselors, therapists, and even other coaches on hand for the client. At the very least, you can give the client the web addresses of search engines where they can conduct a tailored search of their own for a coach, such as ChristianLifeCoaching.com, ChristianCoaches.com, or CoachFederation.org.

QUESTION:

Are you at peace walking away from a client?

Referring can feel like a dilemma because it means sending away business. Although you will lose money by refusing to take on a client who isn't a good fit for you, the reality is that the departing client will likely recognize your goodwill and advertise your virtues in the marketplace. Ultimately, your decision to refer that client to someone else may result in connecting with more clients who are better suited for your services.

Ethical Approach

There are three basic approaches to ethical behavior:
1. outcome-based = *consequentialism*
2. code-based = *deontological*
3. care-based = *Golden Rule*

One isn't necessarily more ethical than the other, and your moral values will influence your choice of approach.

Consequentialism

An outcome-based coaching premise centers on gaining the highest utility for the client. A coaching encounter based on *consequentialism* looks to maximize the benefit to the client. In this approach, the coach helps the client facilitate a plan that puts the client at the highest gain. Another name for this coaching style is *utilitarianism*. In other words, the coach lets the client determine what is right and wrong by helping the client anticipate the consequences or outcomes. In this sense, the coach might advocate the axiom: "If it feels good, do it." Obviously, this takes on a relativistic approach. Although you might not agree with the client's decision and action plan, you give them the space to own the results. Since the client—not the coach—carries the responsibility for the outcomes, the client solely owns the results. As the coach, you would say to yourself, "Whatever the outcome, it's the client's responsibility, not mine."

Deontological

A code-based or *deontological* process defines ethical practice as right or wrong regardless of the outcomes or results. Ethical behavior, therefore, becomes definable. One can weigh and measure ethical behavior on a predetermined scale, while standards and definitions measure the client's progress. In this sense, *the ends do not justify the means.* If it is wrong, it is wrong. A code-based premise might appear at first glance to be limiting. Today's culture promotes a certain liberty to go beyond the regulations, to interpret freely the definition of right and wrong. *Sometimes you just gotta break the rules, right? Maybe you just need to bend the rules or ignore them, just this once.* The deontological approach to ethics would discourage such relaxation of professed morality.

The deontologist believes that an ethical code and law are essential elements. Like air, ethics make it possible to breathe. Without a code of ethics, the coach would suffocate professionally. While the constraints imposed by an external governing body might feel restrictive, from the perspective of the code-based approach, the net result of adhering to such a code gives the coach confidence. Furthermore, a clearly defined code of right and wrong can be freeing for your clients. Janice Lavore-Fletcher of the Christian Coach Institute writes, "A code of ethics allows your clients to establish a sense of trust and confidence in you, as they can know ahead of time how you will deal with sensitive issues and gray areas" (Lavore-Fletcher 2013, 1).

Golden Rule

The third approach to ethical coaching behavior is care-based and widely known as the Golden Rule. Even though you will not find the Golden Rule in the Bible per se, Matthew 7:12 comes close: "So in everything, do to others what you would have them do to you" (NIV). In essence, you don't want someone to cheat you, misrepresent you, or hurt you. Why, then, would you cheat, misrepresent, or hurt someone else? You don't want anyone one to take advantage of you or pull the proverbial rug out from under you. If your clients or colleagues perceive that they have had such an experience with you, you have not followed the Golden Rule.

In his book, *There's No Such Thing as "Business" Ethics: There's Only One Rule for Making Decisions*, John Maxwell reveals this secret: "I think many people are seeking direction. The Golden Rule can provide that. It never changes, even as circumstances do. It gives solid predictable direction every time it's used. And best of all, it actually *works*" (Maxwell 2003, 29). You can actually *decide to do to others as you would have them do to you*. It's a moment-by-moment choice. No one can make you behave unethically. It's up to you.

> **Did you know?**
>
> In a poll of 1,100 college students, 77 percent believe that CEOs should be held personally responsible for a business crisis that they helped create. Of those same surveyed students, however, 59 percent admitted to having cheated on a test, and only 19 percent said they would report a classmate who cheated (Merritt, 2002, para. 8).

Factors That Muddle the Issue

Sally wakes up one morning with her head swimming. The Golden Rule has been always been her operative ethos. Now she wants to abide by a professional code. However, the idea of imposing her moral standards on her clients troubles her, even though she intends to initially coach Christians. After much thought and prayer, she realizes that, at a minimum, she must advertise herself for who she is: a Christian coach.

Regardless of whom you decide to coach or which ethical approach you determine to use, it is your obligation to identify yourself as a Christian. The word *Christian* means Christ-like.

This label declares to the world that we will love others as Christ has loved us (John 13:35). If we are truly followers of Christ, we should proudly wear the label of Christian, not for social or political reasons, but because we want to be associated with Him.

As we do not want to hide the light of God (Matthew 5:14-16), we look for opportunities to advertise the goodness of God. This might mean mentioning your Christian worldview in the initial conversations you have with potential clients. Or perhaps your promotional materials state that your practice is God-owned, Holy Spirit-controlled, and Christ-centered.

Fair Disclosure

For the ethical coach, fair disclosure means hiding nothing. For Sally, that means she should openly disclose her worldview to her clients. Fair disclosure is one of the basic operative principles to which oversight organizations, such as CCNI and ICN, expect professional adherence.

You should advertise what you are and what you are qualified to do. If you have a credential, you should show it. What is behind that credential is definable on that organization's website. Coaches like Sally also want their biblical worldview to be clearly definable. If biblical principles shape your mindset, then *fair disclosure* dictates that you communicate this to your clientele. During the coaching conversation, the Christian coach integrates the biblical worldview to enable clients to see their potential and to act according to God's will for their lives. As professionals coaching from a Christian perspective, "the biblical worldview is given priority over existing theories of human nature, motivation, personal change, growth and development and frames the perspectives by which coaching is offered" ("CCNI Definition of Christian Coaching" n.d.). From the CCNI point of view, the Bible trumps any other code of conduct devised by man, and Jesus remains the model citizen.

Which of My Values is Relevant Here?

The more Sally reads about ethics, the more she realizes that "getting it right" is about putting ethical understanding into practice. This is not always easy when good things compete for her attention. For example, she wants to be a good mother to her teenage daughter, *and* she wants to be a good coach. She is already beginning to see that these two "goods" might occasionally conflict with each other.

Two Perspectives in Balance

Most research on ethics approaches the topic from one of two perspectives: philosophical or behavioral. *Philosophical ethics* is an academic discipline that looks for the deeper meaning, the distinctions between good versus evil, right versus wrong, and moral obligation versus free will. A philosophical-type of discussion on ethics asks the question: How should we then live? *Behavioral ethics* centers on the actions that influence those ideals. A behavioral-type of discussion on ethics asks the question: What do I do to act ethically? Both thinking and doing dictate our ethical decision making. Ethics, then, is a balance between ideals and actions, principles and practices, values and virtues.

IDEALS   **ACTIONS**

Ideals and Actions

You have an ideal to help the client discover, improve, and move forward. It's all about the client. Doing something that benefits you more than the client creates an imbalance of ideals and actions known as a conflict of interest.

CASE STUDY

Your client has a skin rash. It just so happens that you have a box of fine herbal cream that your aunt mixes in her garage. Your aunt really depends on the income from her salves since your uncle passed away two years ago. You think this lotion might be exactly what your client needs. Should you try to sell the cream to the client?

PRINCIPLES   **PRACTICES**

Principles and Practices

You have the guiding principle of treating all clients fairly. You do not cheat or steal from your client because doing so would be a dishonest practice. You also have the principle to run a business with integrity. Therefore, you do not steal clients from another coach. Doing this would be an unfair sales practice. You have the principle to give credit where credit is due. Therefore, you do not steal materials from another coach, or anyone else for that matter. Doing this would be copyright infringement.

CASE STUDY

You feel that you run your coaching practice with integrity and honesty. You go to the local office supply store and buy a cart in which to carry your business supplies. When you get home, you realize that you received two boxes, inadvertently taped together, from the store. In other words, you paid for one cart but got two for the price of one. Your brother could really use the second one. What do you do?

VALUES   **VIRTUES**

Values and Virtues

You have a strong sense of family values, so you do not schedule clients for weekend appointments. Doing this would be contrary to your sense of priority. You have a strong sense of honest gain. Therefore, you return the $20 your client dropped in your office. Not doing this would go against your sense of honor. You have a strong value of appropriate physical behavior. Therefore, you don't hug your clients. Doing this, you feel, would be improper.

CASE STUDY

Your son's team made it to the finals. Unfortunately, the game was rained out and the league rescheduled it for a time when you are supposed to meet with your busiest client. Since you can't be in both places at the same time, you will have to miss one or the other. Which do you choose? How do you go about making the decision? What reason will you give to your son or client for not being there?

Exercise

- Are you able to turn down a coaching contract when the "fit" is not right?

- What did you learn about ethics and morals growing up?

- What level of ethical standards is enough for you as a coach?

- How will you advertise your Christianity?

- By what standards, if any, do you coach?

What Are the Dangers?

Sally reads some case studies and realizes that the answers are not always simple or clear cut. Sometimes, she thinks she knows the right answer and other times she feels as if she is merely guessing. After all, who can say for sure what's right or wrong? The more she studies and reads, the more confusing ethics seem.

The Obvious Choices Are Easy

Most of us would not want to do something that is obviously wrong. It would be a mistake to fill up with diesel when your car takes gasoline. It would not be smart to throw boiling hot water straight up in the air at -40° Fahrenheit or Celsius in the hopes that it would come down as snow. (This experiment results in a common emergency room ailment in Alaska in the wintertime.) It would be a mistake to tell a Canadian he is not an American because he does not live in the United States of America. Some mistakes are more obvious than others, and all of us can tell stories about foolish choices and verbal blunders.

Deciding what's "right" becomes sticky, however, when the apparent choices are not necessarily wrong but don't feel right either. You may sense that none of the options is appealing and, therefore, believe there should be a better way—but you can't put your finger on it. You believe you know what to do, and still, something nags at you. Where can you get help? Ask a coach! A fellow coach can help you explore alternatives that are not immediately apparent to you.

Choices between right and wrong can be difficult enough, but decision making becomes infinitely more challenging when the choices are between right and right. Sometimes, you must choose between two good values that are in alignment with your core values. For example, Sally can spend an hour making cookies with her daughter, or she can take an unexpected client call for an hour. Spending time with her daughter is good, as is earning money to support her family. How can she know what to do? She can pray for guidance.

As Christians, we depend on the peace that the Holy Spirit gives us to help monitor our righteousness barometer. Prayer is our first source of direction. Additionally, we can review our priorities, read a book, or call a mentor or coach for guidance. In the end, we make decisions based on what we feel is best, in alignment with the kind of people and coaches we want to be.

When we look at the risks, as well as the tools to help us choose between two good options, intuition and relativism should be considered.

Intuition

We are all familiar with that feeling we get in the pit of our stomachs when considering an impending decision. This feeling is intuition. We have an instinct about what is right, but we still feel uncertain.

When the stakes are high, we tend to think that more information will help us make the right decision. However, additional information rarely leads to us changing our initial opinions. There are times that intuition can serve you well, but what is most needed is a well-formed decision-making process that will allow you to have peace about the possible outcomes (see chapter three). One of the biggest factors here is time. Even if you end up going with your gut, you'll find more peace in a thoughtful decision that is reinforced with rationality and affirmed with prayer over a reasonable amount of time than in a decision that feels hurried.

QUESTION

Can you recall a recent decision in which you let reason supersede your gut feeling and later regretted it?

The words below are posted in an elementary school and offer some excellent advice regarding thinking and acting ethically.

Think first; keep cool.

Size up the situation. Is there any baggage being brought to the conflict?

*Think it through
(consider consequences)
then …*

Do the right thing!

What a wonderfully simple explanation for ethical decision making and careful planning! The basics to righteous coaching often involve little more than slowing down and examining the alternatives.

Relativism

Relativists don't see ethics as right or wrong in an absolute sense. For them, expressions of whether an act is ethically correct or incorrect are statements of opinion, not truth. Relativists regard each instance as acceptable or unacceptable only in the context of the societal setting in which it occurred. Therefore, the net result of relativism can be referred to as *situational ethics*. What might be correct in one situation is not correct in another. Relativism could also result in unilateral ethics, imposing standards on just one party.

As a relativist, if you want to fib or cheat during the coaching process because you feel the end product will be better than the sum of its parts, you are justified in doing so. The problem becomes one of approach. Do you interpret the code for yourself or are there broader approaches accepted by your peer professionals? The latter is what Enlightenment philosopher Immanuel Kant (1724–1804) declared as the "categorical imperative" based on universal law. Innate to this approach is adherence to the ideas of basic human rights and fairness. Kant hoped that the good person would act in accordance with the moral code of the day because he simply respected and honored the current code. Kant postulated that mankind wanted to adhere to the laws of the day. Right is right because it's right. Right? The problem with Kant's perspective is that actual ethical behavior must be self-imposed. Such a self-imposed righteousness makes the judge (you) solely responsible for your correct behavior. So here you stand in the same danger zone where the Pharisees and Sadducees stood in Jesus's day. In Matthew 12:37 Jesus stated, "For by your words you will be acquitted, and by your words you will be condemned" (NIV). What you say *does* matter. How you coach *does* matter.

What Are the Opportunities?

Sally often prays about the possibilities of becoming a professional life coach. She is encouraged by the standards and ethics of ICF and CCNI. She describes to her sister what a life coach does, and her sister emphatically replies, "Yep, that's you. That's who you are." Those words encourage Sally, but she still wants the green light to come from above. She wants to know coaching is her calling.

Coaching Is a Moral Tool

Coaching is a tool, a skill, a profession, a process for allowing clients to find their way and move forward. Your integrity as a coach will influence your clients. The very nature of your coaching will reflect your ethical standards as you help the client form a framework for aligning their goals and aspirations with the will of God. You are to be a beacon of hope for your clients. You are to be light and salt to your clients (Matthew 5:13-16). When you base the contexts of your questions on biblical principles, it releases the Holy Spirit to speak into your client's life.

For good or for bad, who you are and how you operate model your values to your clients. By the same token, the ethical professional is a beacon of righteousness for the community.

People look up to those who stand for moral goodness and integrity. And when a coach is immoral or unrighteous, his or her behavior speaks even louder. A dishonest coach reflects poorly on the entire coaching industry.

Coaching Is an Industry

In recent years, coaching has become an industry and profession in its own right. Coaching standards provide a baseline for efficient exchange and cooperative activity amongst all members of this profession. These standards exist to ensure that the coach does not abuse the coach-client relationship. The industry regards the trust and vulnerability of the client as sacred.

What would happen if the industry did not respect the coach-client relationship? If a client had a complaint about the level of service he is receiving from a coach, to whom would he voice his concerns? The internal review boards (IRBs) of ICF and CCNI exist for the purpose of accountability. In order for a Christian coach to honestly call herself a professional, she must stand up for a code of conduct and be accountable to it. In fairness to the client, a coach should belong to an organization that will hold her accountable. In this way, the client knows that he has a place he can go in the event that the member coach behaves in a disreputable manner.

Coaching Is a Ministry

Innate in Sally's consideration of coaching as a calling is the aspect of ministry. She knows she is a good listener and is able to hear the story behind the story. At the same time, she knows she has a lot of wisdom and life experience to share. Coaching as a ministry, however, allows the client to discover his own solutions without the coercion or manipulation of the coach. How can Sally do this?

One way is to use the client's vocabulary. In other words, talk in such a way that the client understands what you mean without further explanation.

This shows that you respect the client's way of talking and will not force him to adjust to jargon he may not understand. This is where knowledge of what the client is going through is useful for the coach. When the coach has been there (either by experience or knowledge), the coach is able to communicate in such a way that resonates with the client. Accepting the way the client chooses to communicate allows him to express himself freely without fear of judgment or misunderstanding.

Make no mistake: Coaching is a ministry. Time and again, clients express that one of the greatest benefits they receive from coaching is the feeling that someone is *really listening* to them.

Who Will Know?

Sally types the word "coach" into a search engine and discovers that the designation "professional coach" yields quite a few different job descriptions. Besides the sports designations, there are dog obedience coaches, wellness coaches, conflict coaches, and dating coaches, to name a few. There does not seem to be any rhyme or reason behind the title "coach." It appears that anyone in the helping professions is entitled to call herself a coach if she wants. Who decides what it means to be a coach?

Anyone Can Call Herself a Coach

Unfortunately, many people who call themselves coaches have never received any training in the ethics of coaching, let alone perused a code of ethics. The word *coaching* nowadays simply sounds good; it seems hip and cool. And because it is not a protected professional designation, anyone can call herself a coach.

Please note that it is not my position that coaching should go the way of licensure and state control. To the contrary, the coaching industry can very well self-regulate as long as ethical coaches are trained, credentialed, and monitored in such a way that there is no need for court cases to look after industry misdemeanors.

Coaches who adhere to a well-established standard can claim professionalism congruent to the level of that standard. Obviously, the higher the level of standard, the greater the professionalism attributed to that standard-bearer. In this way, the practice of non-directive coaching can avoid state-imposed regulation as long as coaches adhere to the rights of the client and encourage autonomous decision making.

Being an Imposter

Most of the time, no one will ask you (or even care) about the meaning of the initials behind your name. The simple fact that very few of your clients will check out the validity of your credentials does not mean you should give yourself any title you want. Like other untruths, making up or overstating credentials will catch up with you. When it does, you risk exposure as a phony. As the words widely attributed to Abraham Lincoln state, "You can fool all of the people some of the time, and some of the people all the time, but you cannot fool all the people all the time." Fooling people is *not* the goal of the ethical coach. Besides being dishonest, false advertising is punishable by law; the courts call it fraud. The Bible calls it bearing false witness against yourself.

How Do I Do It Right?

Sally wants to get it right. After studying the various ethics codes, case studies, and the Bible, she is convinced that there is a method to the madness. A few operative imperatives like "Do what is best for the client" help her sift the wheat from the chaff. She has also realized that it is possible for her to form her own set of operative principles. Ultimately, she would like to find a group of like-minded professionals with whom she can exchange experiences.

Do No Harm

Most adults would not knowingly harm another person. Certainly we, as professionals, take a type of Hippocratic Oath to "do no harm" when we enter the coaching arena. For knee-jerk decisions, ingrained, operative principles influence our behavior. For time-consuming decisions, deep-rooted values influence our behavior. Business psychologist and coach Claire Townsend states: "At its most basic, ethics is a system of moral principles that affect the way in which people make decisions and lead their lives" (Townsend 2011, 142).

We can't talk about behaving ethically without talking about behaving morally. We can't talk about behaving morally without talking about principles and values. If these principles and values have never been standardized in our lives, then our thoughts are likely to be tossed to and fro (Ephesians 4:14). Chapter two will continue the discussion of correct moral behavior.

Ethical Owner's Manual

Sally likes the ideas proposed in the book, *Ethics for the Real World: Creating a Personal Code to Guide Decisions in Work and Life*, by Howard and Korver. They propose that you write an ethical owner's manual for yourself. Sally feels that she will operate her coaching business better by having a document that walks her through the dilemmas and decisions she must make as a small business owner. If she could take some of the codes she has read and put them into her own words, she feels that she would automatically act with a higher sense of integrity. She feels that setting a standard in writing would build a platform that allows her avoid potentially unethical or ethically debatable situations (Howard and Korver 2008, 115). Simply walking away from trouble is often the best procedure. Nonetheless, she will need to make decisions, and not every decision is an easy one.

QUESTION

Does your personal set of ethical standards inspire trust and cooperation?

Coaching Standards

The material in this book is congruent with published ethical codes written by the International Coaching Federation (ICF) and the Christian Coaches Network International (CCNI).

Join a Professional Coaching Organization

Whether you join ICF, CCNI, or any other professional organization, you do a good thing. As an ethical Christian coach, you should desire accountability in your coaching. To become a member, you must agree to abide by that organization's code of conduct. This adherence to a code represents oversight—someone has your back, so to speak. Your membership also allows the organization to provide you with direct access to the latest news, trends, and best practices in coaching ethics.

To attain a credential from organizations like ICF and CCNI, you must be tested on the organization's ethics code and have your coaching observed for quality and adherence to its principles. Both CCNI and ICF provide extensive training opportunities to equip you to answer ethical questions.

Each member must practice the code and see to it that his or her conduct does not discredit or misrepresent the coaching profession in any way. Violators of the code may be subject to examination by the Internal Review Board (IRB) of the respective organization. Someone who transgresses the code is at risk of losing their credentialing and/or being barred from membership. In most cases, however, coaches who violate the code of ethics are able to receive the training and assistance they need to perform at the high level of standards expected of them. Neither ICF nor CCNI endeavor to penalize. Rather, the goal of these organizations and their codes is to empower coaches with information and guidelines that help maintain integrity and professionalism.

QUESTION

When was the last time you read either the ICF or the CCNI Code of Ethics?

Autonomy

The purpose of written codes is to ensure professionalism and client autonomy. The term autonomy signifies that the client is responsible for his or her own progress. The Professional Christian Coaching Institute advises this operative approach: "The coach manages the process; the client manages the progress." The net result of this non-directive coaching is that ethical behavior for the coach involves allowing the client to own the results.

For ICF and CCNI, this means a comprehensive trust in the efficacy of eleven core competencies (ICF). In other words, the ethical practice of coaching, as per ICF and CCNI, is to trust the process and to trust the client. Christian coaches also (hopefully first and foremost) trust God with the process and take a biblical approach: let go and let God.

Coaching author Terry R. Bacon claims that there is a notable preference among clients for non-directive coaching. In the non-directive approach, coaches primarily ask questions that raise client awareness. Ultimately, the client defines a goal to achieve and devises an action plan to facilitate that plan. To maintain the integrity of the coaching interaction, the coach will help the client create a structure by which the client can hold himself accountable (Bacon 2003).

QUESTION

If you were the client, would you rather get advice or determine your own solution?

Chapter Summary

In this chapter, you evaluated the balance of who you are as expressed in what you do and how you do it. You will choose to act with the integrity demanded by the code by which you abide. For the Christian coach, you always have an advocate. The Holy Spirit is the unseen force in the room, whether the client has asked the Holy Spirit to be there or not. When you can hear the prompts of the Holy Spirit clearly, the right way becomes evident. Some decisions demand a choice between rights. Some decisions may seem to only involve a choice between wrongs. Nevertheless, the Holy Spirit brings peace to your mind and heart as you uncover and make the right choice and align yourself with professional, ethical standards.

Besides the ethical codes brought forth by coaching organizations, adherence to one's own personal standards is essential to becoming a professional. The very word *professional* indicates that you profess that you are maintaining a certain standard of practice. Irrespective of a credential, you should behave ethically.

The very essence of ethical behavior is operating according to a set of norms and standards that serve as guidelines. On this basis, we make contracts, form cooperation, and establish trust. Most of us follow such a set of principles and values intuitively.

This concludes the story of Sally, the aspiring life coach. Sally recognizes that learning to behave ethically will take some time. Although she herself is a life coach, she contracts with another life coach to help her explore the depths of her personal values. She hopes to eventually be able to formulate her own written ethical code that aligns with that of ICF and CCNI. More than anything, she wants her newfound profession to help her minister to her clients in a way that allows them to grow closer to God. She is confident that when she masters the practicalities of running a small business, her coaching career will thrive.

What Would You Do?

Scenario A: You are undertaking life coaching, and your client tells you he is very unhappy in his marital relationship. He is planning to leave his wife, yet he is afraid to take the step. From an ethical perspective, how do you approach the coaching process?

Scenario B: You are also a massage therapist. One of your fellow massage colleagues asks you to coach her. What are the ethical considerations here?

Scenario C: You are just starting your coaching business. You want to base your business on sound biblical and ethical practices. What is your first step?

Scenario D: You get an email claiming that you can become a certified coach in three easy steps by enrolling in a program, no experience necessary. If you signed up for the program, how would you ensure that such a program would not leave you with the feeling of being an "imposter"?

End of Chapter Questions

- How does your calling (a.k.a. life purpose) guide you in your ethical practice?

- What questions do you have about ethics?

- What hazards do you foresee in your ethical practice?

- What does the Bible say about ethics?

- What is your operative ethical approach: outcome-based, code-based, or care-based?

CHAPTER 2
ESTABLISHING A MORAL BASIS FOR COACHING

*"Try not to become a man of success,
but rather try to become a man of value."*

—Albert Einstein, (1879–1955)

A strong moral foundation is the basis for standing on principle when doubt and fear plague our decision making. In this chapter, we will look at the components of strong moral character. It's not enough to know what is right and wrong when it comes to being a good coach. There are values and principles that guide us to a higher level. The moral high road is not a path of arrogance—quite the opposite. Practicing biblically based morality is the way to humility. When we stand firm and don't allow popular choices to sway us, we can act with integrity and honesty.

The Christian coach seeks to be consistent with the values he professes. This consistency becomes apparent to the client, who will then want to emulate the morality of the coach. The dangers and pitfalls that await us are numerous. This chapter will help you understand why morality is the foundation of solid ethical practice.

After reading this chapter, you will be able to do the following:

- identify the values that dictate your behavior;
- explain why you coach the way you do;
- distinguish moral living from ethical practice;
- evaluate moral choices based on biblical principles;
- discover your moral compass.

Frank's Story

As a young man, Frank spent a lot of time in church. He liked the singing. He liked the playground in the back. He liked the interactive Sunday school lessons, but he did not enjoy the sermons the pastor preached. Later, he learned that this same pastor received a dismissal for "reasons of impropriety."

Now, Frank is working in a company that allows him a certain amount of latitude. He thinks of himself as connected and in tune with society. He works hard to create an environment that is accepting of everyone. He wants to maintain a high level of personal performance, but senses that something he had as a boy is missing. Frank reads a lot of newspapers and magazines, but he discovered that the Bible provides something that news and entertainment media doesn't. In fact, reading the Bible leads to a renewal of his relationship with God. He wants this relationship to be inspirational to others. He wants it to both *be* real and *look* real. He is not interested in practicing "fake" religion.

Frank attends a local church where the people seem warm and inviting. However, not everyone there exemplifies moral living. This confuses Frank, and he begins looking to the Bible for answers. He quickly learns that the people of the Bible often made mistakes. Nevertheless, God had a plan for them, and they were much better off when they followed that plan.

Common Challenges

Frank reads in the Bible that he should love his neighbor. He thinks about the guy next door and supposes that they get along pretty well. Sure, the neighbor does things that are annoying at times, but most of the time, Frank doesn't think about him. Frank now wonders if he has the ability to be consistent in his "love" for people like his neighbor.

Behaving Morally Comes and Goes

Our moral capacity waxes and wanes. Making morally correct decisions is part of our daily grind. Sometimes it's easy. Other times we have to work at it. The amount of attention we give to moral issues often depends on the urgency of the dilemmas we confront. Frank finds it easy to recognize moral issues when he reads in the newspaper about the tragedies that many people experience. He finds it even easier to be morally conscious while listening to a sermon about the Good Samaritan, for example. However, Frank realizes he usually doesn't think about morality at all. It is not even on his radar, since most decisions he makes are not actually moral ones.

The human propensity to give morality a rest brings about an interesting question. Can we be morally upstanding if we do not continually have trials and tribulations to test us? The founder of the Institute for Global Ethics, Rushworth Moulton Kidder, says some people have a "drowsy morality" (Kidder 1995, 43). Their morality is in a perpetual state of sleepiness. Trouble and tragedy are effective ways of waking people up to ethical behavior.

Thrill Seeking

Frank is a "man's man." He likes motorcycles—loud ones. He never gave that a second thought until he read in his biker magazine about riders who intentionally modify their exhaust pipes to irritate people who complain about the noise. This shouldn't be, he thinks. Frank believes that motorcycling is a way to experience the thrill of riding down the open road with the wind in his face. This is a thought that makes him wonder: *Are there any moral implications to riding without a helmet?*

Having fun and seeking adventure is part of human nature. Humans, especially children, like playing with danger and pushing limits. There is an indescribable thrill that comes from pushing ourselves to the very limits. There can also be a lot of pain if such an edge-seeking experiment results in falling off a cliff or out of a tree. Nevertheless, experimentation is how we learn what we like and dislike. There is a natural tendency to do things that bring pleasure and avoid things that bring pain.

The client-coach interaction should not be a place where the coach experiments to find out what he likes and dislikes. The ethical coach must do only what is in the best interest of the client. A coach should not put a client's well-being in jeopardy merely for the sake of satisfying his curiosity, thereby treating the client as a "guinea pig." The client-coach relationship is not a place for the coach to exhibit greed, anger, envy, lust, or self-interest. On the contrary, the coaching conversation is a place for the client to experiment, to discover, to uncover, and to reveal.

QUESTION

How can a coach allow a client to experiment?

Threat

Frank is working with a small blowtorch one day when he sees something wiggle in his garage. Immediately, he points the flame at the moving shadow and kills the snake in seconds. Only after he calms down does he realize that it was a harmless garter snake. This bothers him greatly because he has a "live and let live" attitude toward animals.

Sometimes threat blocks our ability to make a moral decision. When danger lurks nearby, our automatic survival mode kicks in. We often depend on our emotions to guide us when threatened, and we rely on well-practiced habits to guide us through those moments. This physiological response squelches logical and rational thoughts in order to survive the immediate danger. We subconsciously table our innate desire for long-term gain for a time when safety returns and actively weigh each moral decision on the scales of maximizing good and minimizing bad, optimizing reward and minimizing threat.

At the Heart of the Matter

Frank has always said, "Well, that's just the way I am," when he did not fit into the moral pictures painted by other people, especially pastors. Recently, he read in Psalms 51:5 that he has a sinful nature that he inherited at birth. Now, he is beginning to wonder how he might be able to change that.

Morality Is Both Nature and Nurture

We, as humans, can be more kind and altruistic than any other living creature. Conversely, we can also be more cruel and mean-spirited than any other living creature. We have an innate tendency to be honest, but lying comes just as easily if we think it is to our advantage. In the long term, we tend to care about the welfare of others. In the short term, however, we often think only about ourselves.

On a day-to-day basis, moral righteousness is a moving target. For most people, there is tension between doing what is right (morals) and doing the right thing (ethics). The good news is that you are not alone. There are many people in your life that can help you and give you moral guidance. More than anything else, the Son of God is there for you, always making intercession on your behalf (Romans 8:34). Christ said He would help us:

Anyone who intends to come with me has to let me lead. You're not in the driver's seat—I am. Don't run from suffering; embrace it. Follow me and I'll show you how. Self-help is no help at all. Self-sacrifice is the way, my way, to finding yourself, your true self. What good would it do to get everything you want and lose you, the real you?

—(Luke 9:23–25, The Message)

QUESTION

Who is in the driver's seat when it comes to your coaching business?

Moral Awareness

Our ability to be morally aware depends first on our ability to acquire knowledge about morality. We can do this either intellectually or in combination with the conviction of the Holy Spirit. Then we must develop the skill to use this knowledge in the right way, at the right time, and with the right words. We need both knowledge and skill to determine how the human principles that are generally accepted by society apply to our personal value system.

We all know, for example, how it feels to hurt. We feel sympathy for those who are victims of violence because we know that violence causes pain. Similarly, we desire to treat others fairly because we know how it feels when others treat us unfairly. Without this knowledge, we might behave crassly, rudely, or cruelly. Moral awareness is a value no ethical coach can do without. If the coach isolates himself from the discomfort of social awareness, he limits his potential to react compassionately and empathetically with his client. A callous coach is an ethical complaint case waiting to happen.

Factors That Muddle the Issue

"Truth can appear as lie; straightness can appear as twisted"

—*Tao Te Ching,*
Verse 45

Immoral Awareness

Frank reads in 1 Corinthians 6:18 that sexual immorality is a sin. This bothers him because he knows very few people wait until marriage to have sexual relations. Society as a whole condones many things as correct that the Christian coach should regard as non-biblical. Just because "everyone is doing it" does not mean that it is the right thing. For example, to the average U.S. citizen, sex between consenting adults is perfectly acceptable. A biblically based worldview, however, limits intercourse to married couples. Although most professional ethics codes advise against a sexual "dual relationship" (a physically intimate relationship between the coach and client), it happens all too often.

There are many things that your neighbors, friends, and even family members practice on a regular basis that you may feel are morally wrong. The norms of society give clients implicit permission to behave immorally or even amorally; to what extreme will you allow those norms to dictate acceptable behavior? It is crucial for you to know how much decision-making freedom you will extend to your client before you take a stand or make an objection. When you carry the label "Christian coach," you also carry a responsibility to know and follow a biblically based code of conduct.

QUESTION

Have you downloaded any music lately? Did you also pay for it?

CASE STUDY

A quintessential example of a moral dilemma comes from the last century. The judicial system convicted numerous "good citizens" for crimes against humanity after World War II, despite their defense that they were simply acting in accordance with the laws of the land—Nazi Germany. This defense did not hold up against the principles of a sound conscience and the sense of justice held by decent human beings.

Decades later, a Sunday school teacher in the United States asked his students if they would have hidden Jews during the Nazi era in Germany. Most of them emphatically answered yes to the question. I happened to be visiting the class that day, and I responded that I hoped I would have, but I really didn't know if I would have had the moral fiber and courage to do so. After having lived in Germany for twenty-three years, I know a small number of people whose grandparents defied the Nazis and paid a steep price for it. I also know many people who wish their grandparents had defied the Nazis. Perhaps most telling, however, is the large number of people who would prefer that you never ask them about this dilemma.

QUESTION

When cultural norms allow (even insist on) immoral behavior, how does the Christian justify standing on the moral high ground?

Indeed, it might very well seem that everyone is doing something that the Bible defines as morally wrong. Professor Tim Bond writes, "Ethical maturity is tested when we decide whether to follow an established norm or to re-evaluate the norm and be accountable for the adoption of an alternative response" (Bond 2013, 329-330). In other words, it's easier to go with the flow. But what is easy isn't always right.

Goes to the "core" of what Jesus taught
example of Peter
we don't "measure up"

" Would you hide Jews? "

31

Coaches who do not believe in God have a hard time accepting a set of standards based on the Bible. These coaches hope that there is an ethical view based on facts that everyone can accept. This would be great if it were possible. Relativism, dualism, and situational ethics become the tools of the trade for the eclectic, secular coach. However, as a Christian coach, your clients will be better served if you are authentic and stand up for your standards.

Note

Not all Christians interpret the Bible in the same way. Though it isn't imperative that all Christian coaches agree on personal, ethical standards, we do need to agree about ethical *practices*—those things that keep the client's interests in the forefront.

Human Nature

The more Frank reads the Bible, the more convinced he becomes that he is a sinner saved by grace. He particularly likes The Message version of the Bible because of its relatable style. During lunch one day, he reads this passage:

We continue to shout our praise even when we're hemmed in with troubles, because we know how troubles can develop passionate patience in us, and how that patience in turn forges the tempered steel of virtue, keeping us alert for whatever God will do next. In alert expectancy such as this, He will never leave us feeling shortchanged. Quite the contrary—we can't round up enough containers to hold everything God generously pours into our lives through the Holy Spirit!

—Romans 5:3-5, The Message

Think of all the good people you know. Hopefully, the number of people who come to mind is substantial. Now, think of all the not-so-good people you know. For most of us, this number is miniscule compared to the first. Most people do not look for opportunities to lie, cheat, or steal. Wrong things happen because we make immoral choices, not usually because the choosers are intentionally amoral. Wrongdoing happens when the person's actions are out of sync with his values, whether they are society's values or, in the Christian's case, biblical values.

Actions aligned with values create virtues. Our morals become sturdy and resilient when they are hammered by testing on the anvil of patience.

Therefore, patience during trouble is part of one's daily moral exercise program.

Keeping Up with the Times

One of the reasons Frank reads the newspaper so much is that he wants to feel connected to the society in which he lives. He wants to know if the baker down the street had a fire or if the local football team is advancing to the play-offs. He has a smartphone with many apps that give him access to the latest news in real time.

From a societal perspective, the needs we deem as "essential" change over time as conditions, social and economic arrangements, and technologies evolve. For example, our great-grandparents could hardly have imagined the need for all the communication devices we carry around today. It's much the same with the coach who has access to information via technology that would have been unthinkable a century ago.

It may be a challenge, but the ethical coach should keep up with the times, at least to the point of understanding new opportunities and threats. These new developments may affect his value base and, consequently, his moral decision-making ability. As the world around us continually readjusts and equalizes, we need to occasionally reaffirm and recalibrate the connection we have to our value base. Like much of the software we use, our moral software needs updating from time to time. One of the best ways to do this is to stay plugged into a fellowship of believers.

Tip

The best way to avoid trouble is to stay out of its path. Maxwell (2003) writes, "If you know that you are especially susceptible to a pleasure that would tempt you to cross an ethical line, put yourself out of harm's way. When you see it coming, cross to the other side of the street" (p. 78).

Habit

Where Frank works, he is allowed an hour for lunch. However, there is no oversight. No one cares or notices if he takes an hour or an hour-and-a-half lunch. As a new employee, taking a few minutes extra at lunch concerned him. Now, he hardly thinks about it.

Repeatedly doing an ethically or morally questionable action normalizes it. Actions that once evoked feelings of remorse or guilt can begin to arouse feelings of entitlement and even shrewdness. As an ethical coach, you should regularly evaluate your actions. Take an honest look at the decisions you have recently made and measure those against your value system. If a misalignment exists, you might need to reconsider your position. Some of your habits may need to change. You may also discover that some of your values need to change. Even if your underlying circumstances did not change in the past five years, for instance, *you* have changed and have hopefully become more professionally mature than you were five years ago. Adapting one's values always requires a lot of energy and sometimes a bit of pain.

In the past, Frank only read the Bible sporadically. The church he now attends has provided him with a Bible-reading plan that he uses daily. Although the pastor suggested reading the Bible the first thing in the morning, Frank finds that he is more consistent if he reads it during his lunch break. It's become a habit. Frank is also considering working on his "habit" of taking extended lunch breaks.

QUESTION

How have you changed
in the past five years?

CASE STUDY

You go to a client's office every Tuesday morning. You also have another client whose office is about a half-mile away. When tax time comes, you contemplate whether to declare the expense as one round trip or two round trips. You ask your brother-in-law if you can do that, and he shrugs his shoulders. You ask your accountant if you can do that, and she shrugs her shoulders. You decide it is two trips and declare your deductions accordingly. After doing this for five years, a new coach comes up to you and asks if he can declare two trips in the same type of scenario. How might your answer change if you reevaluated this habit?

Exercise

- How badly do you want patience as one of your virtues?

- Who is in the driver's seat when it comes to your coaching business?

- Could you work with a client that you did not like as a person?

- How are your actions in conflict with your values?

Which of My Values Is Relevant Here?

Frank has told his co-workers that he is a Christian. He is concerned, however, that his life and actions might not reflect his faith. He doesn't want to flaunt his Christianity, but neither does he want to "hide it under a bushel" (Matthew 5:15, KJV). He believes that actions speak louder than words. At the same time, he wonders if his co-workers may potentially misinterpret his actions

Authenticity

A *fake* is a copy, a duplicate, a facsimile of an original. The professional coach is authentic—the real deal. No one wants to hear: "Oh, that's Tom; he's a fake coach." We want to be known as genuine!

The desire to fit in and go with the flow seems to snare teenagers in particular. Unfortunately, many adults do not depart from this habit. Being authentic means having standards that make you stand out. In this way, you rise above the chaos to show a fixed point that others can look up to. You can be a beacon, a bright spot on the horizon.

Most successful people claim that the ability to "be yourself" will ultimately carry you further and faster than any other quality. That said, everyone—and every coach—should have standards by which to operate.

QUESTION

Does Jesus stand in your way
or is He the way for you?

An authentic coaching relationship gives the client personal choice and control. In this relationship, the client has the right to sort through his challenges and opportunities without the coach impeding him. An authentic coaching relationship is one where the client is free to prioritize his values and make new life choices. The coach facilitates so that the client can own the resulting success. The authentic coach does not take credit for the client's success.

Character

Most of us are very concerned about image and have a certain profile we want to maintain. We might even hire an image consultant to assure that the world sees the right picture of us displayed. Image is indeed important because a poor image can affect sales. Attractive people are more likely to sell than are less attractive people (Maestripieri 2012). Beauty, however, is only skin deep, as the old adage attests. Outward appearance is merely a covering of the truth inside.

A business concerned only with looking good is less likely to make correct ethical and moral choices than one that makes decisions based on code and character. If you want to be successful over the long haul, ensure that your character is unassailable. Your character goes much deeper than the surface—it reveals your heart. Your character is the sum of the way you think, feel, and behave. A coach referred to as a man or woman of character is a coach who has gained a reputation for *consistent* moral living. He conducts himself in a way that is above reproach.

QUESTION

How important to you is your image?

Moral Fiber

People of strong moral fiber are resilient to the pressures of being popular and "cool." They do not bend to every new wind of doctrine. They are not blown around by cleverness and tricks (Ephesians 4:14). An abundance of moral fiber results in strong decisions based on principle. More often than not, a lack of character—rather than a lack of moral clarity—lies behind unethical decisions. A man of character knows that something is wrong and does not do that thing. On the contrary, a man who lacks moral fiber

Note

After a semester of case studies and deliberations in an ethics course for anesthesiologists, one of the students asked the instructor for a bottom-line takeaway. In other words, what operative principle should help to keep a practicing anesthesiologist from making an unethical decision? The professor thought for a moment before he replied, "Don't buy a big house."

In essence, if your financial obligations are so high that you feel compelled to accept a business contract that goes against your better judgment, then you are overextended. Here again is an ethical principle that should help you stay within the realm of the good and walk away from the bad: *live within your means.*

knows that something is wrong and does it anyway.

Strong character means persevering in accomplishing goals. Such a person holds out for things that last and have purpose. Weak character leads to the distraction of short-term rewards. Such a person longs for trinkets and toys, instant pleasures, and immediate gains. The ethical Christian coach has a calling to be a person of strong character. Having a good name is better than having silver or gold (Proverbs 22:1).

QUESTION

What compromises would you be willing to make for a million dollars?

What Are the Dangers?

Frank reflects on his early childhood church experience. He never really understood why his parents forced him to go to church. All of his friends had to go to school, yes, but few of them had to go to church. As a teenager, he decided that church people were narrow-minded. There was a big world out there, and Frank felt boxed in by those touting the Ten Commandments. To him, churchgoers just wanted to see and be seen. *Didn't everyone know that many of them were the biggest sinners in the neighborhood? Were they blind to that? Was there not more to church than just singing spiritual songs?*

Compliance vs. Rebellion

Being *obedient* and being *conservative* are not the same. Neither are the terms *rebellious* and and *liberal* interchangeable. One should not confuse risk avoidance with obedience or risk loving with rebellion. The media glorifies rebelliousness and portrays the rebel as pushing forward, thinking for himself, making his own decisions, being his own man.

In this sense, the ethical coach can be both obedient and rebellious. You can adhere to the codes and standards of the coaching industry by making an autonomous choice. Here the question of "free will" comes in. The Bible commands us to behave in a certain way yet allows us to choose whether to obey. The Christian coach should not advocate blind obedience but, rather, willful obedience. Often non-Christians perceive a Bible-believer as being so obedient to God and the church that he cannot make his own decisions. The sinner saved by grace knows from experience that this is simply not the case.

Healthy rebellion against society happens when a person stands up for unpopular and potentially counter-cultural decisions. Indeed, standing up for what is right is admirable. In the same way, not every act of protest is a conscious declaration of dissatisfaction. It is also possible that the protestor is overwhelmed with frustration and simply needs to vent that frustration publicly. The ethical coach develops systems for dealing with his frustrations and does not use the coaching conversation as a platform for venting his political or social views. The coaching conversation is not the place to recruit disciples to one's favorite cause. It is a place where the client can choose to identify and support the cause or purpose that will propel him forward.

QUESTION

How much "free will" do you exercise in your coaching?

Complacency

For the coach to be ethically mature in his approach to decision making, he needs to put all the options on the table. Good, bad, or indifferent, he should consider all the choices available. It is too easy to make a decision based on circumstantial or superficial evidence. Without coercion, manipulation, or prejudice, the ethical coach evaluates

the possibilities and then voluntarily decides to proceed with a good decision. Moral decisions are not made by rote but through careful consideration of the facts.

Coaches should not become complacent or simply hold a position because it seems to be the accepted way to behave. Rather, a renewed realization of the tension that exists when deciding between moral choices keeps us from becoming morally lazy; it keeps us alive and fresh. A moral dilemma can be large or small, important or inconsequential, urgent or secondary. One thing is certain: moral dilemmas are ever present. Authors Howard and Korver write, "Small things, no less than the big ones, reveal unresolved conflicts. In fact, the big ethical topics of the day often figure far less into our daily lives than a host of small persnickety ones" (Howard and Korver 2008, 74).

QUESTION

What distinguishes a small conflict from a big conflict in your coaching business?

Ethical Blind Spots

I recently backed my car into a post. *Crunch*! In my time as a licensed driver, I have now done this four times. There's a blind spot on the back right side of a vehicle that I continually need to watch. There are two dangers when a blind spot exists: Either I am unaware that I have a blind spot, or I have forgotten that I have a certain blind spot. Ethics professor Dennis J. Moberg states, "Ethics blind spots exist when people fall victim to common, but defective or incomplete, perceptions of moral attributes" (Moberg 2006, 415). In any case, falling victim to a blind spot is a question of not taking the time to evaluate the circumstances before acting.

In threatening situations, humans tend to revert to primitive behaviors without flexibility or compassion. Emotions mask our perception, and we behave as if on autopilot. Our reactions during times of challenge or crisis are guided by our embedded response structure. Like pilots, we can train ourselves to immediately respond to potential danger with quick and correct actions and reactions.

QUESTION

What are your moral blind spots? How might you prepare to respond to them?

Did You Know?

Some years ago, I met a pilot instructor for 737 jets. I told her the only joke I knew about flight instruction. Question: "What's the #1 rule of the pilot? Answer: "Always keep the blue side up." My assumption was that this was an obvious explication of the basics of flight. The sky is blue, and it is better to have the blue side above you than below you.

The instructor neither laughed at the joke nor agreed with my assumption. She explained to me that the rule is quite serious. This rule refers to the horizon indicator on the plane's instrument panel. The blue side is the sky and the black side is the ground. In wartime, many fighter pilots crashed into the ground when they thought they were actually pulling up and gaining altitude. A pilot cannot solely depend on what he sees out of the window; he has to pay attention to his horizon indicator.

Immediately, I thought of the horizon indicator as analogous of the Bible. We might be confused and feeling upside down. The Bible will always show us the right direction of things. In times of trouble, God will show us what is up and what is down. The Word of God is a lamp to our feet and light onto our paths (Psalm 119:105).

What Are the Opportunities?

"Would you tell me, please, which way I ought to walk from here?"

"That depends a good deal on where you want to get to," said the Cat. *"I don't much care where …"* said Alice.

"… so long as I get somewhere," Alice added as an explanation. (Carroll 1865, 89)

The decision-making process is not always easy. We have choices to make and paths to determine. Standing still is also an option. Who or what will show us the way?

Calling

One day at lunch, Frank reads this verse: "Show me the right path, O Lord; point out the road for me to follow" (Psalm 25: 4 NLT). He realizes that he has never asked God to show him the path to take. He doesn't want to end up just *somewhere*. He wants to be in the place God has called him to be and to follow the way God has called him to follow.

Investment advisors often say that people spend more time each year planning their two-week vacation than they spend planning their retirement. A small-business owner might fall into the same trap. We want to retire and have a nice life, but we don't really care how we get there. We seek guidance, yet we don't like being told what to do. We look to maps to show the possibilities, yet we demand the right to choose our own paths.

For the Christian, one's compass is his calling. During the initial call, I tell my clients that one of my highest values as their coach is helping them find their *calling*, or purpose in life. During the course of the coaching relationship, I will circle back to this idea. Whether the client believes in the Bible or not, finding a sense of purpose gives the client a goal, a destination.

Oftentimes, religious people feel that a calling is not truly possible without the hope of eternal salvation as incentive for good moral behavior. While the assurance of one's ultimate future is comforting to the believer, there is also the hope that the present can be happy. Enjoyment of life is important to the believer (Ecclesiastes 9) and the non-believer *(carpe diem)* alike. Your task is to make every day meaningful for yourself and to assist your clients in doing the same.

QUESTION

With regard to your calling, what does "seize the day" mean to you?

Who Will Know?

Frank decides to stop over-extending his lunch breaks. He feels he needs to do this to maintain integrity in the workplace. He tells his supervisor that he will stay within the sixty minutes allotted to him, but his supervisor responds, "Look Frank, you are one of the best workers we have. Nobody is going to care if you bend the rules every now and then. Don't worry about it."

Integrity

We act with professional integrity when we do what is consistent with our values. A person who says one thing and does another is divided and inconsistent. This is also called being "two faced" or "speaking with a forked tongue." Jesus referred to such people as being "wolves in sheep's clothing" or hypocrites (Matthew 7:15). The word *hypocrite* comes from the Greek and refers to an actor wearing a mask, i.e., pretending to be what he is not.

Most people are only concerned with hypocrisy when someone else actually sees it, reasoning that *if nobody sees it, nobody cares.* A lawyer in Germany once told me that most laws in that country only punish the person who gets caught. The expression in German "*Wo kein Kläger, da kein Richter*" translates: "Where there is no accuser, there is no judge." The perpetrator thinks that he is under the radar—out of sight, out of mind.

Sooner or later, however, a lack of compliance to the law seems to catch up with a business. Ignoring unethical practices will eventually destroy the reputation of a company. Putting one's head in the sand will only provide a dark and dismal view of impending danger. Furthermore, we know as Christians that Someone is indeed watching. The man of integrity knows that he will stand before God one day and be held accountable for his actions (2 Corinthians 5:10).

QUESTION

How important is transparency in your coaching practice?

CASE STUDY

You know the report is due on Thursday, and the person expecting the report is demanding and unlikely to forgive a late delivery. You also know that new information that could affect the outcome of the project may be available on Monday. Nevertheless, you submit the report on Thursday and make no mention of the anticipated new information. Withhold the information and turn it in on time, or be late with the report and present a more complete picture: What would you do?

Obedience to a Fault

When you obey the rules despite knowing that doing so will lead to a negative outcome, you are contributing to the problem and not to the solution. Former International Coach Federation President Diane Brennen calls this "malicious obedience" (Brennen 1996, 152), i.e., people do as they are told regardless of the outcome their actions will bring. This is not the type of rebellion that an ethical coach should exhibit. It is a poor excuse to say you were just following the rules when you knew beforehand that the result would be harmful. Can you really claim innocence when you knew your behavior would hurt more than it helped?

Your clients could be in similar situations. As a coach, you can point out the danger of malicious obedience if the client goes down the path of obedience without considering the outcomes. When you bring such dilemmas to the forefront of the client's mind, you help that person define his or her true values. That is good coaching!

How Do I Get It Right?

Frank wants to get it right. He wants to know what the truth is and to be truthful. He is tired of going his way; he wants to align with God's way. He would like his life to be a good example of what the Lord can do when He is in control. Frank's prayer time becomes less about telling God what he wants and more about listening to what God wants. Frank puts a sign up on his desk at work: "I am God's work in progress."

Wearing Biblical Glasses

"We don't see things as they are; we see things as we are." This anonymous quote, often attributed to the Talmud, expresses that we look at every situation from our own perspective. We can only see things as well as our eyes are able to see them. A person who lacks the ability to see correctly cannot legally drive a vehicle. Spiritually speaking, we are not fully able to see correctly (1 Corinthians 13:12), yet God entrusts us with the control of our spiritual vehicles (i.e., lives). He tasks us with knowing what is right and wrong. In terms of ethics, we should know the difference between moral versus immoral, ethical versus unethical, and legal versus illegal. How accurately we see these distinctions depends on the quality of our ethical eyesight. To stretch the analogy, a biblical worldview acts like a set of glasses.

The secularist would argue that the Bible-believing Christian does not see things naturally because he is wearing biblical glasses. The fundamentalist would argue that the secularist cannot see things clearly because sin has tainted his worldview. The secular coach keeps ethics in perspective by aligning his actions with his declared ethical principles and values; the concepts of right and wrong are strictly from his own perspective.

The Christian coach keeps ethics in perspective by aligning his principles and values with his biblical worldview, endeavoring to see things from God's point of view. The Christian's ethical actions are thus a function of his desire to please God and not just an attempt to live morally upright in the sight of man. In 1 John 5:3 it says, "Loving God means doing what he tells us to do, and really, that isn't hard at all" (The Living Bible).

QUESTION

Are you wearing biblical lenses?

> **Danger Zone** !
>
> The mature individual assumes ownership of his mistakes but does not continually beat himself up for them. Taking responsibility for one's mishaps and deficiencies is essential for growing as a professional coach.

Lead by Example

A coach who is in a position of leadership holds the special honor of being an example for others. For good or ill, people look to leaders for their behavioral cues. For example, whether one accepts or denies the consumption of alcohol as morally correct, drinking to a point of drunkenness is unacceptable, biblically speaking (Ephesians 5:18). A leader coach who has alcoholic tendencies but frequently visits bars will soon find a group of other coaching buddies who are all too happy to join him. "Hey, if Tom can get drunk any time he wants, so can we. After all, Tom is the leader of the local coaches' roundtable group. He's cool."

Now, imagine that Tom stops going to bars and asks the same followers to hold him accountable for his abstinence. Tom promises to do the right thing. "I promise that I will no longer get drunk or encourage others to do so." The pledge to correct his mistakes becomes an example for others to uphold. Accountability reinforces his words.

Standing on and leading from the moral high ground requires a solid foundation built of values and principles. Accountability is a cornerstone in that foundation. When you make yourself accountable to another person for correct ethical behavior, you make a pledge to behave in a morally correct manner.

Moral Example

When a client assesses a coach's character, she wants to know two things: 1) How well developed are the coach's core values, and 2) how congruent are the coach's actions with those core values? (Kidder 1995, 42). Ultimately, the client looks up to her coach. She wants to become more like her and, therefore, she wants to spend more time getting to know her.

There are several things you can do as Christian coach to make your moral message obvious:

- Profess a clear statement of faith in God and belief in the Word of God.

- Exhibit fairness in your treatment of others (e.g., with your spouse, children, coworkers, and other professionals.)

- Take care of yourself and show respect for your own mind, soul, and body (a.k.a. temple, 1 Corinthians 6:19). Without self-care, we cannot adequately care for others.

- Listen well with few, if any, interruptions. Exhibit respect and compassion.

- Epitomize responsibility and accountability.

Client Care

Coaching is a service. We serve our clients and have their well-being as the higher priority. Yes, you must look after yourself as a business owner. However, the care your client receives should come before the benefits you receive. Client care comes before rights and rules. This is a level of care where the building, maintaining, and restoring of client relationship takes precedence over one's duty to perform obligations.

The innate belief that your clients can and will achieve their goals encourages and substantiates an authentic relationship with them. To me, it is antithetical to "bad mouth" a client under any circumstances. I cannot secretly, and certainly not publicly, regard any of my clients as weird, strange, a rapscallion, or even lazy. In my mind, all of my clients are good people. I sincerely believe that they have the potential to improve and succeed. I would not be able to coach a client if I felt otherwise. It is not my place to judge a client's intentions or ability to achieve (Matthew 7:1).

Reflection

Often, we hear and see things we don't like in a client's words and behaviors. When this happens in your practice, stop and consider what is bothering you and why. Is this because the actions or thoughts of the client go against your moral grain, or do you see in the client's behavior a part of yourself that you do not like? What part of the client's behavior makes you feel angry, impatient, or awkward? Such reflection provides insight into those areas where you might still need healing or improvement. The quicker you can get this taken care of, the sooner you will be able to serve your clients to the fullest.

Chapter Summary

In this chapter, you have looked at the components of morality that affect coaches. You see here that moral choices go beyond codes, rules, and even standard practices. Morality is, at its core, your default sense of right and wrong, even when it's just you and the Holy Spirit in the room.

You will make choices based on a number of variables. The question that should linger with you when making decisions is whether you feel comfortable with the face you see reflected back at you in the mirror. Are you feeling like an honored child of the King, or are you feeling like a fake? Obedience to the law or to a code of ethics will not make you feel light and without burden. Having strong moral values and knowing that your coaching practice reflects your values will give you peace and the confidence that you are a coach of integrity.

The Bible will guide you. It will be a light unto your path. The Holy Spirit will inspire you. You will be able to stand up for what you believe with conviction and honesty. You are real. You are genuine. You are clean. For you, the greatest thrill will come from hearing the words: "Well done, my good and faithful servant" (Matthew 5:21).

It is entirely likely that you do not agree with all of the values and principles presented in this book. That's perfectly okay. I am confident that you can operate within the framework of good coaching if you have had the patience to read the book to this point. What is not okay is trying to practice coaching without standards purposely integrated into your coaching business. In the end, we only need to agree on one point—Jesus Christ is the Way, the Truth, and the Life. No one gets full access to God without coming to grips with Jesus (John 14:6, paraphrased).

This concludes the story of Frank, the aspiring ethicist. Frank realizes that Christians are not perfect, yet God has called them to righteous living. His daily regimen of prayer and Bible reading keeps him aware of the moral dilemmas that surround him. He hopes one day to also teach Sunday school—maybe to rebellious teenage boys. He would like them to know that there is a real way to be on the right path. Frank knows that his decisions pivot on what God wants—not what he wants. He is excited about sharing what he has discovered with others.

What Would You Do?

Scenario A: You are talking to one of your good friends. She explains that a sense of heaviness has been plaguing her since her father died. Since you have a gift of compassion, your spiritual antenna immediately goes up. As a coach, you know you can help her put together a plan to move forward and find release from this burden. You also sense that she may need counseling, therapy, or even inner healing first. What is your next step?

Scenario B: A client of Jewish faith hires you as a coach. He says that he needs a coach who understands how faith interplays with all decision making. In the initial call, he says that he admires and respects the teachings of the prophet Jesus Christ. How do you react to this?

Scenario C: A potential client wants to hire you because her current coach is not meeting her needs. You are under no obligation to inform the first coach that the client wants to shift to you. Will you inform the first coach or let it be?

Scenario D: A taxi driver overhears his passenger talking on his phone about a drug payment. He says, "Yeah, I got the money right here." After the passenger leaves the taxi, the driver notices that the moneybag is still in the back seat. Should he run after the man or take the money to the authorities?

End of Chapter Questions

- Is the "blue side" up in your life?

- What is the basis of your moral foundation?

- How do you know what is right and what is wrong?

- What can you do to ensure that your blind spots don't cause accidents in your life?

CHAPTER 3

ETHICAL CHOICE — THE FOUNDATION OF ETHICS

"Honesty is the best policy."

—*Benjamin Franklin, (1706-1790)*

In this chapter, we will examine the decision-making process. Good decision making is the result of years of experience making and learning from one's choices—good and bad. Likewise, we can learn from *others'* choices. Imagine the added benefit of an ethical coach being able to help his client avoid bad decisions.

With the goal in mind of helping our clients learn to make good decisions for themselves, we will look at the factors that influence an ethical decision. Several dangers can readily cause clients to make bad decisions. The good news is that we can help them stop the cycle of bad decisions and begin restoration by teaching them how to make good decisions.

After reading this chapter, you will be able to do the following:

- Identify the factors that bring about ethical decision making.
- Explain why you feel frustrated when a decision is hard.
- Distinguish between good and bad decisions.
- Evaluate various decision-making styles.
- Discover a course of action for good decision making.

Elena's Story

Elena has been working for Vasserwerks for just over ten years. For the most part, she is happy with the work she does, yet feels there is more she can accomplish professionally. She constantly finds herself at odds with her boss about matters of procedure. One evening, a professional recruiter contacts her and tells her of a position opening up at Jago's. Not knowing how to respond, she tells the recruiter to send the job description to her via her private e-mail account.

For the next few weeks, Elena becomes engrossed in the details of the job at Jago's. Her due diligence research on the firm leaves no stone unturned. Jago's certainly seems more innovative and dynamic than her present firm. Surprisingly, what bothers her about the new job is the higher salary that it offers. Now she has a dilemma. Both are good jobs. They are each located within a tolerable driving distance from her home. Both of these jobs offer security and responsibility. Both are a good fit for her.

Elena looks within herself to find what really motivates her to do her job. She sees that ambition has been a primary factor so far. She will work harder than anyone else if that's what it takes. She has never been happy with little, and she wants more out of life than what she had when she was growing up. In a rare moment of deep reflection, she realizes that she is afraid of being poor again. It is not that she craves the things money can buy; rather, she fears the diminished number of options caused by lack of money.

Common Challenges

Elena feels the pressure of making the right decision, as much depends on the direction she will take. Whichever way she chooses, she knows she will expend tremendous amounts of mental energy. It's not so much the risk of wasting time deliberating each alternative that concerns her. What concerns her, more than anything else, is making the right decision.

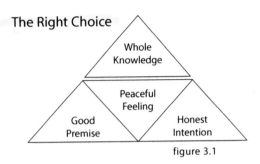

The Right Choice

figure 3.1

Right Choices

Making decisions is an everyday activity. You could have cereal or toast for breakfast. You could drink orange juice or coffee. You could also just skip breakfast altogether. Indeed, making good decisions on a daily basis could simply be the result of having a good breakfast or not. When your body is well nourished and your mind well rested, this increases the likelihood of your thoughtful engagement in a solid decision-making process.

The best choice becomes evident when we reflect on God's purpose for our lives. The components to making good decisions include having the right knowledge, honest intentions, and a good premise. With the complete picture we can feel at peace with our decisions (see figure 3.1).

A *good premise* is one that brings about a satisfactory result. A *peaceful feeling* is one that rests easily in the heart. The Holy Spirit confirms this with a sense of ease, even calmness. An *honest intention* is one that is sincere and free from deception. These are three intrinsic components of a right choice. On top of this basis goes the extrinsic component of *whole knowledge*. Whole knowledge is the collection of facts, background, and experience that one needs to complete the picture. Whole knowledge is where logic, rationality, prudence, and even common sense come into play. We all struggle with the common challenge of keeping the big picture in mind when making a right choice.

When we know God's will, then the Holy Spirit functions as a navigator, leading the way (Proverbs 3:6). The right choice is one that engenders peace and the confidence that the hand of providence is at work. What we want to avoid is a choice that only satisfies—in other words, that only meets a minimum level of acceptability. It is a constant challenge for us, as Christians, to make choices that align with God's perfect will for us. You are probably familiar with the phrase, "The good is the enemy of the best." Expressed in terms of decision making, "The good-enough decision is at odds with the right choice." There are many good possibilities. Which one is the best choice? Ultimately, making the best decision is a matter of humility and willingness to submit to God's perfect plan.

Analysis Paralysis

Elena keeps weighing the options. She could continue to work for Vasserwerks or move to Jago's. She wants to make an informed choice. It seems, however, that her research into the topic never ends. There seems to be no limit to the depth of information that relates to changing jobs and moving up the corporate ladder. She also notices that delving into the background of these companies keeps her busy and occupied. Besides, as long as she is still looking into the factors that relate to the decision, she doesn't have to make a choice.

The human brain deciphers, at best, five to nine alternatives simultaneously. Limiting options to three choices makes it easier to come to a decision; too much information and too many options can lead to overthinking and indecision. This happens when the action center of the brain, the prefrontal cortex, becomes overloaded. I like to compare the prefrontal cortex to the Random Access Memory (RAM) of a computer. This is the part where computations and calculations occur. Like the RAM in your computer, if you try to cram in too much information at once, it could freeze up. Your brain tells you: *Not enough memory available to complete this operation. Quit one or more applications to increase available memory, and then try again.*

Zugzwang

When the decision maker is in a position where only a loss seems possible, we call this *Zugzwang*. The German word Zugzwang describes the point in a chess game when a required move results in the loss of one of your favorite pieces. The alternative would be forfeiting.

We must make sufficient effort to ensure that the best possible choices are on the table. Too many viable positive alternatives competing with one

> **Tip**
>
> The ethics of good coaching involve allowing the client to fully own the decisions she makes— even bad ones. The coach has no stake in the outcome.

another causes a predicament. Too few viable alternatives competing with one another causes frustration.

It's often frustration that causes people to seek out a coach. Good coaching helps the client explore the best alternatives or discover new ones. Like Elena, a client may feel compelled to make a decision—ready or not. The desire to move forward compounds the client's sense of frustration, particularly when he or she believes that indecision creates grave consequences (Schulte 2010). In order to coach a client effectively at such a juncture, the coach guides the process but not the decision.

At the Heart of the Matter

Elena's boss makes overtures one day about a promotion. He mentions that the downtown office might need a new manager. This would put her on the same level as him in the company hierarchy. He practically asks her if she would be interested. He mentions her performance evaluation scheduled for next month as a good time to discuss the possibilities.

The Timing of Decision Making

Decision making and problem solving are not the same. To solve a problem, one needs to find a solution. To make a decision, one needs to make a choice. Energy is often wasted when too much time is spent looking for a solution when actually making a choice is the best way to go. General George Patton once said, "A good plan, violently executed *now*, is better than a perfect plan next week." However, in order to consider the alternatives completely, one needs to take time—a lot of time.

Having a good feel for the timing of a decision is one of the most beneficial abilities a wise decision-maker can develop. Sometimes the quick decision is best; sometimes it might take years before the best ideas surface. Evidence reveals our gut feeling (i.e., intuition) is spot-on more often than not (Haidt 2001). The ability to make the quick decision (the correct reflexive reaction) is essential in clutch situations. A dog musher I know says that he stops his team immediately when the "halt" bell goes off in his head. Only then does he see the moose on the trail or the crack in the frozen lake. He has learned that when he neglects that inner voice, he ends up regretting it.

Elena feels trapped. She feels that Jago's is probably the right decision but remains unsure. Instead of forcing a decision, she goes sailing on her cousin's boat. Sailing always helps her clear her mind and allows her to contemplate the deeper issues of life without overthinking. After several hours at sea, it becomes clear to her that no matter what her decision is, she needs to make it soon. She sets her performance evaluation meeting next month as the benchmark date to make her decision. Immediately, she feels a sense of peace that she is moving in the right direction.

Ethical Decisions and Ethical Dilemmas

In its most simple form, an ethical decision is a choice between right and wrong. Given that some of the choices are legal and some of the choices are illegal, the ethical decision should be apparent. For the Christian, obeying the law should be a simple choice (Titus 3:1). More often than not, the decision you face is not a legal, ethical, or even a moral one. It's a practical one.

A conflict arises when multiple choices overlap. The origins of the word dilemma come from two Greek parts: *di* = two and *lemma* = fundamental proposition. Having two parts, it makes sense that a dilemma is the conflict that arises when there are two conflicting good choices or two conflicting bad choices.

Let's look at different types of dilemmas.

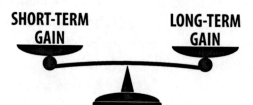

SHORT-TERM GAIN   LONG-TERM GAIN

Short-Term Gain versus Long-Term Gain

Are you looking for a quick return or a long-term gain. In the short-run approach, you can become famous if you are the first person to achieve something; you can establish yourself as an innovator and a pioneer. In the long-run approach, you can better plan, adjust, and sell; you can establish yourself as a steady rider and a harvester.

CASE STUDY

Your normal speaking fee is $1,500. A colleague has asked you to speak at the convention of a non-profit organization where potentially hundreds of prospective clients will be attending. They tell you up front that they are unable to compensate any of the speakers. Do you stand on your reputation of being a high-quality speaker worth the money, or do you forego the money in order to get the chance to speak to people in your target group?

BEING JUST **BEING MERCIFUL**

Being Just versus Being Merciful

You can pass judgment because sin is evident. Your reputation is that you tell it like it is.

You can also show forgiveness because sin is unavoidable. Your reputation is that you are a compassionate soul.

---CASE STUDY---

You find another coach has been continually pilfering your proprietary graphics from your website. Which is the better way in this case: justice or mercy? Do you sue her for copyright infringement, or do you just write a cease-and-desist letter?

REVEALING THE TRUTH **STAYING LOYAL**

Revealing the Truth versus Staying Loyal

You can reveal someone's sin because exposed sin shows reality. Doing so makes you a whistle blower. You can also conceal someone's sin because unexposed sin saves the person embarrassment. Doing so makes you seem like a team player.

---CASE STUDY---

Another coach in your firm bills his clients for unrelated expenses. You mention it several times, yet he continues his practice of over-billing the client. Truth or loyalty: which is better? Do you mention it to the firm's owner or not?

BENEFIT TO INDIVIDUAL

BENEFIT TO COMMUNITY

The Benefit to the Individual versus the Benefit to the Community at Large

Sometimes, one of the available choices helps one person but leaves others short. Other times, the decision that best serves the greater good short changes the individual because the benefit is distributed among many people.

─── **CASE STUDY** ───

You belong to a coaching contract organization that distributes work to its members. One day, a company offers you a contract that involves coaching thirty people; however, this offer is for you personally. If you give that contract to your organization, at least four other coaches will benefit and you will only get six of those thirty contracts. Will you share the caseload?

Indeed, a dilemma might involve *more* than two variables. This is when decision making gets really sticky. As a Christian coach, your ability to know the nature and complexity of the dilemma will determine the speed and accuracy of your ethical choice. As coaches, we practice reflectivity with our clients because it helps us stay on top of the ethical dilemmas we face personally. Ethical reflection means becoming aware of the alternatives to various dilemmas. The next step is making the correct ethical choice. When it comes time to account for your decisions, you should be able to delineate the thought processes that went into the formulation of your decision. Simply saying, "Well, it seemed like a good idea at the time," does not represent the level of responsibility expected from a professional coach.

Factors That Muddle the Issue

Elena feels that leaving her company now would put Vasserwerks in a difficult situation. She has been responsible for starting several initiatives that still need her attention. Can she ethically justify abandoning those young initiatives? To make matters more complex, she has developed many close friendships with her colleagues during the past ten years. She just can't seem to get her head around the idea of leaving all this behind.

The Heart and the Brain

The feelings behind a decision often muddle the logic behind a decision. We talk about decisions as being of the heart. "Keep thy heart with all diligence; for out of it are the issues of life" (Proverbs 4:23, KJV). The heart is where life ebbs and flows. The heart is eternal. A pastor I know often says, "Ask not *why* things happen to you. Ask *when* they happen, 'how will I react?'" When your life becomes unstable, that is when your true behavior patterns surface (Luke 6:45-46). When your cup is jostled, the contents tend to spill out. This always made me think of the software programmer's creed: "Garbage in, garbage out." Certainly, there is an entire sermon in those words.

The brain, too, recognizes the importance of the heart. The brain dedicates

---

Did You Know?

A fictional tale is told in management seminars about a young manager who was to replace a retiring executive. The younger man approached the older, venerated leader and asked, "Sir, I know you are a legendary leader in this company. Could you give me some advice as I try to fill your shoes?"

The older man pondered the question and responded: "Three words: Make good decisions!"

"That is good advice," the young man replied as he wrote this down.

"And what is the key to making good decisions?"

"One word," the veteran executive replied, "Experience."

"And how do I get this?" the eager young man asked as he scribbled "experience" on his paper.

"Two words," the retiring man answered, "Bad decisions."

The younger man looked surprised, and the older man asked, "Any other questions?" (Morris, n.d., para. 5)

a set of neuropathways to processing moral decisions. Results of fMRI (functional Magnetic Resonance Imaging) scans during real-time experiments show moral decision making runs entirely through the emotional centers of the brain rather than the logical ones (Grayling 2010, 123).

Mirror Neurons

Another factor in the decision-making process is that it is human nature to copy what we see other people doing, irrespective of whether that behavior is right or wrong. The innate cause of this phenomenon is in the microscopic parts of our brain cells called *mirror neurons*. Consider what happens when one monkey sees another monkey behaving a certain way. The mirror neurons in the brain of the watching monkey fire up in the same way as the performing monkey (Grayling 2010, 124). If the performing monkey scratches his head, the watching monkey begins scratching his head. Quite literally, it becomes *monkey see, monkey do*.

The increased intelligence humans have over monkeys should allow us to distinguish whether what we are watching is right or wrong. However, without a moral code as a filter, people simply do what they see others doing; without a moral code, they don't know right from wrong and simply imitate behaviors.

Which of My Values Is Relevant Here?

Elena's cultural background is more collectivistic than individualistic. She very much feels as if she is the product of the village in which her parents raised her. She feels a strong sense of community. In light of that experience, how can she turn her back on the company that has helped feed her family for all these years? She grew up hearing one primary rule: "Never turn your back on family." Yet, she believes that moving to another company will increase her status and thereby make her family even more proud of her. Isn't it a good thing for her to become a role model for young women from underprivileged environments?

Social Framework

Ethics, and particularly Christian ethics, are a product of our social framework. How, when, and where we learned about Christ and Christian behavior significantly affects our view of ethics. Traditions shape the way we think and, consequently, how we feel.

The kind of environment we grew up in plays an integral role in shaping our values of strong family, integrity, honor, and loyalty.

The first time I went on an overseas mission trip, I was shocked to discover that much of what I thought about Christianity was actually a result of the religious practices of the churches I had attended in the United States. Other countries practiced Christianity in very different ways than I did. This certainly did not make them any less Christian or less devoted. Upon reflection, I could see that individualism and pragmatism, traits that Americans value, are reflected in our religious practices in the United States. The cultural environment of the country I visited shaped the way its inhabitants practiced Christianity. In the same way, our social framework shapes and filters our decision making.

Here is a short list of some of the filters that influence our decision making:

- Culture
- Religion/morals
- Heritage
- Education
- Socio-economic status
- Intentions
- Motives
- Needs (self/organization)
- Values (self/organization)
- Consequences (local/global)

We all walk around with these filters. Our age, gender, geographic location, and level of professionalism influence these filters as well. So for example, if you're a teenager in China, your filters will be quite different than if you're an octogenarian in Finland or a thirty-something in the United States. Professional coaches, just like everyone else, develop a framework influenced by friends, family, teachers, leaders, and other role models. To state the obvious, one's point of view is a question of perspective. We all see things differently. You are likely to experience an ethical conflict with someone else when your perspectives do not line up. Both of you could be full of integrity and even righteousness by religious definitions and still be unable to see things eye to eye or agree on every point. The same can go for your clients.

For example, your client may feel that he hates his job, but what he really hates is spending so much time away from his children. Furthermore, he might feel that his boss is 100 percent in disagreement with him on an issue. When you coach around the issue, your discussion reveals that he agrees on the *what*, *why*, *when* and *where* but simply disagrees with the *how*. The tension with his boss is tangible, and the level of discomfort is extreme, even though in reality he agrees with 85 percent of the situation. This is what Patterson,

Grenny, McMillan, and Switzler (2002) call *violent agreement*. In this situation, your task as the coach is to help the client center his efforts on bridging the 15 percent gap. You may achieve this simply by getting him to envision the boss's perspective. In other words, you assist the client in taking an imaginary walk in the boss's shoes.

Rules

To cope with viewpoints, we develop rules for establishing a common framework. Similar to playing a game, you can play by the rules or not. Sometimes it seems that rules constrain us. In reality, rules give us the freedom to play. Rules are designed to restrain us from cheating although plenty of people choose not to play by the rules. Even so, you cannot play this game without other people. Stated simply, without other players, there is no game. Consequently, the rules prevent all of the participants from seeking an unfair advantage.

Like children, new coaches must learn the rules (i.e., ethical codes) of the profession. In grade school, teachers and hall monitors ensure that everyone plays nicely and fairly. Proper training and ethical codes set forth by organizations like ICF and CCNI provide similar guidance. Coaches who have graduated from their initial training should have a strong sense of what is professionally correct and what is not.

Ethically mature coaches are those who have not only internalized the codes of conduct but have also made these values instinctive. After years of successful experience, such automatic moral choices by the coach become increasingly subconscious rather than conscious. As Christian we call this innate discretion *discernment*. Discernment means going past the surface of the situation and finding the nuances of wisdom underneath. Discernment is wisdom in action.

Coaches need discernment now more than ever before. In my positions with both ICF and CCNI, I have watched the codes of ethics change with the times. As people from various cultures and diverse values join the mix of members, the framework of the ethical code adapts and adjusts accordingly. We do not rely solely on interpretations from the past to guide us; rather, we attend to the events that are affecting the code now and tomorrow. This does not mean that the aspiring coach should wait and see how the governing body interprets the code in its latest revision. The time for forming your framework for ethical Christian coaching is today, not tomorrow.

Exercise

- The client says, "I love you." Your reflexive reaction is …

- Is it a good idea to make bad decisions for the sole purpose of gaining experience?

- How do you respond under extreme pressure? Write down a good example. Now write down a bad example.

- What forms your social framework?

What Are the Dangers?

Elena's mother is facing foreclosure on her house. Ever since her mother developed some health problems, she has not been able to hold down a steady job. Elena is thinking that she might be able to help her mother with the extra money she would earn at Jago's. On the other hand, her current company might offer her a promotion. That could also mean extra money. Are these really the only two ways she can help her mother?

Threat

As pointed out in chapter two, the difference between moral and immoral decision making is often threat. Our sense of right and wrong hinges on how we feel about a situation. We intuitively gravitate toward things that stimulate our sense of reward. Consequently, we naturally shy away from things that threaten us. Best-selling business authors Doug Lennick and Fred Keil describe the human tendency to avoid risk this way: "As far as our brains are concerned, there are no shades of gray. We are either excited and pursuing rewards or fearful and trying to avoid danger" (Lennick and Keil 2011, 50).

A client who feels backed into a corner will almost certainly feel threatened. We all know that a cornered animal has the potential to come out fighting. When you are coaching a "cornered client," you are standing in harm's way. Watch out! The client might inadvertently lash out at you.

How do you know if you're at risk of a client lashing out at you? David Rock, founder of Results Coaching Systems identifies five "domains" as survival issues. The astute coach should be aware that a coaching conversation that dances into one of these domains has entered into a type of danger zone. Rock uses SCARF as an acronym for these five areas: Status, Certainty, Autonomy, Relatedness, and Fairness (Rock 2009, 195-196). People feel threatened when any of these areas are at risk.

The remedy for threat is trust. We will look at forming trust more in the next chapter. For now, suffice it to say that you don't want to embarrass, unsettle, endanger, or otherwise threaten a client. The results might be disastrous if the client decides to fight you instead of battling the underlying problem.

Too Few Alternatives

Elena reanalyzes the benefits of working for Vasserwerks. She then reanalyzes the benefits of working for Jago's. After repeated analysis, she agonizes that neither one of them appeals to her sense of purpose. She looks deeper and deeper into the possibilities but finds nothing in either company that satisfies her sense of calling.

You might feel threatened because you see no other choice. This is the frustration of Zugzwang that we looked at earlier. Ironically, there are probably alternatives you are unaware of in this situation. You feel forced into a decision without realizing that, intentionally or unintentionally, someone has withheld the knowledge of a better alternative from you. In other words, not all the cards are on the table—the dealer has hidden some of the cards up his sleeve. It seems that he dealt you a bad hand, and you are limited to poor options. Without knowing there are better options available, all that remains is a *sucker's choice*, based on the false premise that there are the only two, undesirable options available. The dichotomy of two bad choices paralyzes your brain, which works overtime to decipher the information between two bad choices. Why is this? David Rock explains, "Because the brain is built to avoid threat, people tend to work hard to reinterpret events to meet their expectations" (Rock 2009, 141). You don't want to entertain the thought that someone might be cheating you or withholding information from you. Therefore, you feel compelled to decide between the cards on the table.

The Sunk-Cost Effect

Elena becomes increasingly anxious. She fears that leaving Vasserwerks could cause her to lose everything she has worked so many years to achieve. Better a bird in the hand than two in the bush, she tells herself. She feels trapped.

Continuing in a course of action solely out of fear of losing one's investment is what economists call the sunk-cost effect. The decision-maker is not willing to risk losing the sizeable investment of time, money, and effort that have already gone into a venture, so rather than pursuing an alternative endeavor, the person stays in a less-than-satisfying situation.

The sunk-cost effect can challenge us in regard to ethical behavior if we're not careful. For example, getting clients to sign up for your coaching services takes time, effort, and money. Giving up this investment when a potential client isn't a good fit for you takes moral courage. Having a big house and then downsizing to a smaller one takes moral courage. Very few people are willing to move backwards without someone forcing them to do so. Part of our human nature is to want more—more stuff, more security, more prestige, and more recognition. Being unwilling to let go or take a step back puts you in a position of *needing* more and more clients. That need can make it difficult to refer a client to a coach who may be better suited for his or her needs.

In Luke 12, Jesus tells a story about a farmer who wanted to tear down his barns so that he could build bigger ones to hold more stuff. The farmer in this passage is depending on his own resources to make him happy and to give him the good life. Jesus calls this man a fool.

When I was a junior in college, a theology major friend of mine once set out to irritate me and a group of our friends. Using 2 Peter 3:10 as his premise, he wanted to remind us that nothing was permanent except the Kingdom of God. What he was doing was responding to any point of the conversation with the phrase: "It's all gonna burn." You'd say, "I need some new jeans." He'd say, "It's all gonna burn." You'd say, "The hamburgers in the cafeteria are soggy." He'd say, "It's all gonna burn." Do you see how this could get a little exasperating? For the past thirty-five years, however, this phrase has stuck with me. "It's all gonna burn." It's *all* stuff. Just *stuff*. One day, yes, on the day of reckoning it is *all going to burn*. Most of what we are afraid to lose is just stuff. The Bible says the following:

Do not store up for yourselves treasures on earth, where moths and vermin destroy, and where thieves break in and steal. But store up for yourselves treasures in heaven, where moths and vermin do not destroy, and where thieves do not break in and steal. For where your treasure is, there your heart will be also.

—Matthew 6:19-21, NIV

QUESTION

What are you not willing to lose?

Habits

Our brains work to create habits and routines that we can perform without much mental energy. We form habits to increase efficiency and reduce wasted time and resources. These rote practices become ingrained in our behavior patterns. Without habits, we could all be guilty of thinking too much. The danger of habit in ethical decision making is that we could make a mistake out of practice or routine even if we know there is a better way. We might agree to an ethical practice as being correct but behave contrarily by doing what we have always done. For example, one may always file a tax declaration late because of a pervasive procrastination habit.

When we enter the new behavioral territory and explore new ways to act, the brain can disconnect from the habitual solution and allow for the possibility of a new solution to form. If your habit is unethical, a cleansing might be in order. Forming a new habit that is ethically clean may take a bit of scrubbing and washing. Consider this fair warning that you might get soap in your eyes and feel the uncomfortable rub of abrasive cleansing. However, the result will be a clean conscience.

> *"Create in me a clean heart, O God; and renew a right spirit within me."*
> —*Psalm 51:10, KJV*

Fear

The opposite of trust is fear. Fear causes us to shut down or run away. Trust enables us to receive. Trust relaxes the limbic system and allows higher-level cognitive processing to occur. Fear puts the amygdala on alert and sends warnings throughout the body. Trust opens up. Fear closes down. Trust is warm. Fear is cold.

The task of the coach is to set up an atmosphere of trust—one in which the client feels safe. If the coach were to set up an atmosphere of fear, the client would feel threatened by the coach. This could cause grave results. When fear is the dominant emotion in the brain, the adrenal system releases large amounts of cortisol and adrenaline. The brain's cortex becomes masked. When fearful, the limbic system bypasses the parts of your brain responsible for higher-level thinking, planning, and decision making. When the amygdala senses danger—be it physical, emotional, or psychological—you go into "survival mode" to ensure your own safety. Survival mode results in five strategies for dealing with danger:

1. *Fight* — We attack.
2. *Flight* — We run away.
3. *Fellowship* — We seek the company of like-minded people or friends.
4. *Fracture* — We go to pieces.
5. *Freeze* — We immobilize.

When we are in one of the above states, it becomes difficult to perceive, behave, or do any long-term planning correctly. Our primary task is returning to safety. Unless a parental instinct takes over, we disregard even the safety of others. Cortisol controls our hearts as they start to pound wildly and our blood pressure rises. Over time, we become worried sick—literally! In this sense, *fellowship*, *fracture*, and *freeze* are variations of *flight*. Unless we train ourselves to react differently, we usually enter into *fight or flight* mode when we are afraid.

The flight mode might show up in your client as an unusual silence. Suddenly they are afraid to talk to you. The fight mode, on the other hand, could manifest as arguing or backlashing against you as the coach. When that happens, you need to retreat to a place of safety. When you are under attack, try to help the client identify the person or situation from which they are really trying to fight or flee. The client should not be fighting or fleeing from you. When adrenaline levels return to normal, it is safe to continue. What happened during the fight or flight reaction may be a revelation for the client as well as an opportunity for them to become more aware of how they react.

The ethical considerations here are synonymous with the coach's task to respect the client. While too much fight or flight during one coaching conversation may indicate the client is in need of a therapist or pastor, a healthy willingness to fight forward or flight (retreat) backwards is often part of the coaching practice. The Christian coach should not be afraid of the client's fear. Rather, the objective is to assist the client in determining whether he is fighting or fleeing the right issue. It is, therefore, somewhat normal for a client to get upset every now and then. However, the ethical coach should be wary of repeated drama centering on a reoccurring issue. This could be an indication of a pathological disorder. If that is the case, the client might need to engage a licensed counselor.

QUESTION

Are you looking forward to the next time a client gets angry during a coaching conversation?

QUESTION

What is your tendency when afraid—fight or flight?

What Are the Opportunities?

As a new coach, you may find that many aspects of running a business are unfamiliar to you. How you make decisions and what you decide will greatly influence the type of business you run. This, in turn, will influence the type of clients you attract. Therefore, your motivations play a big role in the degree of success you can expect. Let's start off here with a quick motivational check:

- Are you interested in coaching professionally?
- Are you interested in making money at it?
- Are you interested in acquiring clients?
- Are you interested in referring clients to someone else?

Did you answer yes to all of the above questions? Perhaps you waffled a bit on that last one. The key to long-term sustainability in the coaching profession is referrals. If one hundred people were to refer you as a coach, you would probably have more business than you could handle. So how do you get referrals? Satisfied clients will refer you to their friends, co-workers, and family members. Ultimately, you earn referrals by proving your ability to help clients help themselves to move forward. When the client does not feel comfortable referring you—or worse,

actively tries to discourage others from working with you—then you have a problem. For whatever reason, if the client does not feel you are worth the money, she will not recommend you to her friends. Training, experience, and practice can help you become a very good coach, but if your ethical practices are deficient, your clients will not recommend you. Simply put, good ethical behavior pays in the long run.

QUESTION

If you have a problem with the allocation of your business resources, from whom could you seek advice?

Motivational Questions

By now you might be asking yourself, "Is there any simple way to look at ethical dilemmas?" The answer is yes. Depending on your frame of reference, one or more of the questions below may be the key to unlocking your ethical dilemma. Simply looking at a decision from the perspective of another person can often help solve the mystery. Let's explore some motivational questions that may help us locate the desperately needed hidden nuggets of wisdom:

What would Jesus do?

Great question. The problem is that most of us feel quite lowly compared to

Tip

Focus on what you really want. By focusing on what you want for yourself, what you want for others, and what you want for the relationship, you align your mind to your core values. This allows you to find your bearings and set your mind on problem solving rather than fight or flight. It is your decision. The only emotions you can directly control are your own.

Everyone does it, right?

Well, what if *everyone* really did what you're proposing to do? Would that be good? This is a high-road question. While one person doing one shady thing only one time might not produce a substantial negative impact, there would be mayhem if everyone did it all the time.

Before going into panic mode due to lack of insight, you should check whether the answer to any of the above questions would suffice in your decision-making process.

Him. His level is so high that it seems unreachable.

If I were to ask my mother, what would she say?

Pretty good question. However, most of us would rather move to Alaska in the winter than ask our mothers for advice.

If my son were facing the same decision, what would I want him to decide?

Okay, if you can break the dilemma down to a form simple enough for a child to understand, this is a good question.

If all the media and press published my decision, would I feel comfortable with that?

Aside from the potential confidentiality issues, this could be a good come clean approach.

CASE STUDY

You meet regularly with a group of other professional coaches. You have a client that you are unsure about and want to share some of the details about the client with the group. Perhaps one of them could give you some insight. This is a common practice in a clinical environment. Is this ethical?

The Decision Is Emotional

All decisions are emotional decisions. You only add logic and rationalization after you feel your decision is the right one. In order to evaluate the situation, you need to assess the circumstances. Family, culture, values, education, and experience all become decision filters. To this, you add your emotional needs and wants and carefully assess whether you feel safe or threatened. However, your ability to stay cool and objective is directly proportional to the heat of emotion you are experiencing. A certain degree of vulnerability is at play when a decision is on the table. When everything is hunky-dory, you can move forward seemingly without thinking at all. In fact, you make most of your decisions at a subconscious level.

QUESTION

Do you argue with yourself?
If not, try it.

Bringing the client to a safe place where they can make good decisions is the task of the coach. Ethics Professor Richard Rowson notes, "If they [the clients] are in shock, stressed, experiencing strong emotions, or just very tired, people often find it difficult to think clearly about complex matters" (Rowson 2006, 108). The ethical coach allows space for the client to be weak. It is almost as if the coach is letting the client argue. However, this argument is not with the coach but with himself.

Such arguments can be very emotional indeed.

Most of the time, there are alternatives. There really is hope when all feels hopeless. Helping the client find that hope is essential for him to move forward. Expert coach and ethics mentor Teri-E Belf once told me the following story: "I am reminded of a client who came in saying: 'I have lost all hope.' I said, 'Some part of you chose to come here today. That suggests there is some hope. Speak to me from that place, please.' He did and we had an amazingly useful meeting as I reminded him to speak to me through that place. Halfway through, he needed no more prompts."

Giving your client hope for the future is the essence of ethical coaching. Regardless of the dilemma, God is in control. When a client is feeling hopeless, I like to share the following verse: "May the God of hope fill you with all joy and peace as you trust in him, so that you may overflow with hope by the power of the Holy Spirit" (Romans 15:13, NIV).

Who Is Going to Know?

If you never tell anyone that you need to make a decision about something, no one will know. There is no pressure to declare a decision when no one else knows about it. However, deciding not to decide is also a decision. Realizing that you don't need to make the decision now can sometimes break the analysis paralysis. You can make it later or not at all. In six days or in six months there could be better information or resources on which to base the decision. If information is hidden or missing, sooner or later the truth will reveal itself and allow us to make a better decision. We often forget what economists call the *phantom*

alternative—making the decision to change nothing. In contrast to zugzwang, deciding to do nothing is always an available option. In other words: You can decide on A, or you can decide on B, or you can decide on C, or you can decide to change nothing (the phantom alternative).

A person in Elena's situation might feel compelled to make a change for all the right reasons. However, what Elena hasn't yet considered is staying in her old job with her old boss and her old routine. No, this might not be the best choice for her, but it might not be the worst one either.

How Do I Do It Right?

One of the best-known ethical codes is the Hippocratic Oath, which dates back to about 400 BCE. The idea to "do no harm" rings true for all professions. Doug Lennick and Fred Keil write, "Failure to act in concert with our values and goals is worse than worthless. It is a failure of the core principle of responsibility. It does harm to everyone we care about—family, coworkers, and community" (Lennick and Keil 2011, 79). Never is it the declared intention of a coach to hurt, harm, injure, mislead, or deceive. We profess that we will do right by our clients and therefore declare ourselves members of the professional community. Reflecting on one's operative creed goes as far back as Socrates. Most of the questions posed in this book are Socratic questions. That is, their intention is to draw out thoughts or ideas that your mind has previously forgotten or discounted. Indeed, I do feel that your professional creed can be objective and not subjective. I also believe that the Bible is the source that will confirm your operative professional creed. As a Christian—i.e., someone who endeavors to be Christ-like—the way you decide and the way you behave should never be in conflict with the Bible. You should uphold the Ten Commandments and the Golden Rule. Indeed, such obedience calls us Christians to Deontology (actions based on adherence to rules).

We should want to do right and promise to do so. For this, we have a duty to respect others, keep promises, be honest, and help others when possible. A Christian deontologist should endeavor to have the moral qualities that are above reproach.

Self-Efficacy

The power to believe that you can accomplish what you set out to accomplish is self-efficacy. For this to happen, you first have to be ready to make a decision. Second, you have to want the result. The more you want the result, the easier it is to make the decision. There is an old joke that I often think about when it comes to decision making:

Question: How many behavioral psychologists does it take to change a light bulb?

Answer: Just one. But the light bulb has to *want to* change.

Forcing the client to change before he is ready is an exercise in futility. By the grace God has given us, we *own* the decisions we make. We make them without force or coercion. At the same time, effective coaching is encouraging. Henry Ford is credited with the saying, "Whether you think you can, or you think you can't—you're right." More poignant is the story of the little engine that could. Take a moment to remember that famous line from our childhood reading: "And then she said, 'I think I can. I think I can. I think I can.' And she hitched herself to the little train" (Piper 1930, 32).

The amazing thing about the Holy Spirit is that He is a complete gentleman. He will never force you to decide one way or another. The choices you *make* are the choices *you* make. You own them. Author John Maxwell notes, "No matter how much pressure there is, you can't allow others to force you into making unethical decisions"

(Maxwell 2003, 61). As this relates to ethical coaching, we circle back to the premise of acting in the client's best interests. Simply do what is best for the client. You will know you've made the right decision when your choices are able to withstand the fires of testing.

> If anyone builds on this foun-
> dation using gold, silver, costly
> stones, wood, hay or straw, their
> work will be shown for what it is,
> because the Day will bring it to
> light. It will be revealed with fire,
> and the fire will test the quality of
> each person's work.
>
> —1 Corinthians 3:12-13, NIV

Chapter Summary

The simplest way to avoid an ethical problem is not to have one. Easily said, right? Acting with integrity, respecting autonomy, and treating people fairly should not conflict with other ethical obligations. In this chapter, we have looked at the various components to good and ethical decision making. You have seen that right choices are dependent upon good information gathering. More so, emotional principles and solid values serve as the foundation of good decision making. There are many factors that can limit a good decision and even influence the coach to behave unethically. In the end, however, a decision is required, even if the decision is to make no decision.

Elena feels the tension of her job choice in the pit of her stomach. Old job at Vasserwerks, new job at Vasserwerks, or new job at Jago's? Those are her options. As her performance review date looms closer, she decides to try something she has never done before. She goes on a fast. After seeking advice from her priest on the best ways to fast, she goes several days without food. As she becomes hungry to the point of desperation, she realizes that money, status, or even the food in her refrigerator will not satisfy her need to feel fulfilled. She decides to stay with Vasserwerks and pursue the position downtown if her boss offers it to her.

What Do You Do?

Scenario A: Just as there is more than one way to catch a fish, there are many ways to acquire clients. As a coach, you can get clients by luring them away from other coaches, baiting them with special discounts, or by simply waiting. What is the most ethical way to "catch" clients? How do you decide what your client acquisition strategy will be?

Scenario B: Your client tells you she will sue you if you do not refund all the money to her that she spent on coaching with you for the past year. How do you go about making the decision as to how you will respond to this threat? What outside factors might influence your decision?

Scenario C: If you ask the client to refer you to others, he might think that you are greedy and you are only using him for your personal gain. If you don't ask the client to refer you, you might not have a client base big enough to sustain your business. How do you go about deciding whether or how to ask for the referrals?

Scenario D: Your family raised you to believe that customers and vendors will always try to cheat you. Your father repeatedly told you that in matters of money, people are not to be trusted. How do you decide whether to enter into a business contract?

End of Chapter Questions

- Do you find it more difficult to make an ethical decision when you know that no one will find out?

- What elements are necessary for you to make a good decision?

- What conflicts do you see when you consider the allocation of your resources?

- Doing what is best for the client might mean that you have to give up on other things. What would those things be?

CHAPTER 4
DEVELOPING AND MAINTAINING TRUST

"Never be afraid to trust an unknown future to a known God."

—*Corrie Ten Boom, (1892-1983)*

In this chapter, we will look at the effects of *trust* on coaching. Trust is a fundamental part of building a communication bridge between the client and the coach. To build that bridge, the coach must be worthy of the client's trust. Mistrust or fear causes communication to break down, essentially burning that bridge of trust. How—and to what extent—the coach maintains the confidentiality agreement is the cornerstone of this bridge. Trust is also a two-way street. We will look at the ways the coach can trust the client and the ways the client can trust the coach. The most successful results come when both parties trust the Holy Spirit. Without trust, we cannot push our clients outside their comfort zones.

After reading this chapter, you will be able to do the following:

- define trust and know its effects;
- explain the workings of the brain around trust issues;
- distinguish between trust and mistrust;
- evaluate a client's propensity toward trust;
- discover how much you trust the Holy Spirit to perfect the client.

Amir's Story

In the past ten years, Amir's efforts as a lobbyist have benefited several areas of the Middle East. Amir is now looking for a new coach. He has already had two coaches who really helped him move forward and gain valuable insight into his values and practices. However, in each case, he felt that the coach betrayed his trust. Because he holds a high-profile position as a political activist, confidentiality and anonymity are a must.

He wants to find a coach he can count on. He really doesn't care whether the coach is Christian, Muslim, or Jewish. He does feel that a coach with a strong religious background would be able to respect the sensitivities of the issues he faces. The coach should be able to understand where he is coming from—literally. Amir contacts an international coaching contracting agency that encourages him to develop a set of questions to use when interviewing a potential coach. They also send him several profiles of coaches with religious affinities. He enjoys looking at their websites and comparing the various ways the coaches present themselves. The degree to which the coach exhibits a high level of professionalism greatly influences his decision.

Common Challenges

Professionalism

A professional is someone who offers sufficiently high-quality work to be worth the hire. We distinguish between the amateur and the professional in this way: the pro is one who does the service at a level worthy of getting competitive compensation ("the big bucks"). For example, you might say, "My son is a professional artist." This implies skill, training, recognizable quality work, and integrity. To call yourself a professional implies that you believe you have a high level of distinction. The *profess*ional professes to quality. The professional not only professes a higher standard, but the professional also *practices* a higher standard.

Can someone watch a few videos about coaching and claim to know all about it? Hardly. Can someone practice coaching for many years and call himself a professional? Well, maybe.

> **Note**
> A 360-degree assessment tool asks questions about you from the perspective of your superiors, your peers, your subordinates, and your clients. There are numerous 360-degree assessment tools available. The Booth Co. administers my favorite (boothco.com.)

Again, this depends on the practitioner's definition of quality. Certainly, if clients continually pay the coach for his services, he must be offering some level of quality. Certifications that verify his credentials also speak to the quality of coaching he is able to offer. This, of course, leads to a discussion about the validity of a professional certification if there is not a rigorous testing and screening procedure behind it. We will examine this topic in detail in chapter nine. Nevertheless, the ethical coach should have a definition in mind as to what professionalism means.

As you consider your own professionalism, rank yourself on a scale of one (lowest) to five (highest) on the extent that you ALWAYS:

Keep confidentiality	1—2—3—4—5
Honor anonymity	1—2—3—4—5
Respect privacy	1—2—3—4—5
Tell the truth	1—2—3—4—5
Remain unbiased	1—2—3—4—5
Assess honestly	1—2—3—4—5

Unless you are extremely down on yourself or have an above-average sense of self-awareness, you most likely marked a four or five on each of the traits above. Most of us innately regard ourselves as being people of integrity. If you would like another person's perspective, ask your friends, family members, coworkers, clients, or boss how they would rate you on each of those traits listed.

All Men Are Created Equal

Amir believes all people should receive fair treatment. Having grown up in the United States, he is acutely aware of discrimination due to his heritage. Skin color, religious background, and sexual orientation should not influence the way his new coach treats him. He is not looking for a coach who agrees with him. He is also not looking for a coach who relates to him. He is looking for a coach who can follow his way of thinking and help him move forward. He wants a coach who will challenge him and help him think with renewed clarity.

When you are honest and fair, the client can be hopeful that you are a person of integrity. Such a coach holds dear the principle that "all men are created equal, [and that they] are endowed by their Creator with certain unalienable Rights" as stated in the Declaration of Independence. This does not mean the practice of coaching is uniform, static, or inflexible. Quite the opposite, coaching is quintessentially flexible, dynamic, and full of variety. You must know how to adapt to the client's context and know when and how to treat people as individuals. There is nothing wrong with having different prices, different operating hours, and different terms and conditions in your offering. With all that in mind, there is something wrong if those differences discriminate against protected minorities.

At the Heart of the Matter

Confidentiality and Anonymity

Amir's last coach was always happy to share his knowledge. One of his favorite expressions was, "I happen to know something about that." Unfortunately, he would also include political insider information he learned from Amir with other clients in his "I happen to know" statements. Amir found out about this one day while working out

at the gym. Another insider there was talking about a political initiative that was not public information. As it turned out, this insider learned about it from Amir's soon-to-be-former coach during a prayer breakfast. Soon after that, Amir ended the relationship with that coach.

The client's right to privacy is sacrosanct. The client should be able to trust that you will not communicate his beliefs, behaviors, or opinions to anyone else. In short, nothing the client tells you is up for discussion at the dinner table with your family or your Sunday school class (see Proverbs 11:13). Your job is to maintain this confidentiality unless the client explicitly gives you permission to share the information or legal constraints dictate otherwise. The client's right to privacy means he is free from unwanted public dissemination of his information in any form.

Privacy also includes the client's right to be left alone. When the client forms a working relationship with you, she must trust that you will keep her information secret. Obviously, disclosing the client's name is taboo. However, revealing the context of the client's data in such a way that others can guess who you're talking about is equally taboo. For example, the client has good things to say about you, and you want to post her remarks on your website or in a promotional brochure.

With permission (preferably in writing), this is possible. However, revealing a client's identity in any form without her permission might serve as the basis for a negligence claim in a court of law.

All coaching ethical codes require a contract between the coach and the client that spells out the level of confidentiality expected. Both parties should sign this contract in advance of the coaching. Basically, you must promise that you will keep your client's secrets. However, there are times when keeping a secret for life is not necessarily in the best interest of the client. If a divergence from the norm of total silence is a possibility in your coaching, you should stipulate this in your contract. For example, a corporation sponsoring coaching for its employees might require disclosure if the coach learns that the sponsored client has been misappropriating funds. In chapter six, we will look at the elements of a good coaching contract in more detail.

Factors That Muddle the Issue

Required Disclosure

Even though the coach promises to keep client information confidential, occasionally the law or a moral imperative may compel you to reveal something to another person. In most cases, the information revealed in a coach–client relationship is not under any legal protection. In an unregulated industry such as coaching, there are no laws requiring a coach to honor a code of silence. However, it is morally and ethically imperative that the coach maintain confidentiality. In most states, laws stipulate disclosure when someone is in peril. If a client tells you she is planning a murder or suicide, for example, you would be legally and morally obliged to inform either the police or other influential persons. If your client reveals to you that he is hiding a kidnapped thirteen-year-old in his basement, you would be obliged to inform the authorities of this. Again, most states and municipal laws require disclosure when there is legitimate reason to suspect significant harm. It is your duty, as a professional coach, to know how these laws read in your legal venue.

Confidentiality Does Not Go Both Ways

While your client has the benefit of confidentiality in the coaching relationship, the private information you tell a client does not have the same protection. Your client has the right to publish, preach, or talk about whatever you said in a coaching conversation. She can mention your name as her coach in any circle she chooses and reveal anything she wants to about you. For example, if you tell the client you are going skiing in Colorado next week, she is perfectly within her right to mention your trip to her friends on Facebook. Confidentiality is not a two-way street.

Recordkeeping

Many people would like to get Amir's cell phone number. Although he realizes he cannot hide from the public, he doesn't want just anyone calling him in the middle of the night. And since one of his fellow lobbyists found a swastika burned into the grass on his front lawn, Amir doesn't want his address to get into the wrong hands.

There are two sides to recordkeeping. On one side, many coaches take copious notes of the words, nuances, and ideas brought forward by the client in a coaching conversation. Other coaches might only occasionally jot down a point or two, but largely do not make any record of the exchange in any definitive form. Some coaches will take notes on paper and shred them immediately after the coaching meeting is finished.

If you were to have to prove your involvement in the development of a client, your notes would become important evidence. On one hand, having no orderly record of a client's interactions might appear as negligent if your practice were involved in a court case. On the other hand, if you don't have notes or records, there would be nothing to subpoena. An attorney can subpoena any records you keep, but only a court order actually requires you to provide the information. Before releasing any client information, you'll want to get a signed release agreement from the client.

Keep records in such a way that you can represent the interests of your clients fairly and honorably. Ethics expert Jory Fisher, for example, encourages the client to take her own notes and upload them to her personal file of Jory's online coaching platform. Jory also offers to record the conversations so the client can listen to them later. Obviously, she keeps these digital files under lock and key.

Another aspect of recordkeeping to keep in mind is that the IRS requires you to substantiate the amount of coaching you do. Credentialing agencies also ask for the names and contact data of clients so that they can verify your volume of coaching. That's it. More recordkeeping might be a good idea but is not required.

Statute of Limitations

All contracts fall under a *statute of limitations*—a timeframe within which a complaint can be filed against you in court—in every legal jurisdiction. In the United States, this ranges from three years in Alaska to ten years in Louisiana and everywhere in between. In England, the limitations are generally six years with no limitations for a fraudulent breach of trust (Limitation Act of 1980, chapter 58, part 1, section 21). Generally, the IRS has ten years to collect taxes you owe them, but you normally do not need to keep your financial records past six or seven years depending on the type of record in question. It is your duty as a professional coach to find and use a data storage solution applicable for your situation. Consulting a local tax advisor and/or a lawyer is a prudent idea. Bottom line: keeping records for seven years is a good benchmark.

CASE STUDY

As a coach, your practice is to take about a page worth of notes on your laptop during each coaching phone conversation. You like to write down the ideas and intentions that you hear from the client. You subsequently upload these notes into the client's digital file for safekeeping. One day, you receive a subpoena for all the records you have for a particular client. You review the notes you have taken and decide that the words you recorded were your ideas and thoughts and not those of the client. To make things easier, you delete the client's digital file and tell the court that you no longer have any notes for that client. Have you behaved ethically?

QUESTION

What is your practice of keeping tabs on your clients?

Getting Permission

The freedom to use someone else's words is usually a matter of simply getting permission. You might be surprised how willing your clients are to give you an endorsement. For example, I have *carte blanche* permission from several of my clients to use their names and recommendations in any format. This is the exception, however, not the rule. Most of the time, I need to get a specific allowance from the client to use his comments about me for a specific purpose. A prudent practice is to get permission in writing, even if it is a simple e-mail or text message. For instance, if you want to use a client's name in advertising or publications, send him an email to which he can reply with his approval. You can even offer to use an alias: "Thomas from Pittsburgh." This demonstrates in your presentation that you honor the anonymity of the client.

Identity Protection

No one who is listening to or reading anything you say about a client should be able to figure out the client's actual identity. This is true whether you're talking to one person or to a group during a lecture. For example, during a presentation, I might say, "I have a client who is a pastor in Fairbanks." Insofar as there are more than thirty pastors in that city, his identity remains hidden. But saying, "I'm coaching a pastor in Two Rivers," would be too specific because there are only four pastors in Two Rivers.

In the same way, coaches should obtain permission for passing on contact information to another party. Whenever possible, clients should agree to the coach sharing their information.

Let's look at some examples:

Example A: A company's Human Resources Department contracted with you to do the coaching for its employees. As such, the HR manager is your contact point for all data exchange. Now, the accounting department manager is calling and requesting details about the clients. Any sponsor (i.e., company, parent, spouse, supervisor) has the right to know that the money is well spent, but the first person to inform the company's representative about his or her progress should be the client. For the coach to reveal any information, the client needs to agree. The best way to handle this is to include permissible avenues of disclosure in the contract established at the beginning of the coaching relationship. Alternatively, you could tell the client about the request and he or she could contact accounting.

Example B: A prospective client is a friend of someone you have already coached. Mentioning your former client would be a good way to establish credibility with the new client. This is not a problem as long as you already have the former client's permission to do so.

Example C: A client has a health issue that one of your professional colleagues—who is an expert on this type of ailment—would serve well. The best choice would be to refer the client to your colleague directly or to get permission to contact the colleague for the client. Either way, the client should agree to allow her contact information or health concern to be shared.

Example D: A client offers a service you feel would benefit one of your friends. You can recommend the service to your friend without revealing that the provider is actually one of your clients. You could also get permission to reveal to your friend your association with the client. Alternatively, you can ask the client to contact your friend and use you as a reference.

QUESTION

When have you really wanted to share something that a client has told you?

Exercise

- Do you trust the Holy Spirit to come up with the best solution for your client?

- Define for yourself the word "professional." Start with: "I am …"

- What types of information obtained from a client should you keep confidential?

- Is there a topic that is a deal-breaker for you as a coach?

Which of My Values Is Relevant Here?

Amir considers himself a person of faith. He has seen too much in his life that he cannot explain without acknowledging a higher power. When he looks at all the complexities around him, he cannot deny the existence of God. While he doesn't consider himself very religious, he would describe himself as believer in the one God, maker of heaven and earth. He wants his new coach to understand what it means to rely on God as the author and finisher of his faith. He wants his coach to understand what he means when he says that he trusts God for everything.

Trust

The word *trust* has its origins in the German word *trost*, which means to comfort, to reassure someone that everything is all right. Where there is trust, there is a sense of confidence and comfort in the (or your) relationship with another person. Coaching is an intimate place that the coach and client share. Trust implies that the client feels you have their well-being at heart, and it is imperative for an authentic coaching relationship to occur.

In chapter three, I noted that trust is the opposite of fear. When we trust someone, we depend on that person to be who he or she claims to be. Likewise, if we trust in a company or a thing, we believe that it will do what its advertising or image claims. If I look at a chair with four legs and solid-looking construction, I trust that it will hold me when I sit on it. But I also know looks can sometimes be deceiving, and as a cautious adult, I've learned to test a chair before plopping down.

Skepticism develops when evidence seems askew with our sense of reality. Cynicism evolves when mistrust becomes the person's reality. *Forming a true coaching relationship based on anything other than trust is an exercise in futility.* Psychotherapy researcher Dr. Tim Bond writes, "Trust is a relationship of sufficient quality and resilience to withstand the challenges arising from difference, inequality, risk, and uncertainty" (Bond 2007, 436).

We cannot touch or measure trust. It is an intangible quality based on client risk and coach obligation to not disappoint the trust-giving party. There is no confusion in trust. It exists, or it doesn't. If any inclination towards mistrust exists, then true trust is not present. Giving someone your complete trust is one of the most difficult things you can do. We have all had our trust abused and hate the feeling of betrayal. Trust is easily broken. Trust is fragile. However, trust can also be amicable and friendly.

Faith

Faith assumes complete trust. A deed done in good faith is one where all involved perceive the intentions and actions to be honest and integral. Faith, if you will, is a higher level of trust. Faith is blind trust, the trust in the unseen. The word "faith" is often used to describe our trust in God but faith is a more comprehensive form of trust. We trust God to be true to His Word and to keep His promises. Ethically, we know God is just and has our best interests at heart. We can hope that our clients will trust us as we conform our practices to a higher ethical code. Moreover, we can hope that our clients will have faith in us as we conform ourselves to the image of Christ.

What Are the Dangers?

Amir feels like a wounded animal. He still has difficulty believing that his previous coaches could have betrayed his trust. He feels unsure about what he can do to overcome his fear of betrayal. The only thing that comes to mind is to try again. This makes him feel vulnerable and weak. He decides that he will give a prospective coach three months to prove trustworthy to him.

Betrayal

Trust usually takes a time to build, and it can be destroyed in mere seconds. Trust expert Shabbir postulates that it takes about the same amount of time to rebuild trust the second time as it did to build it the first time.

There is, however, a level of trust that transcends the immediate. A type of permanent trust can develop when confidence in the other person is so high that a bridge forms over troubled waters. Despite bad days and minor betrayals, the trustee keeps on trusting, ignoring mishaps and minor malevolence. Shabbir writes, "There is an element of belief that one day that person would do as you have perceived. It is as if you have already seen the actions that person would do one day. That is trust" (Shabbir 2010).

Most cases of client trust betrayal involve a coach with a loose tongue (Proverbs 21:23). Coaches often find themselves in a quandary about something a client said, did, or will do, and may mention something in passing without considering it a transgression. It is important to keep in mind that gossiping about a client is careless. Treating the information the client gives you with care is a way of showing respect. Betraying trust comes at a cost and must be avoided with the exception of a situation when it is in the best interest of the community at large to disclose a client's private statements.

A good example of such a situation would be a client sharing that he wants to go on a shooting rampage, and the coach thinks he might really do it. The coach needs to react quickly. However, before going to the police or the media with a client's information, the coach should know her options. If the client is directly posing a threat to another person, then the situation becomes more critical. If the client is threatening to hurt himself, then the dilemma becomes tangible. The coach should have a good "what if" scenario worked out in her mind for such situations. It is incumbent on the coach to know the local laws and practices for how, when, and where to disclose such information. In some places, the law requires professionals to report impending danger. In other places, the regulations leave such matters to the discretion of the individual coach.

Ultimately, the coach makes decisions based on the firm belief that she is doing what is best for the client. This is a value judgment that the coach needs to be prepared to stand by before someone blows the whistle. In such situations, having a mentor coach becomes invaluable. We will discuss this more fully in chapter nine.

The Trusting Brain

If there is a strong emotional connection between two people, the propensity to learn from each other increases dramatically. It is simply easier for the brain to make decisions when one deems the other person reliable, truthful, and fair (Paine 2000, 320). As already mentioned, the brain in survival mode does not trust. Fear, stress, uncertainty, and doubt all stimulate the limbic system to exude danger signals to the body. Research shows that when a person feels trusting and opens himself to the feeling of comfort that comes with trust, the brain emits high levels of serotonin (5-HT) and oxytocin (Zak 2008). When the level of trust increases, the brain produces even more oxytocin. In other words, people who feel trusted become more trustworthy as a result of increased oxytocin levels in their brains.

Recall also the discussion in chapter one about mirror neurons—the monkey see, monkey do syndrome. When the coach trusts the client to be creative and resourceful, the client trusts the coach to be the same. In contrast, without a high level of oxytocin, people tend to behave more rashly and become more willing to punish others even if it hurts them to do so. Mistrust causes a decrease in oxytocin levels and can cause us to become defensive.

What Are the Opportunities?

Trust Is a Reciprocal Relationship

At the Professional Christian Coaching Institute, a favorite saying among the faculty is "trust the client, trust the process." When you trust the client to make untethered decisions, you don't have to manipulate, coerce, or even give advice. Trusting the process means recognizing that the client owns the results. The client is smart enough to know what works for him and what doesn't. Former ICF president Diane Brennen says that holding the client in unconditional positive regard creates trust, openness, and honesty. "It allows for deep dialogue" (Brennen 2008, 244). Therefore, it follows that trust is a cornerstone in the relationship-building process with the client.

Trust Is Good; Control Is Better

It was Vladimir Lenin who is thought to have coined the phrase, "Trust is good; control is better." My spin on the idea is this: *Trust is good; control is expensive.* It takes a lot of effort, regulation, laws, bureaucracy, and time to actually control whether someone is doing what they promised. The coaching relationship simply works better when both parties trust each other to do what they said they would do. This goes for all coaching interactions, and especially for the initial written contract.

A coaching contract can be as specific or nebulous as comfort dictates for both parties. If there is a point in the agreement that makes one party nervous or uncomfortable, client and coach should completely discuss the issue and spell it out clearly. When trust is high from the get-go, there is little need to spell out all possible contingencies and foreseeable conflicts. Additionally, high-trust contracts are more streamlined and call for fewer external verification processes because both parties expect the other to act honorably. People prone to high trust prefer a more intuitive negotiating style. In contrast, research done by Professor Yu-Te Tu shows that people who are less trusting tend to prefer a more factual and analytical approach to negotiation. (Tu 2014, 263). Indeed, trust is a prerequisite for negotiating and working with clients.

Who Is Going to Know?

Hiding the Truth

For the client to be able to explore new emotions and unacknowledged or unrecognized truths, the coach has the task of creating a safe, open, and honest relationship with the client. As an ethical coach, you should always tell the truth. However, you don't always have to tell the truth immediately. My Professional Christian Coaching Institute colleague, Susan Whitcomb, likes to say, "Truth is never optional; however, the timing and technique are." It is possible that the present situation is about as good as it is going to get, and waiting to tell the truth might be the best option. That said, telling a client something you know to be false would be lying. If you purposefully omit information that is relevant to the client's situation or intentionally fail to correct a misperception, that lack of disclosure will likely be construed as deception.

Very often, clients hire a coach because that coach has specialized training and experience. The client wants to glean from the coach's knowledge. Does this mean that the client hired the coach to give advice? No, it does not. However, neither does it mean that the coach should hide the truth. What it means is that the coach is able to help the client create a platform for discovering the truth. Sometimes, the ethical consideration of a matter is relevant and significant. Not telling the client about potential marital impropriety might save the client from much grief. However, revealing potential infidelity to the client might save him much embarrassment. What, then, becomes the coach's role in such situations? The answer depends on the type of relationship established with the client. I have numerous clients getting business coaching from me; in a business relationship, such knowledge

DEVELOPING AND MAINTAINING TRUST

is irrelevant and not part of the coaching agreement. Any expressed infidelity that the client shares with me has little effect on our coaching conversations. Other clients getting life coaching from me really need to understand the intentions of their significant others. Only then can they fully explore the possibilities before them. The coach's job, therefore, is to help the client set up a platform on which he can discover the truth relevant to his situation. Truth-finding in coaching is a discovery process.

<hr/>
QUESTION

You believe that the client's wife is cheating on him. Do you tell the client?
<hr/>

The Dark Side of Trust

There is a dark side to trust that is described by authors Skinner, Dietz, and Weibel. The dark side of trust is when the client tells you something about which you are uncomfortable knowing. Going back to the infidelity example, the client tells you that he is cheating on his wife. What do you do with this information? "A scenario of inappropriately placed trust *can* become a poisoned chalice if requests for that trust are contrary to the trustee's better judgment and create an uncomfortable obligation" (Skinner, Dietz, and Weibel 2014, 212). For this reason, some coaches build a provision into the confidentiality clause of the coaching contract that provides for a certain amount of whistle blowing. For example, I've seen confidentiality clauses that allow for the release of secret information after six months or maybe even six years. Personally, I have never had to rely on a contract to guide me on this point because my clients always seem to desire to come clean. Often, they are actually looking for a means to confess their sins. What is important here is planning ahead of time for what you will do if a disclosure issue comes up. By pre-planning scenarios for extreme situations, you are ready and able to deal with the dynamics a client brings to the session. Obviously, one of those scenarios might include terminating the coach–client relationship if you feel uncomfortable keeping his secrets.

How Do I Do It Right?

Amir is excited about finding the right coach. To his surprise, he notices that profiles of women coaches appeal to him more than the profiles of men. This intrigues him. Normally men with his cultural background do not look to a woman for help. He notices that the profiles he has viewed so far show the women as strong in terms of empathy and the men as strong in terms of direct communication.

Empathy

Understanding and sharing the feelings of others is the essence of empathy. Most of us simply assume that our feelings and our pain are obvious to others. Unfortunately, this is not the case. For example, men and women could perceive your personal situation differently. "Men don't experience empathy with someone who is in pain or who has been unfair, whereas women do" (Rock 2009, 183). On one hand, many coaches will intuitively know the client's feelings before the client himself is even aware of his emotions. These coaches speak to the heart of the client. On the other hand, many coaches base their perceptions only on the spoken word of the client and purposely leave speculation out of the picture. These coaches speak to the client's head. Both approaches are useful to the client and

form the basis of the niche in which the coach ultimately specializes. On the ethics side of empathy, the essential thing to remember is that a coach may not coerce a client. A client has the right to make his own decision without the fear of emotive coercion by the coach.

Direct Communication

When coaching, we often perceive something that might be useful to tell the client. We call this direct communication, and it is an encouraged competency. Understanding how and when to share such insight is an entirely different proficiency. Addressing an issue right away works well in some situations. Sharing a direct observation later (not immediately) works better in other situations, which is why many coaches take notes that they can refer to when the time is right. Either way, the coach should provide feedback to the client in a way that it is constructive.

The client should know that you are on her side and respect her decisions. Having a basis of trust is essential when giving feedback to the client. In life coaching, an observation of the client's values is often a good starting point for direct communication. A permission question is one that asks the client whether this would be a good time to interject an observation through direct communication. The client should feel equally comfortable saying yes or no to your request for permission. The direct communication should then proceed, using vocabulary that affirms the client's strengths and abilities (Rock and Page 2009, 358).

Calling for Back-up

When it comes to giving the client comments about the ethics of her plans, we need to stop and check whether such feedback is really in the client's best interest. Most of the time, our own ethical barometer will guide us (Carroll and Shaw 2013, 353). We need not rush off as soon as we hang up the phone to call the ICF Assist Line or our mentor coach with our perceived predicament. Our own gut feeling, our first reaction, our intuition is usually enough to gauge the potency of the problem. There are times, however, when we really should seek counsel yet hesitate too long or simply don't do it. Instead, we rationalize a way to handle the situation. As hours and days go by, this rationalization becomes right in our own minds regardless of what is in the code of ethics or what our mentor coach might have recommended. Studies show that once we make a difficult decision, we tend to prove to ourselves logically that it was indeed the best choice (Smith 2012, 24). More often than not, the human tendency is

to avoid controversy and take the path of least resistance.

Again, do what is best for the client, not for yourself. If you need advice and reassurance from an outside source, get it. Negligence results from needing to do something yet doing nothing instead.

Trusting the Holy Spirit

As a Christian coach, your additional task is to allow the Holy Spirit to be a part of the coaching process. At CCNI we say, "The centerpiece of Christian coaching is the client's awareness of where God is leading a person" ("CCNI definition of Christian coaching," n.d.). Practicing building awareness brings your professional coaching to another level. Not only do you profess quality, but you also profess Christ (See 1 Corinthians 2). There are two words in the banner of Christian coaching. You must honor *Christ* first and foremost, and you must also honor *coaching*. In terms of trust, the Christian coach should be able to trust the Holy Spirit to finish the good work He has started in the client (Hebrews 12:2). Ultimately, the Holy Spirit is in charge of perfecting the client, not the coach.

QUESTION

Do you trust the Holy Spirit to come up with the best solution for the client?

Chapter Summary

When we trust our client, we endorse her character the way it is; we affirm her capabilities without judgment. Hence, we endorse her status in general terms as well as within a given social network. We respect our clients for who they are in Christ and demand no changes. The change that transpires during a coaching conversation is a change instigated by, through, for, and within the client.

In today's culture, we move in many different circles—our lives are interconnected. Gone are the days when a person could isolate himself to the point where trust became unnecessary to survive. Integrity is necessary for the professional to maintain any level of public trust. Likewise, it is necessary to behave in accordance with the acknowledged values and objectives of professionalism. Ethical coaches keep promises, maintain confidentiality, and practice professionalism. The ethical coach is sensitive to the vulnerabilities of the client and recognizes that a client in fear is a person in need of careful attention.

Amir knows he will find the right coach in time. He actually enjoys the process of interviewing each of the coaches. He finds most of them to be amicable and accommodating and none try to push him to contract for their services. So far, each of the coaches he has talked to has volunteered to help him find the right coach by offering referrals. Coaching, it seems, is not a one-size-fits-all industry.

What Do You Do?

Scenario A: Your good friend asks you to coach her husband. After several sessions, he reveals that he is having an affair. What are your responsibilities to him in terms of confidentiality? Would you feel obliged to inform your friend, his wife? Even if you say nothing, how will your relationship with your friend change?

Scenario B: I'm in a peer group for coaching training. Sometimes I play the role of the coach, sometimes the client. Often we get together with the entire class that includes students not in my peer group. My peer coach reveals some information about me to the entire class that I shared while playing the role of the client. Is this okay because everyone in the class is in the same boat, or has the peer coach violated my right to privacy?

Scenario C: The client comes to you with a proposal to build a deck for you behind your backdoor instead of paying money for your coaching services. Could a conflict of interest exist here? What if the resulting deck is shoddy and displeasing to you? Bartering has been a financial practice since before the invention of money. However, earning money and paying taxes has become a part of our lives. When the coach can internally justify the goods-for-services exchange, then he has fulfilled his moral obligation. However, he must also justify the external obligation for paying the taxes on the value-added new deck sitting outside of his backdoor.

Scenario D: A human resources professional, who is also an internal coach, learns that three of her clients will be let go in two months. She has several meetings with them before that date—should she tell them? Company policy typically trumps client confidentiality. Coaches need a reminder that if a company pays them, they might also be bound by the policies of the company. They need to know the company rules in advance and, if a conflict should arise, which rules apply. The coaching contract should clearly state all of these stipulations.

End of Chapter Questions

- During a coaching call, does it sometimes feel that you can't wait to give the client your opinion?

- Your client says, "I'm going to kill myself." How do you react as a coach?

- What level of professionalism are you content with in your coaching?

- To what extent do you truly trust the Holy Spirit to do the good work He has started in the client?

CHAPTER 5
MULTIPLE ROLES AND RELATIONSHIPS IN COACHING

"We must learn to live together as brothers or perish together as fools."

—Martin Luther King Jr., (1929-1968)

We all come from different places. This chapter focuses on how our cultural backgrounds, beliefs, and even our experiences might create tension that could lead to conflict. Religion and heritage are strong foundations upon which many people build their worldview. When the ways and means of staying true to one's mindset clash with one's practice, the result is a conflict of interest. Nowhere in the coaching relationship is there more evidence for this than in a dual relationship. A coach may find that he plays several roles in his life that conflict with his coaching role. Here we want to look at the ways in which a coach can mitigate or avoid the impact these roles have on the coaching relationship. We will examine specific dual roles that could occur within the context of internal coaching, group coaching, and team coaching. Finally, we will learn a few conflict resolution strategies.

After reading this chapter, you will be able to do the following:

- find ways to deal with dual-role conflicts;
- explain the difference between playing by the rules and living by the rules;
- distinguish culture sensitivities in the context of conflict;
- evaluate the need for possible delegation and mediation;
- discover how adhering to one's values can create conflict.

Father Kahill's Story

Father Kahill is a jack-of-all-trades. Not only does he function as priest and regional inspector for his parish, he is also a town council member and the coach of the local T-ball team. He seems to be everywhere, and everyone knows him. He is a servant leader and a pillar of the community he loves. People call him "Father K" and come to him for all kinds of advice and counseling. In the past few years, however, he's found that using the coaching approach gets better long-term results. He calls this service "talking." He does not charge for his services directly, as his role as clergy takes care of his needs.

Recently, he has noted an increasing number of people asking for favors. In other words, Father Kahill often feels forced to provide services beyond normal expectations. Another matter of concern: a culturally different population has moved into his parish. These folks bring a rich sense of family that Father Kahill cherishes. At the same time, they have greater expectations of him than he has previously experienced. Indeed, his private sphere seems to be decreasing as his growing responsibilities increase.

In order to be fair to all of his parishioners, Father Kahill resolves to find a way to equalize his efforts to help people. It's not that he wants to do less; he just wants to do things more equitably. He sets out to discover a means of balance and fairness.

Common Challenges

A lady in Father Kahill's parish likes to visit his office on Tuesdays to tell him stories about the old country. After several weeks of this, he realizes that her needs are more than strolls down memory lane. Father K has determined that she is looking for a way to find her place in this new world. The coaching approach serves these conversations well.

Heritage

The search for one's roots is a matter of keen interest to many clients. Indeed, each of us is a product of our past. A sense of heritage gives a client an emotional anchor and feeling of belonging. Stories and memories from the past are important to clients and one should not take them lightly. Cherokee Elder J.T. Garrett recounts an anecdote from his childhood:

> One day many years ago, when I was still a little one, I was sitting with my grandfather by the edge of the Oconaluftee River. He was sitting on a rock enjoying the afternoon sun while I was playing in the water.
>
> "What do you see?" he asked me.
>
> "I see the water," I said.
>
> "What else do you see," he asked.

> "Well, I see the fish," I answered, because there were little minnows swimming around in the water.
>
> "What else do you see?" he asked.
>
> "I see the rock," I said.
>
> "What else do you see?" he asked again.
>
> "Well, I don't see anything else." I answered.
>
> "No," he said, "What you see is a reflection of the whole world before you." (Garrett and Garrett 2002, 20)

Each of us is a reflection of the world we have experienced. Each of us bears the marks and scars, blessings and pleasures of a culture, worldview, and perspective unique to us individually. The coach is conscious of the cultural differences the client brings to the table and endeavors to respect and honor that mindset at all times. More specifically, if a coach were to disrespect or dishonor a client's cultural values, a conflict is in the making.

The coach will always find some of the cultural norms and values of his client to be a bit out of his comfort zone. My coaching colleague Bryan Pettet says, "All coaching is multicultural coaching." Many clients regard their genetic heritage as an important factor in the explanation of their specific behavior. For instance, the client may attribute her frugality as a trait passed down from her parents. The client's convictions, attributable to his worldview, might affect others factors that are more general. For example, a client who sees himself as a product of creation will reflect a naturalist's point of view. The respect he holds for God's creation is central to his worldview.

Lost in Translation

One of Father Kahill's coaching clients likes to mix English with her native language. At first, Father Kahill was unsure that he could coach her at all. Yet, as the relationship progressed, he noticed that the client would find deeper meaning to words she used as she struggled to find the right English words. The process of searching for words promoted the discovery of the nuances of ideas. The challenge for Father Kahill was to give the client time for her exploration.

You may interpret the words your client chooses in a much different way than she intended. For instance, the client might describe her relationship with her boss as "okay." You interpret this to mean above average or satisfactory. She, on the other hand, thinks of "okay" as being just below average and

unsatisfactory. Another problem could be one of transliteration. The literal meaning of the words does not equal the affective meaning of the words. This often happens when the two speakers have a different base language.

Here's an example of a potential problem involved in interpreting someone else's language into your own. The following quote is in the original German: "*Was der Mensch ist, wozu er lebt, was er werden kann oder sollte, hängt von dem Weltbild und Menschenbild ab, das ein Individuum in der Auseinandersetzung mit seiner persönlichen Geschichte und der Kultur erworben hat*" (Migge 2010, 42). The literal translation is as follows: "What man is, why he lives, and what he can or should become, depends on his worldview and mindset. He is an individual in tension with his personal history and his acquired culture."

The essence of the original quote does not entirely come out in my direct translation. It really needs a more free translation to communicate that man "lives in the tension between his personal history and his present lifestyle." I use this example to show that regardless of one's familiarity with a culture, mindset, or even language, the coach will subjectively translate the interpretation of what the client says and means.

QUESTION

How comfortable are you with the tension of multicultural coaching?

A Biblical Worldview

Clients expect Father Kahill to refer to the Bible. However, some of them become a bit miffed when he asks, "What does the Bible say about that?" They would much rather that he quote a Bible verse than think themselves through a biblical example. Nevertheless, Father Kahill feels strongly that the coaching initiative needs to come from within the client.

Sometimes, the client will make moral judgments that may or may not align with your understanding of a biblically based worldview. If coaching with a biblical worldview is your objective, you might experience some tension when the client believes differently. If that's the case, what should you do?

If you feel that the client's worldview is contrary to the Bible, you have a few options. First of all, you can encourage the client to explore the Bible for herself. Secondly, you can ask permission to share your view of the Scriptures regarding the point in question. Third, you can refer the client to a pastor/priest/rabbi or other spiritual counselor.

Ultimately, the client will make an evaluation based on the values she holds to be obligatory to her own culture or subculture. Even though the client might feel that she is making her decision consciously, it is more likely subconscious. Those inbuilt moral templates fashioned by her environment, relationships, and experiences will subtly influence her decision. Helping the client to create awareness involves having the coach help the client see beyond her fixed perceptions of the world, looking instead to a wider, more ecumenical worldview. However, when not done with respect and honor for the client's background and heritage, the coach is setting himself up for a discrimination case.

QUESTION

When a client is notably different from you, how do you respond to them?

At the Heart of the Matter

Values

Our past and present experiences intertwine to create a value system. This value system affects our actions. Values dictate the nature of our thoughts. Principles dictate the nature of our actions. Combined, values and principles determine our behaviors. Decision-making processes develop and fully establish themselves by the time a person reaches adulthood.

Coaches need to be aware of how unconscious thoughts influence their own thinking process. Most of our reactions as coaches are preprogramed expressions that formed long before the coaching conversation actually began. The ethical coach is aware of his value system and recognizes the role it plays in the coaching relationship. The coach needs to be fully present in order to self-manage without allowing the emotions of the client to overrun him. When the coach knows and stands firm on his values, he has an anchor for the times that the client seems ungrounded.

TIP

Values dictate the nature of our thoughts. Principles dictate the nature of our actions. Combined, values and principles determine our behaviors.

QUESTION

When was the last time you made a list of the values that motivate you?

Divergent values

Father Kahill hears things about the people he loves on nearly a daily basis. This encourages him to pray for them. Often, people come to him with ideas and plans that are diametrically opposed to his values. Most of the time, the non-directive coaching approach serves him well, and the client can move forward within his or her own value system. Other times, the client's intended goal is so far off Father Kahill's belief system that he has to refer the client to someone else. He keeps a list of professionals handy for just such occasions. He wonders about the best and most expedient way to refer his clients to someone else. He decides that he will bring this up in the next meeting of the local business owners.

Our values originate from many places. A professional code, research, experience, peer coaches, mentor coaches, supervisors, and many other resources help the coach form a basis for confident, justified, and ethical decisions. However, the things we hold worthy of respect determine the value we give them. What happens when one of the coach's strong values is opposed to that of the client's?

Let's pick a relatively benign example to illustrate. You, the coach, are a vegetarian. Not eating meat is a strong value to which you adhere and practice. A potential client who is a butcher comes to you for coaching. In fact, he is a slaughterhouse worker. You simply cannot get your head around his profession and suggest that he look for another coach. You can't just leave the butcher to hang out to dry, however; that would be abandonment. As a professional, you should have in your toolbox a list of qualified references for when you feel that you are not able to continue coaching a particular client. Preferably, your list of other coaches will be easily accessible and available to the client, and he will appreciate your assistance in helping him find the right one.

QUESTION

What are some values a client might have that could conflict with your own?

Similar Values

The more typical dilemma facing the Christian coach is not divergent value systems but similar ones. As my colleague Michael Pfau asserts, the more you identify with the client's situation, the more likely you are to get "hooked" into the client's dilemma. Your ability to coach objectively is hampered when this happens. People of your church, social club, or other subculture might have so much in common with you and you might know them so well that a precarious "dual role" develops. You become friend and coach. "The client's culture, maturity, and presenting problem are probably some of the most important factors determining the appropriateness of establishing a dual relationship with a client" (Zur 2007, 39). The ethical coach needs to know when the situation lends itself to a correct coaching relationship and when it doesn't.

Factors That Muddle the Issue

Creating Awareness Can Create Conflict

The ethical Christian coach is not only concerned with having an awareness of his own values, but also endeavors to help the client create deeper awareness of her values. The coach helps the client discover new thoughts, new beliefs, and new perceptions. By helping the client see her enemy's perspective, for example, the client might actually develop a sense of empathy for the other person's experience. This might bring the client to a state of tension as she begins to sympathize with the viewpoints of her opponent. If the client has a more choleric personality, there might be some hostility involved in the coaching session. A client who feels tense is not in a place of safety.

It might be useful to note here that certain personality types are prone to conflict avoidance. Those include people who by nature prefer to avoid conflict, those who are very detail oriented and/or compulsive, and those who have a tendency to be highly sensitive. The coach should not try to force the client to see things in a new way.

The Risk of Religion

People often seek out Father Kahill because he is a priest. The piety and the sanctity of the church give many clients a sense of comfort, even protection. Father Kahill, however, is acutely aware that there are wolves in sheep's clothing, and that not all men of the cloth are men of integrity. Many people enter the doors of his church skeptically and even afraid at times. Nonetheless, he is happy that new people seek him out to talk. In every initial conversation, he wants to convey how sincere he is about the client finding her own way. At the same time, he needs the client to be aware of his dependency on God's Spirit to direct and guide the conversation.

Can a client trust a coach to be impartial when the coach bases his coaching on the Bible? There is much skepticism behind the hiring of a coach who has "found religion." Usually, animosity or acceptance of a biblically based coach results from the prospective client's past encounters. In my experience, a client vetting a coach is often quite forthright and direct with their questions. Say, for example, that your initial conversation with the client goes something like this:

"I am looking for a coach with strong Christian values." *Good thing, that's me.*

"I see on your website that you are a 'biblically based' coach. I don't think my Human Resources Department is going to be overly enthusiastic about contracting with a religious fanatic." *Well, I am not ashamed of the Gospel of Christ. Indeed, the Bible affects my worldview in a significant way. Whether it will affect your worldview is entirely up to you.*

It is a fair assumption that the vast majority of coaches believe no one has universally established one single source, belief structure, or ethical foundation as the sole basis for all moral conduct. Most people see followers of a religion as being above average in their ability to make morally correct decisions. By definition of their religious beliefs, faith-based coaches have a built-in dual role as an ambassador of that religion. Rowson states, "Religion gives [believers] a worldview that has emotional and intellectual coherence and a sense of purpose: as individuals they know who they are, where they are intended to go, and where to look for guidance on their journey" (Rowson 2006, 23). However, Rowson's analysis leads to the conclusion that when a person with only one basis of ethics acts in a professional capacity, he might not be fully trustworthy because he is not open to seeing things from different perspectives (Rowson 2006, 37). Rowson might argue that the Christians are *blinded by the light*, so to speak.

John 1:5 shows us that as Christians, we see this light as the creative force

that allows us to discern God's perspective on an issue. This *true* perspective comes as a result of living according to the code that Jesus gave us (John 8:32). Rowson does not discount the validity of a religious professional being able to act in a correct ethical manner. However, he does admonish the religious professional to be upfront with his beliefs so that consumers of his services know what they are buying (Rowson 2006, 37). I agree.

To date, the majority of my clients are not Christians. However, ALL of my clients know that I am a Christian and that I base my highest values on biblical principles. In other words, I see no reason why my religious beliefs should create a dual-role conflict. I can be an ambassador for Christ *and a good coach* at the same time.

QUESTION

Are there any points of your religion with which you disagree?

Look at the following quote from Boss (2008):

It is easy for religious ethics, once set adrift, to become grounded on the rocky shores of cultural relativism. When this happens, religion can become a destructive force by sanctifying cultural customs that are unjust and limiting one's conception of the moral community. (p. 187)

Boss's criticism is that religious efforts to win converts sometimes compromise values for convenience. Let's say a missionary arrived on an island where the natives worshiped trees as gods. The missionary could twist the Gospel to sound like Christ should be their God because He died on a tree. Sorry, but in my hermeneutics, it is possible to compare Jesus to a lamb, a ransom, or even a rock—but not a tree. The ethical Christian coach should not reinterpret the Gospel to accommodate a client's perspective. Doing so would not only exhibit a lack of integrity; it could border on sacrilege.

No Harm, No Foul. Right?

When a Christian coach does not play by the rules, he or she dishonors the name of Christ. In the broader sense, actions contrary to biblical truth contribute to the impression that Christians are hypocrites. The biblical worldview professed by the Christian should be more than a label. It should also be more than a habit. Having a strong religious base allows us to think and behave in certain ways without much deliberation or debate. The secularist will argue that the Christian coach is merely mirroring the behavior he sees relevant in his Christian subculture. What a nonbeliever cannot see is that the Christian is hopefully behaving in a certain way due to the influence of the Holy Spirit.

Without the added influence of the Holy Spirit, the coach is left to his own devices. When a Christian coach does not practice what he preaches, it reduces his ethical witness to what is called an *a priori moral theory*—his thinking is a product of study, not witness. When this happens, the coach believes he is right, yet does not get confirmation from the Holy Spirit. This implies that the coach believes he is good because he wants to be good. Without the intention of wrongdoing, there is no wrong done. No foul, no harm, right? Wrong (Hosea 4:9; Matthew 23:27). A professional does as he professes. He professes to do good because the ethical code, the biblical code, and the active prompting of the Holy Spirit confirm his actions.

Exercise

- What areas and aspects of your life will you not allow a client to infringe upon?

- How do you preplan to remove yourself from potential conflicts of interest?

- You really like one of your clients and feel that she would be a good person with whom to share your problems. Would that be overstepping the line?

- Can I coach two people from the same organization?

What Are the Dangers?

The town where Father Kahill lives and works is not very large. In fact, he feels that he knows almost everyone by sight and most by name. It is entirely possible that a prospective client will interact with him on several levels. For example, Thomas regularly comes to Father Kahill just to talk. Thomas regularly attends Father Kahill's church services, is the dad of one of Father Kahill's T-ball kids, and is his banker. Father Kahill has laid out a firm written coaching contract with Thomas. In this agreement, both client and coach have promised to point out immediately when there is an overlapping role or conflict of interest. When such things come up, Father Kahill asks Thomas whether he is comfortable continuing. On very few occasions, Thomas has felt inhibited sharing something with Father Kahill.

Dual Roles

A dual role is when you have two relationships with the client. On one hand, you are her coach; on the other, you are something else, such as Sunday school teacher, boss, family member, friend, or the sole supplier of her favorite maple syrup from Saskatchewan. Can you be both? Yes, you can. Can it create a conflict? Yes, it can! If the supply of maple syrup from Saskatchewan

is particularly low and the client wants to end her coaching relationship with you, then the client might fear that you will withhold the syrup if she does not continue the coaching.

Yes, you can offer both services to the client. The cleanest way to do this is to clearly delineate, preferably in writing, the separation of each role before the coaching relationship begins. Here's a personal example. In addition to being a coach, I am also a certified assessor of a 360feedback survey. If a client of mine wants to take the survey, she should know that I am able to administer the 360: (1) at no extra cost to the client, (2) for administrative costs only, (3) with an exorbitant upcharge. I spell this out before the client feels manipulated into getting something that she did not bargain for.

QUESTION

Are you an MLM distributor? If so, how does that affect your coaching?

Let the Reader Beware

Conflict of interest from a dual relationship resulting in a disadvantage to the client is the most prevalent reason for a complaint against a coach. If you're not careful to guard yourself against conflict of interest from a potentially inappropriate dual role, you may find yourself in front of a coaching review board. One of the other more common complaints against coaches is that they behaved inappropriately, either physically or businesswise. The pursuit of a physical attraction or undue monetary gain can set up a dual role relationship, which affects the coach's ability to be objective and the client's ability to be transparent.

QUICK QUIZ

Can you have sex physically, by telephone, or in cyberspace with a client? No, you can't.

Can you have sex physically, by telephone, or in cyberspace with the client's sponsor? No, you can't.

Can you accept a personal, professional, or monetary advantage from a client or sponsor outside of the compensation agreed to in the coaching contract? No, you shouldn't.

Can you be the instructor of the client in an educational setting? Well, maybe. Let's look at some decision-making criteria for such gray areas.

How Close Is Too Close?

It is inevitable that your client will share some connections with you, especially in the arena of life coaching. Let's say your next-door neighbor's friend's second cousin's boss's daughter wants coaching on Thursdays. *Eh?* It's getting a bit convoluted, isn't it? Let's see if I can offer a few guidelines here. You can assess the appropriateness of the coaching relationship with the following questions:

Firstly, will the coaching relationship take advantage of or harm your client in any way?

Secondly, are you as coach subjecting yourself to an unfair limitation?

Thirdly, could your potential bias and lack of objectivity limit the coaching relationship?

Father Kahill feels that giving a parishioner biblical counseling and coaching at the same time would limit his ability to serve the need of the client. Consequently, he will don either his counseling hat or his coaching hat, but he will not switch hats within one conversation. He wants to be fully present when someone is talking to him. He does not want the client to be confused in any way as to the objective of the conversation.

In the realm of psychotherapy, Zur has some suggestions for the clinician, which are also good questions for a coach to ask before entering a dual relationship with a client. Here are four risk-benefit analysis questions:

1. What are the potential risks of entering into the dual relationship?
2. What are the potential benefits of entering into the dual relationship?
3. What are the potential risks of not entering into the dual relationship?
4. What are the potential benefits of not entering into the dual relationship? (Zur 2007, 43)

Informed Consent

We want to avoid all conflicts of interest, but we also know that they are inevitable. It is the responsibility of the coach to point out such conflicts and get the client to sign off on them. Suffice it to say that entering into a coach-client relationship without considering potential problems is not only careless, but it could also be a breach of the ethical standards.

In a small town or in a niche-specific market, the probability of completely avoiding dual roles may be miniscule. Again, reflecting to psychotherapy, Zur points out that *informed consent* is the basis for the client's decision to proceed with an intervention or not. Informing the client can include making her aware of possible benefits as well as consequences. Implicit in this approach is also making the client aware of exit strategies should she

decide not to continue (Zur 2007, 44).

Since coaching is not therapy, *informed consent* is not mandatory per se. However, communicating thoroughly about the processes and procedures is more than just a good idea. Furthermore, the ICF Code of Ethics mandates that the client has the right to terminate the relationship at any time. We'll look more thoroughly at coaching contracts in chapter six.

Play by the Rules

Follow the mantra: *Do what is best for the client, not for the coach.* When talking about the potential for a conflict of interest, the operative premise is for the coach to know what benefits the client and what benefits himself. These benefits do not have to be mutually exclusive.

Most of the time, what benefits one party benefits the other. There is a win-win scenario in motion when the coach plays by the rules. However, one can only execute the game fairly when there is an organization of professional coaches providing the rules and codes of conduct by which to play.

Furthermore, no organization accepts disloyalty from its ranks. In fact, most organizations will dismiss a member found dishonoring the organization and/or its code of conduct. Therefore, in the broader sense, the honor of the coaching profession is also a responsibility of each professional coach. For the client to truly benefit from the coach, the entire coaching industry should be able to endorse the individual coach. You want all of your peers to be able to point to you and say, "Hey, he's a good coach. You can trust him."

Conflict of Interest

Definition from ICF (2009): "A conflict of interest exists when you have an interest that interferes with your responsibilities as a coach or interferes with your ability to act in the best interest of the coaching profession" (p. 7). Therefore, the coach should put both the interests of the client and of the coaching profession above his own. Any conflict of loyalties could have a significant negative effect on the objectivity of the professional coach. There should be nothing to distract the coach from giving the client the best service possible. If, however, some doubt arises, the coach must discuss the potential conflict with the client and/or the oversight bodies to which the coach aligns himself.

Imagine that someone asks you to coach an employee whose boss is currently your client. Clearly, you might not be able to separate the two client agendas. Then again, you might. Before accepting the contract, you should clearly discuss the ramifications

with the first client (Lavore-Fletcher 2013). For years, I coached a department head that liked the coaching so much he set up coaching with me for several of his subordinates. This went on for many years. During a session, one of these subordinates asked me, "You're not going to tell my boss about this, are you?" My response was, "You know that I coach dozens of people in this building. When have you ever heard me say anything about what your coworkers have told me?" His response: "You haven't."

That is the way it should be.

When I enter the office of a client, I enter with a blank slate. Once, I coached Department Head A, who was having a problem with Department Head B. Ironically, the next day I was coaching Department Head B. His agenda for that conversation was to devise a plan for working through his conflict with the head of Department A. He asked me, "Do you see where I'm coming from on this?" To which I replied, "Yes, I have a very good idea what you're talking about." End of discussion.

What it comes down to is a professional relationship based on fair business practices. One should call into question anything that negatively affects the objectivity or integrity of the coach. This does not mean that all potential conflicts of interest are wrong, immoral, or unethical. It does mean that the coach should have a clean conscience regarding his clients and his coaching business.

Okay, let's take another a short test. Which of the following are legitimate reasons for taking on a new client?

1. The client pays good money.
2. The client is a high-status person.
3. The client makes my numbers look good.
4. The client needs help.
5. The client is a friend/family member.
6. The client is a referral of an influential person.
7. The client works for a company in which you hold stock.
8. The client is within the scope of your target group.

Let's break these down into some nuances:

1. Is money your primary motivator? Believe it or not, it is possible that the client will want to overcompensate you so that he has more control over the coaching relationship.
2. Are you interested in being able to boast that Congressman X or Famous Person Y is your client?
3. You want to sound busy. Would you take on a client just so the number of clients you coach sounds impressive?
4. Okay, but does the client need YOUR help? Would someone else's help be better?
5. Is there a conflict of interest? Are there clearly defined roles?
6. Are you afraid of disappointing that influential person (pastor, spouse, etc.)?
7. Do you not have a vested interest? Doesn't the company's performance on the stock market affect your wallet?
8. This is a good reason. However, one should check whether the target group has protection against unlawful discrimination.

What Are the Opportunities?

In his many years as a coach, Father Kahill has worked with a variety of groups, including youth action groups, marriage and family enrichment groups, and even "buddy" groups with fellow priests. In each case, there are usually sponsors or stakeholders behind the group initiative, and these people want to know how the group is progressing. This is a good form of accountability, and Father Kahill looks at the reporting function as an integral part of his ministry.

Internal Coaching

When an organization or company hires a coach as a permanent member of the staff, internal coaching is the result. The company has a vested interest in the coach. An internal coach can quickly get caught in a quandary between the objectives of the organization and the objectives of the client, who is also an employee of the company. Again, the coaching contract is a key factor in determining the boundaries needed for the internal coaching relationship.

The situations inside the walls of a company can be quite sensitive at times. The coach should define the expectations and clear roles for each stakeholder and spell out the objectives of all interested parties in the forming phase of the contract. The meeting room can fill up quickly with interested stakeholders when the stakes are high—i.e., when the goals of the coaching are significant to the organization's future. I find it best to have all the stakeholders present: the coach, the client, the HR representative, and even the client's boss when appropriate. Usually the atmosphere is upbeat and positive. Expectations are high. As the coach in the room, I want to clearly spell out what I will do and what I will not do. It is the responsibility of the coach to address potential conflicts of interest.

Sponsors Expect Results

In most coaching literature, we refer to the stakeholder paying the bill as the *sponsor*. This could be the client's boss, one or more members of human resources, a person from the corporate development department, and so on. If the client is young, the sponsor might be a parent or a guardian. In business coaching, measurable results often define the objectives for the coaching relationship. For example, the client receives the lead on a project that will obviously cause a greater investment of time than at present. The client also wants to spend more time with her teenaged boys as soccer season gets underway. The extra time for the project and the extra time for her sons are quantifiable figures. The "how" of managing this extra time requirement is the point of befuddlement. Hence, the coach's purpose is to help *un-befuddle* the client's time management.

QUESTION

Whose priorities are more important—the client's or the sponsor's?

Usually the sponsor feels obligated to monitor the outcomes of the coaching relationship. Insofar as the sponsor is paying for the coaching directly or indirectly, this is fair. The key point of ethics for the coach is the reporting of such results. A conflict of interest can arise quickly. Ideally, the client gives regular reports to the sponsor about decisions made and goals reached. Some sponsors want more than this and ask the coach to report as well. There is not an ethical problem with that unless the client objects to the way in which the coach gives the report. Again, a clearly defined coaching contract is the easiest way to make sure that everyone is on the same page. If it becomes evident that one of the parties involved needs a revision to the contract, revise it. If that doesn't work, revise it again.

Group Coaching

When three or more people gather together in a coaching meeting, we have group coaching. This means there is a coach and at least two clients. Is one-to-one coaching more "rich" than group coaching? Yes, it is. I wrote a dissertation on this topic (Marx 2009). My research discovery was that trust is higher when fewer people are in the room. Keeping group numbers as small as possible is a key to unleashing meaningful conversation.

At what point is the group too big? In my experience, the tipping point occurs at about seven or eight, including the coach. A coaching group is usually comprised of a handful of people with like goals and aspirations. By forming a small group, two worthwhile things happen: one, the participants save money by dividing the overall cost into smaller amounts; two, the brainstorming potential in a small group is second to none. By being together with people of like mind, the potential for finding a new twist, or a new perspective or viewpoint, is extremely high. Obviously, the potential to share restricted information outside of the group circle is also extremely high.

In a small group, the expectation of confidentiality is as real as in one-to-one coaching. The problem here is that the group members who have not read this book may not be familiar with the ethics of confidentiality. Looking back to the previous section, we can also imagine that the internal coach will work with small groups. It is entirely possible that these group members will have the same supervisor or manager. A team member might not feel free to speak openly if she knows that someone in the group could inform her boss about her attitude towards the job. A coworker could figuratively hang her dirty laundry out to dry in the next staff meeting. The importance of agreeing to confidentiality becomes paramount in group coaching. The ethical coach should thoroughly cover the ramifications of confidentiality at the beginning of the group-coaching relationship and should refresh this point to its members at regular intervals.

QUESTION

Many coaches prefer group coaching. Why do you think this is so?

A particularly intimate coaching group centers on marriage enrichment. Here, the husband and wife, or fiancé and fiancée, look to coaching to find ways to enhance their relationship. Regardless of the goal of the coaching, the Christian coach should be careful that the process needed is indeed coaching and not counseling. Collins notes that in marriage coaching, it is essential that *both* people are actually coachable (Collins 2002). Again, if the relationship needs healing, the coach should refer the couple to a marriage counselor. In Christian circles, there are numerous services to fill this need. The Christian life coach should be familiar with the offerings in his local area.

Team Coaching

An increasingly popular trend in coaching is team coaching. This is where two or more coaches share the same client or group of clients. The benefits of team coaching are considerable. Clients can effectively utilize coaches with varied areas of expertise to meet their needs. Similar to group coaching, each coach on the team needs to have an understanding of what she can and cannot share about the client. This also includes sharing information between the coaches on the same team. In each case, the client should agree as to what information to relay from one coach to the other.

Who Will Know?

As the resident local priest, Father Kahill often receives gifts. For many of his parishioners, the gifts become an indirect means of compensating him for his services. However, this is not the way the givers in his church see it. These gift givers feel that clergy are an integral part of the leadership structure of the community and they need to care for them. Father Kahill feels that refusing such gifts would dishonor them. Nevertheless, he wants there to be a balance between the givers' expectations of him and the services that he can offer.

Receiving Gifts

A conflict of interest exists when the coach might gain personal or monetary value that comes outside of the coaching contract. This could come in many forms: gifts, free tickets, or the use of a client's cottage in the Pocono Mountains. There is a difference between an unexpected gift and an expected one. When does the gift go beyond, "Hey, I'm thinking about you, and I just wanted to do something to thank you," to "Hey Coach, it is payback time"? The gift could set up a potential situation where you feel obligated to respond in a way that goes beyond the coaching contract.

You've heard the expression: *There is no such thing as a free lunch*. Well, somebody actually paid money for that lunch. As the recipient, you should recognize the possible implications of a request, demand, or some form of indebtedness in the invitation to dine with your client. Their expectation might be that you will do something to pay for the free lunch. You may have even inadvertently asked for the gift. Some of the time, such gifts come disguised as efficiencies. Say, for example, the client agrees with your request to start the meeting thirty minutes earlier so you can attend the warmup session before your son's game. The client has just given you a gift of time, and that could make you feel indebted to her.

QUESTION

The client gives you a $200 pen as a Christmas present. Is that okay?

Giving Gifts

Let's look at the flip side to this. The coach offers something of value to the client that is not in the contract. If we give them a free copy of a book, or invite them to attend a seminar at a reduced price, we are offering a "value-added" gift. As a result, the client may feel unduly pressured to continue the coaching relationship past the point when they would like stop. You might inadvertently establish a sense of obligation with your client by offering value-added services beyond those contracted. A case in point: you regard staying on the phone with a client an extra fifteen minutes as going the extra mile. However, if you do this consistently over a long period of time, you have slowly developed a claim against the client for the unpaid time you gave her. She could perceive this as an unpaid debt. Such a feeling of indebtedness might make the client

feel obliged to extend her contract with you when she'd really rather stop.

Of course, fair marketing practices and incentives are normal in any business relationship. The ethical coach, however, should be sensitive to coercing the client into decisions that the client does not want to make. The rule here is that an expectation of *compensation in kind* might oblige the client to do something that she is not interested in doing. The premise of: "*Give* unto others as you would have them give unto you" does not work for the ethical Christian coach.

How Do I Do It Right?

Most of the time, the tension that arises from a dual relationship conflict can be worked out with heartfelt communication. There is a popular saying in education: *People don't care how much you know until they know how much you care.* In the ethics of Christian coaching, we can make many mistakes. We can mitigate the likelihood of such mistakes creating real conflict, however, when the love of Christ is evidenced in our coaching. As it is written in 1 Peter 4:8, "Most important of all, continue to show deep love for each other, for love makes up for many of your faults" (Living Bible).

When dealing with situations where misunderstanding of cultural norms and values causes tension and friction, the desire to live in peace with all men (Hebrews 12:14) will most often transcend the gap and form a bridge of understanding. Often the cornerstone of this bridge of understanding is having a down-to-earth, open conversation. This does not mean that the coach confronts the client in such a way that the client wants to cower in a corner due to fear. It means that the attentive coach knows the client's areas of sensitivity and approaches with relaxed caution.

Confrontation

When the coach crosses a boundary, he should take the initiative to talk about it. For instance, when the coach has done something to transgress the coaching contract, resulting in a conflict of interest, it is the responsibility of the coach to bring up the issue. Authors Brinkman and Kirschner write, "We're often amazed at how many strategies people employ to deal with each other without first attempting to talk it out" (Brinkman and Kirschner 2002, 58). If talking about a transgression is too uncomfortable for you, try writing a letter or email. A written confrontation should be void of anything that will add heat to the conflict. It is in your best interest to read and reread all such communications before sending them (Brinkman and Kirschner 2002, 206). If there is any doubt about it, let a trusted friend or mentor coach review it before you send it. A well-formulated letter of confrontation states right up front the positive intent of your interest to clear the air. Couching the point behind a bunch of fluff is more likely to confuse the other party and possibly make your communication seem disingenuous.

Have a Feedback System in Place

Empirical research has shown that a report written by a coach to a sponsor is largely ineffective ("Coaching Services Assessment" 2014, 14). Monitoring the changes in the client's actual performance and behavior is the more accurate way to tell that the coaching has been effective. Communication is a two-way street. Besides the opportunities the coach has to communicate directly to the client, there should be equal opportunities for the client to give feedback directly or indirectly to the coach.

All services (in my opinion) should have a closed-loop system for getting feedback from the client. This means that there should be a suggestion box in the back of every church and an online comment section on the website of every restaurant. In coaching, the ethical coach should regularly check with the client as to how he is fulfilling the client's expectations. This can be as simple as asking a quick question at the end of any coaching conversation. "So how is the coaching going for you overall?"

Certainly, after the termination of the coaching relationship there should be an exchange of feedback forms. The client will put in writing what she liked and didn't like about the coaching. She might also mention areas for improvement. Consequently, some coaches send their clients a summary of the coaching relationship in writing.

These summaries mention highs and lows and delineate areas for potential growth. The coach should give such feedback to the client carefully. A note of caution: Keep in mind that if there is anything undiplomatic or derogatory written in black and white against a client, it could possibly reappear in black and white in a complaint about the coach even years later.

Closed-Loop Feedback

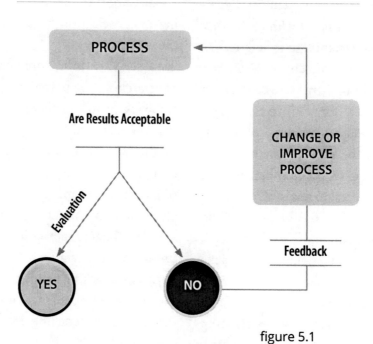

figure 5.1

Chapter Summary

This chapter has examined the various conflicts that occur when the coach enters into a dual role with the client. Such overlapping roles are easy to formulate and might be unavoidable. Nevertheless, the coach must identify and mitigate, as much as possible, any damage that might occur from a dual role resulting in a conflict of interest.

A coach creates a safe space for the client to make decisions. However, the coach should be sensitive to the vulnerability of the client as she navigates through unfamiliar territory. Bypassing the client's right to decide for herself sets up a case of neglect against the coach. If the client were to expose such neglect to others, this could force the coach into an embarrassing defensive position. Conversely, a coach should also be aware of areas that are no-go for the client and keep private matters off limits to the

client. Both parties should respect the boundaries formed in any professional relationship.

Due to his many commitments in the community, Father Kahill knows that he cannot avoid a conflict of interest with his clients. He tries to spell these out as much as possible in the initial coaching conversations, yet he knows that he wears many hats in the community and 100 percent impartiality is not always possible. Father Kahill decides that the best way for him to ensure objectivity is to monitor the coaching relationships continually. He implements a feedback system that he administers online by an organization very far away. In this way, he can have an impartial reviewer look at his work and compile results over time. Father Kahill is pleased that he has found a way to incorporate this form of objective monitoring.

What Do You Do?

Scenario A: You are an internal coach employed by the organization to help other employees improve their work performance. Your client tells you that he is planning to quit and go to the company's main competitor. How do you react and what are your responsibilities to the company in this matter?

Scenario B: You are coaching a client who tells you of new initiatives in his company that would greatly increase their net worth. This looks like a great investment opportunity for you if you buy shares in this company. Would investing based on this information be a correct ethical decision?

Scenario C: Over the course of many months, you find that you and your client have much in common and you enjoy being together. A physical attraction is also evident. What can you do to ensure that there is no significant conflict of interest?

Scenario D: A company hires you to coach several of their employees. Included in this group is your niece with whom you have a fairly close relationship. What would be the best way to ensure that your niece receives fair treatment? Should you exclude her from the group of clients?

End of Chapter Questions

- Do you need a coaching agreement when you are coaching friends or family?

- You are a manager and coach. Should you use a coaching agreement when you are coaching your employees?

- How does your coaching contract reflect the ICF and CCNI Code of Ethics?

CHAPTER 6

ETHICAL USE OF CONTRACTS IN COACHING AND LEGAL ISSUES

"In civilized life, law floats in a sea of ethics."

—Earl Warren, Chief Justice, US Supreme Court,
Address at the Jewish Theological Seminary of America Annual Awards Dinner (Nov. 11, 1962)

Setting up a proper contractual relationship is probably the most important aspect of risk management in the coaching process. In this chapter, we will look at the purpose of a contract and the elements it should include. We will examine the various phases involved in initiating a contract, paying particular attention to the essentials of the first meeting, outlining payment arrangements and schedule, stipulating boundaries, and explaining non-directive coaching. The goal of establishing a contract is to clear up and prevent misconceptions in the coaching relationship. Lastly, we will discuss pursuing the advice of legal counsel.

After reading this chapter, you will be able to do the following:

- identify the key elements of a proper coaching contract;
- explain to clients what coaching is;
- establish parameters for good cash flow management;
- evaluate when and why to seek legal counsel;
- initiate controls for safety and security while coaching.

Fred's Story

Fred runs a coach contracting service, a.k.a. a coaching custom-house. He functions as a contractual broker between clients and coaches. Most of the clients come from the corporate world, but an increasing number of inquiries are coming from the religious sector, particularly churches. He is always on the lookout for quality coaches he can trust who honor their contracts with him. He collects his pay on a commission basis by either adding his mark-up to the invoice sent to the client or by receiving a handling fee directly from the coach.

As his business increases, so do his worries. Christian or not, he seems to have difficulty getting some his coaches to keep their word. For example, although the contracts he sets up are binding for two years, many of his coaches try to circumvent him by contracting directly with the client after just a few months. He finds that this is usually not the result of malicious intent, but more a matter of ignorance regarding the contractual procedure. He decides that the best defense here is a good offense. He sets out to develop a system that ensures coaches on his retainer list are fully aware of the elements and ramifications of a good contract.

The Contracting Process

Fred puts together a flow chart that illustrates the typical coach contracting process. He tries to talk through each step with the new coaches he takes on. He finds that most of the coaches are impatient with this protocol and are anxious to get started. However, if he does not carefully and thoughtfully work through this process, the results are usually cumbersome, at best.

Often, the most confusing part of beginning an endeavor is getting started. For a coach to successfully enter into a contract with a client, certain steps need to be taken. These steps tend to flow in phases as described in Figure 6.1. Skipping or ignoring any of these steps could lead to problems later. A properly established coaching contract acts as a guide for the client and a shield of protection for the coach. Clients expect that the professional coach will have her contracting process ready to go. Although the steps noted below may vary from client to client, the five phases are fairly universal.

Inquiry Phase

Something sparks the interest of the potential client and he wants to find out more. The Inquiry Phase is when the client has raised the question, "What is coaching?" and "How can I benefit from it?" The answers to these questions can occur formally in a pre-arranged appointment or informally as two people converse.

Presentation Phase

In the Presentation Phase, the coach explains his or her services. Many coaches use the same welcome packet and contract for every client. Other coaches customize their presentations for each situation. In addition to your materials, I highly recommend giving the prospective client a live demonstration of a coaching session to help him more accurately understand what he is buying.

Agreement Phase

In the Agreement Phase, the coach and client discuss and agree upon the goals and expectations of both parties. Keep in mind that the agreement is two-sided; both client and coach can decide whether or not to proceed. Personally, I like getting an extensive list of goals from the client after he has said yes to coaching. I feel this is the best time to explore the client's agenda and to immediately identify the coaching objectives for the next several months.

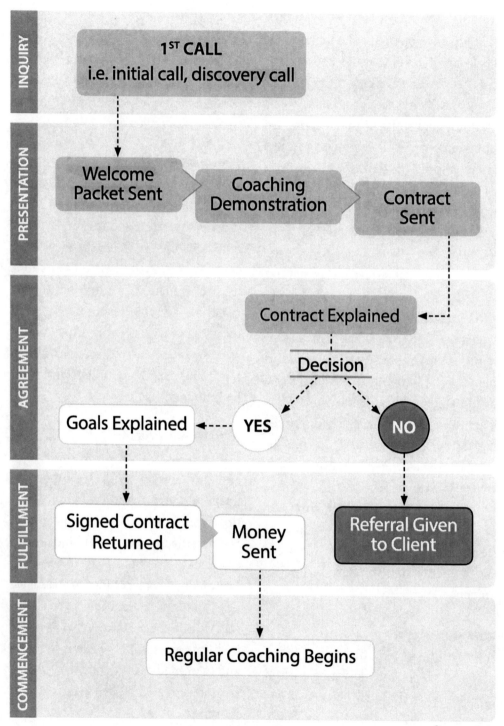

figure 6.1

Fulfillment Phase

In the Fulfillment Phase, the client returns the signed contract and consideration (money) is paid. This confirms the expectations of both parties. I still like to see a handwritten signature and a handwritten date on the bottom of the contract. Technically, the fulfillment phase is not complete until the money has been deposited in the coach's bank account. As discussed in previous chapters, if the coach is not going to enter into a full contract with the client, she should offer a qualified referral. This ensures that the client does not feel abandoned.

Commencement Phase

Beginning a coaching relationship with a solid foundation is critical. From an ethics point of view, a coaching relationship that starts well has the best chance of ending well. Having completed the aforementioned phases with a client, you are ready to begin the coaching process.

Common Challenges

Fred works as a broker and a bookkeeper for his coaches. He expects each coach to take the lead on creating client contracts. He prefers that his coaches list a fixed price on a rate table that is sorted by categories. Nonnegotiable rates are relatively easy to manage, whereas variable elements in contracts can be confusing to many coaches.

Not All Coaching Contracts Are Alike

Coaching contracts can vary significantly. A lot will depend on who the client is and who is paying for services. Both the coach and the client have the right to add or subtract stipulations they feel are important to the relationship. Add a sponsor to the mix, and the number of contingencies can multiply. This is normal and should not be a source of concern. You can change, tweak, and adjust your contracts as much as necessary. A good practice is to have one's documents (e.g., contracts, advertisements, and written operating policies) reviewed by a legal professional. Anything that makes a promise—such as a statement in an advertisement—is part of the contractual process. In the end, you must deliver what you promise.

First Contact

The coaching meetings usually begin after the first encounter with a client. In the literature for coaching, there are many different names for the first contact call. Some refer to this call or meeting as an *initial call, inquiry call, discovery call,* or *exploratory call.* I like to refer to it simply as the *first call.* Avoid the term *intake call,* as that implies a more clinical or mental health application.

Typically, the objective of the first call is to create a partnership. Here, the coach defines coaching, discusses the roles of both parties, and—most importantly—seeks to form a bond. The Christian coach wants to hear the heart of the client and gain a sense of his agenda. Additionally, the coach should evaluate the client's potential for growth and ability to move forward with his goals.

It is possible that the coach may be unable to identify with the client's agenda. The chemistry might not be right, so to speak. Or the coach may determine that the client is looking for emotional or spiritual healing. In either case, the coach should take caution to ensure the potential client in no way feels discriminated against. Regardless of the reason, if the coach and client are not a good match, the coach should offer the person two or three referral names of other coaches or, if more appropriate, to helping professionals such as a therapist or pastor.

======= **QUESTION** =======

How honest can you be with a new client about seeking therapy and not coaching?

Contracts Are Re-Negotiable

An important point about coaching contracts is that they can change. You might need to change the frequency or location of the meetings. For example, if you switch from phone conversations to face-to-face meetings, you could add a clause that asks the client to bring doughnuts to the meetings. (Just kidding.)

Christian Coach Institute Founder Lavore-Fletcher gives the example of changing fees. If a client took a three-month break—during which time you raised your fees—would the original or the new fees apply? Unless you actually re-contract to the new fee, the old one is still the valid (Lavore-Fletcher 2013). For this and other reasons, it is a good idea to state in advance how many meetings a client can miss before a renegotiation becomes necessary.

Payment

As Christian professionals, we have a moral, ethical, and legal responsibility to treat people fairly. We should not treat people differently based on the emotional responses they elicit from us. Nowhere is this a more sensitive issue than when it comes to payment. When, where, and how one receives payment is obviously an important part of the partnership-building process. Clients expect the professional coach to earn money. Most clients are actually uncomfortable with *pro bono*, i.e., "free" coaching. If one considers coaching to be a ministry, they should explain that to the client. Otherwise, the *pro bono* client might not understand that all the rules of professionalism still apply to the coaching relationship. In my experience however, when the client pays nothing, he pays attention to nothing.

Equitable Pricing

It is possible that two or more ethical principles might compete with each other. For example, helping people in need is a good thing. Getting fair pay at a level commensurate with one's experience and expertise is also a good thing. The professional worth her hire should have no qualms about charging for services at fair market prices. A good practice is to have a rate sheet written down and available when you talk to clients. Having set prices helps to prevent you from making up prices on the spot. Creative negotiation methods are easy to forget. You do not come across as professional when it sounds like you are improvising on contractual elements. That said, circumstances and rates can change. For example, it is fine if the coach wants to offer her coaching for $50 per meeting to one client and $250 per session to another client, provided the coach is clear in her own mind about what differentiates the two fees. Is the rate determined by a predefined value or principle or by an emotional feeling?

--- **QUESTION** ---

True or false? All men are created equal.

At the Heart of the Matter

Many of the coaches Fred uses receive credentialing through ICF and/or CCNI. These coaches are familiar with the contracting documents he expects. The uninitiated coach often needs extensive explanation as to the goals and expected outcomes of coaching. He finds that there is much confusion about the definition of coaching even among those calling themselves coaches. Nevertheless, if he is going to enlist a coach, he is also going to ensure that the coach understands what their contract can and cannot do. For those who have never owned a business before, this type of explanation can become somewhat tedious. Still, for those who want to make a living coaching, he finds their learning curve to be short and sweet.

Coaching Contracts

A coaching contract is a document that spells out what the coaching relationship is and what it is not. Both ICF and CCNI ask that the coach give all prospective clients a written contract. The literature on coaching refers to this as the coaching agreement. For the sake of simplicity, in this book, I refer to the *contract* as the document used to describe the coaching relationship and the *agreement* as the agreed-upon agenda for a single coaching meeting.

Therefore, the coaching contract is a specific document that forms the basis for all ethical and procedural actions for the entire coaching relationship. The coaching contract does more than establish the rules for playing nice. The contract should inform the client that he is in charge of his own progress.

Most coaching contracts mention the goal-ownership of the client. The client owns his progress and acknowledges that deciding how to handle the issues and subsequent implementation is his responsibility. Particularly in business and executive coaching, the coaching contract should clearly spell out the goals of the coaching relationship. One could also include the resources needed, the roles of the parties, and a scheduled plan of action. For example, most coaches ask their clients to fill out a prep form and send it to them twenty-four hours in advance, or at least one hour in advance of the coaching meeting. If this is a firm expectation and is included in the coaching contract, both coach and client need to discuss and commit to it. The coaching contract should be signed and sent to the coach before the second call or meeting.

Coaching with a Purpose

There should be a sense of purpose in the coaching relationship. In German, a coaching contract is an *auftrag*. An *auftrag* implies that there is a *commission* in the sense of *duty* or *command* to accomplish something with a purpose. German coach Thomas Schulte notes that without a real *auftrag*, coaching cannot really take place. Without a dire need to change, there might be some pleasant conversations, but there will not be a platform for the client to intensify his purpose and make the necessary changes (Schulte 2010, 26).

The coaching contract establishes the terms by which the coaching interaction will take place and also informs the client of what can and cannot happen within the coaching relationship. Allowing the client to review this agreement before signing it is essential to assuring that he avoids feeling pushed or coerced into signing the contract. Often the details of these contracts contain a certain amount of necessary *legalese*. To go over ALL the elements verbally might be too extensive and cumbersome. The average client is usually familiar with the basics of contracts. Therefore, the task of the coach at the onset of the relationship is to point out those elements that make the coaching relationship exceptional. For example, one could point out the importance of confidentiality and the difference between coaching and therapy.

QUESTION

What should be included in a good coaching contract?

Elements to Include in a Coaching Contract

The important premise for making a good coaching contract is the *sleep-well* principle. The contract should allow you to sleep well at night. If there is something about the logistics of the coaching relationship that is of high value to you, this might be a good item to include in the contract. For example, if a coach desires no client contact between sundown on Friday and sundown on Saturday, he should mention this expectation in the coaching contract.

Some coaching contracts are relatively short, about a page. Others can be two or three pages long. At a minimum, the coaching contract should contain the following elements:

- The coaching contract should clearly state the fee for service and the payment expectations.
- It should describe how, when, where, and how often the coaching should take place.
- It should spell out the client's obligations for missing a meeting.

- It should specify the length of each meeting and permissible variations.
- It should mention the duration of the contract as well as the provisions for ending the contract.
- As previously mentioned, confidentiality and the distinctions between coaching and therapy are necessary elements in the coaching contract.

Additionally, your desire to use the client's data for certification purposes is important to mention if it applies. In other words, a coach wanting ICF's Professional Certified Coach (PCC) designation needs 500 hours of coaching experience. The client agrees that the coach can send ICF his name, contact data for verification purposes, as well as the length and number of coaching hours. If the contract goes through a sponsor or other contracting agent, one can omit the client's name. At ICF, only two people will ever see the client's data; in addition, ICF keeps the data file under lock and key and deletes the file after five years.

QUESTION

What are the sleep-well elements you need in your coaching contract?

Law Takes Precedence over Contracts

A coaching contract cannot and does not supersede the laws that govern a coach's professional conduct. For example, a coach cannot state in his contract that he will hold all information strictly confidential when the law requires otherwise. In the United States, these are usually state laws, but local laws can also apply. It is the coach's responsibility to know these laws and inform the client if they affect the coaching relationship—especially the right to confidentiality. It is a good idea to include a clause stating all client information is confidential unless the client gives written consent to release it or the law requires such information. When a client signs the coaching contract, he acknowledges that the coach intends to follow the law.

Business Contracts

When you hire the next-door neighbor's son to cut your grass, you enter into a business contract. Although it may sound simple, there are many aspects to the negotiation. You discuss which lawnmower to use, the time of day and the day of the week for cutting (You don't want him mowing the lawn at three in the morning.), the quality of service expected, and the security of locking the gate when finished. Finally, you agree on a price.

These are the elements of a simple contract. Few of us would actually put this in writing, although that might not be a bad idea. Essential to the above example is the legal ability or capacity of the neighbor's son to enter into a contract agreement. Due to their status as a *protected person*, the law considers a contract with a minor or the mentally ill *voidable*. This means that either party can cancel the contract because the minor is not capable of deciding on the contract. Voidable does not mean that the contract *must* be canceled— only that it *can* be canceled. Therefore, one cannot force a minor or mentally ill person to fulfill a contract.

When any person agrees to enter a coaching agreement with you, they give you *informed consent*. This consent has three components: Firstly, the person agrees that the coach has adequately informed him as to the contents of the contract. Secondly, they consent to the contract voluntarily; the coach is not coercing them. Thirdly, they are competent as per legal definition; age and mental status does not preclude them from entering into contracts.

QUESTION

Under what circumstances could one make a coaching contract with a mentally ill client?

> **Tip**
>
> It is usually best to negotiate price last.

Factors That Muddle the Issue

Starting a small business is not unlike starting a big business; everything is just on a smaller scale. All businesses face the same risks and dangers regardless of size. A coach who is becoming the sole proprietor of a coaching business is often afraid of making a killer mistake or losing everything due to a careless oversight. This is normal. Chris McCluskey, founder of the Professional Christian Coaching Institute, says, "If you are not a little fearful about starting your own business, you're not in touch with the reality of it. But that kind of fear is part of discernment—awareness of danger—and it's key to exercising wisdom and prudence and sound judgment in your venture (McCluskey n.d., 236)." The key to being in touch with the reality of business is not necessarily knowing what to do but knowing who to ask. Your lawyer, tax advisor, banker, and insurance agent are your best allies.

The Apostle Paul admonishes us to live free from fear. Our attitude should be one of power and love and sound judgment (2 Timothy 1:7). Our contracts should, therefore, reflect our power to do business, our love for God's children, and our sound judgment in business decisions. The qualified coach has the power to be a professional. The sincere Christian has love for her neighbor and herself.

The simple fact that you are reading this book demonstrates that you have exercised sound judgment. At a minimum, reading this chapter means that you have gained some understanding about making contracts. That's a start.

Cash Flow

A new coach can get herself into a predicament by signing a contract that is bad for her business. For example, if you contract for advertising at $500 per month for a year, you had best have the cash flow to cover the $6,000 expense. On the flipside, if you contract with a client for $500 per month for a year, you should be sure that the client has the cash flow to cover the $6,000 expense. Many small businesses implode because they cannot meet their contractual obligations. The coaching may be superb, and the clients may be happy; yet the money is not always there when it needs to be there. A shortage of cash is the biggest killer of new businesses. Having a firm grasp on one's cash flow is one of the highest priorities of risk management. To repeat: Be sure you have the means to pay for something before you commit to paying for it.

QUESTION

Where are you most likely to overspend?

Exercise

- How comfortable are you with your advertisements and contracts? Do you present them without fear?

- How would you define power, love, and sound judgment for your coaching business?

- How often do you review/audit your presentation documentation?

- Consider the following well-known phrase: "The truth, the whole truth, and nothing but the truth." What does this mean to you?

Which of My Values Is Relevant Here?

Recently, Fred got a phone call from one of his new coaches. She was practically in tears because one of her clients told her that the coaching was not bringing the expected results. Fred and the new coach talked for almost an hour. After speaking with the coach, Fred determined that no one clearly defined the expectations for the coaching.

The Promise of Non-Directive Coaching

In the first stages of the coaching relationship, the coach should emphasize the client's future. The client does not need to *bring* anything to the coaching relationship. There need not be a preset or predetermined agenda before the coaching begins. However, the client should understand that the liability for his progress lies with him and not the coach. In its purest form, coaching is non-directive and non-manipulative.

In other words, the coach manages the process, and the client manages the progress. In order to ensure this distinction, my colleague, and founder of Way of Life Coaching Cheryl Scanlan, makes two promises to prospective clients:

1. I will never ask you a question that I have the answer to.
2. I will never lead you or manipulate you. (Scanlan, personal communication, June 3, 2014).

In this way, Cheryl promises to keep the ball on a level playing field. The client can expect, and in fact demand, that he be in charge of the agenda. The ethical Christian coach does not enter the conversation with the expectation that it will go in one direction or the other. The coach will not direct the conversation. The client determines the direction. This is something the client should know about coaching from the get-go.

The Place and Time for Coaching

One Sunday afternoon while Fred was taking a nap, he awoke to the sound of someone ringing his doorbell. It was a coach who wanted to talk about a new contract and happened to be driving past the house. Since he works in a virtual environment, Fred was surprised to see this coach on his porch. Honestly, he also felt that the coach had intruded on his private sphere. More than anything, he wasn't happy that his beauty sleep was interrupted. He realized that he would need to establish certain boundaries with coaches who live nearby.

There are many ways to coach: face-to-face, video conferencing, or by phone. Despite evidence to the contrary (Aoun, Osseiran-Moisson, Shahid, Howat, and O' Connor 2011), many coaches believe that a virtual business is less effective than or not as personable as a brick and mortar business. This might be true (Marx 2009). However, in the United States, Canada, and Australia, coaching via phone or videoconference has proven effective as a viable way of doing business. Regardless of the medium, 95 percent of the time there is an appointment. For the odd occasion that the client wants to call a coach directly without an appointment scheduled, a coach should clarify the no-go times in advance. Office hours, for instance, might be worth mentioning in a contract.

Many of my clients are in Europe, and I now live in the United States. They are at least six hours ahead of me. I explain to them that before 4:00 pm Central European Time, it is unlikely that I will answer the phone or even reply to an e-mail. However, one should exhibit caution here. When the client feels that the coach does not want his inquiries, a feeling of neglect might develop. It is useful, then, to encourage the client to contact you as often as needed, yet within the agreed-upon parameters. The client should feel justified in wanting and getting your services. The coach should make clear what to expect for an average response time when the client leaves a voicemail message or sends an inquiry e-mail. That time could be twenty-four hours, forty-eight hours, or even a week in the summertime.

Note

Professional coaching is not a hotline service for distraught clients. The coach should be aware that the client might form a pseudo-dependency relationship with the coach. Within the ethics of Christian coaching, the coach should become neither a surrogate parent nor a surrogate spouse.

What Are the Dangers?

Fred gets a call from a client who wants to cancel her contract with one of his coaches. It seems that the coach, a former pastor, asked her if he could pray with her. She agreed, but then to her surprise, the coach took both of her hands in his and started to pray. She felt extremely uncomfortable with this and now wants a different coach.

Give Us a Hug

At one time, I had the opportunity to become a youth pastor. I learned that the previous youth pastor had not behaved appropriately. More to the point, he had had sex with one of the teenage girls in his office in the church. When I toured the office, I said that I would not do any counseling of teenagers in that office. The other two pastors were a bit bewildered. I told them that the office had no windows. Particularly, the door needed a window. The next day all three pastors had windows built into their doors.

Clearly, an intimate relationship with a client will taint the objectivity of the coach. This also brings up the question of whether a coach can have a spouse as a client. Besides the potential of a conflict of interest, which contract supersedes the other: the marriage contract or the coaching contract?

QUESTION

Is it okay for the coach to give the client a small hug after a coaching meeting?

Physical Environment

Obviously, there is a reduction of physical threat to the coach when the coaching is mainly online or over the phone. If the coach is working with clients in her home, this magnifies the risk of physical mishap between coach and client. Some coaches charge extra for meeting the client at his office or having the clients come to their offices. Local zoning ordinances sometimes limit the manner in which a person can operate a business from home. Those stipulations aside, legally, ethically, and morally there is nothing wrong with inviting a client into your office for professional coaching. A cautious coach, however, should take the necessary precautions to protect her safety and her reputation. If the client were to *say* that something happened and threaten to take that public, a case of extortion could develop. There is also the risk of damage to a coach's personal and public reputation. To my knowledge, this has never happened. I pray that I am right.

What Are The Opportunities?

One of the more lucrative features of Fred's business is setting up coaching for large corporations. He gets directly involved with the contracting process because he knows that stakeholder satisfaction often results in long-term business. The challenge here is finding the balance between all expectations brought to the table. He prefers to talk with each stakeholder personally before aiding the coach in drafting the contract. Occasionally, a team of coaches is required, and the contract drafts become standardized. This is a lot of work for Fred upfront, but when he does it well, the benefits are significant.

Third Party Contracts

More work is involved when the coaching occurs within the confines of a structured environment such as a corporation. When a sponsor is involved—whether the human resources department or even a parent—a more comprehensive coaching contract is often necessary. Usually the sponsor may expect *empirical evidence* with measurable and quantifiable behavior changes in the client.

One should clearly identify the boundaries of the information exchanged between coach and sponsor. The sponsor should have a good idea as to how he will get the information he needs in order to satisfy involved stakeholders. Most coaching contracts involving a business sponsor seek to clarify *who* will do *what* and *when*. Therefore, the contract often includes a means for accountability and follow-up. Sponsors want to know that coaches can deliver what they have promised and often want to put a system in place by which they can monitor both the performance of the coach and the progress of the client.

QUESTION

Can a sponsored business client have some personal outcomes that the coach won't share with the sponsor?

Who Is Going to Know?

Fred values the integrity of his coaches and their transparency about their work with clients. The other way around, however, is a different story. Recently, a client asked his coach to contract with him directly and thereby circumvent Fred and his commission. It is not the first time this has happened. Normally, this results in a canceled contract and a lost client. Fred wonders if there is any legal action he could take, yet he knows that the court costs alone make going after the client prohibitive.

Tell the Truth

We know that we will always need to tell the truth. Aside from morality, telling the truth is a contractual obligation. Sometimes, however, the way and the extent to which the truth is communicated needs to be reined in. We must not say things that did not happen. That would be lying. We must not leave out salient details when describing an event. That would be fraudulent. We must not replace one truth with another and hope that no one notices the reversal. That would be deception. A lawyer can help us sort out these distinctions and assist in defining exactly how much to say and not to say.

So Sue Me

Most people do not cheat, lie, or break promises made to a friend. Yet these same people sometimes have a different attitude when it comes to reneging on business promises. Say for example, that you sign up for a training course you think will help you professionally. The day before the course begins, you decide that the money needed to pay for the course would be better spent on website development. In your mind, website development is the better business investment for the moment. When the training school reminds you of your contractual obligations, how do you respond? The Christian coach would not say, "So sue me." One should not brush off a legal obligation with a flippant remark. The modern comeback, "So sue me," implies that the battle in court will not be profitable and therefore the school will probably not even try to sue. Just because the other party might not come after you in a court of law does not mean you are free to ignore your obligations. Such a casual attitude towards one's obligations is a blatant disregard for responsibility and does not show integrity.

How Do I Do It Right?

Fred's lawyer has become one of his best friends. The attorney knows his stuff and is willing and able to help Fred through most of the sticky contractual situations that arise. If the lawyer does not know the answer, he usually knows someone else who does. Furthermore, Fred's lawyer becomes an excellent source for the legal questions Fred gets from his coaches. Both Fred and the lawyer are very pleased with the amount of business they do together.

Legal Eagles

Lawyers are—by definition—experts on law but not necessarily on ethics. According to Allen, most lawyers have had little to no training in ethics and one cannot regard them as knowledgeable in ethics (Allen 2006, 1328). Just as your mentor coach is there to help you with coaching dilemmas, your lawyer is there to help you with legal dilemmas. Most of us would rather not take anyone to court, or even threaten to do so. In fact, between believers, we are admonished to settle our differences out of court (see 1 Corinthians 6).

The easiest way to avoid legal problems is to avoid any claims at all—either from your side or against you. This means that you do business in such a way that no one is likely to sue

you and that you are unlikely to sue anyone else. Should someone make an accusation against you—or should you accuse someone else of breaking a contract—your goal should be to stay out of court. The best defense is no defense when it comes to litigation. In other words, avoid going to court, if possible. Settle the dispute without a lawsuit.

As a last resort, go to court knowing that the outcome will always be a gamble. For the Christian coach, a lawyer who helps you pursue peace and goodwill is a good ally to have.

QUESTION

What is your plan for settling a dispute with another believer?

There Is an Exception to Every Rule

Another reason for consulting a lawyer might be to determine whether the problem is one of ethics or law. If there are situations in which a coach questions whether her actions are legally justifiable, then she might need a legal expert. As previously mentioned, the coach might build into her coaching contract an exception regarding confidentiality, for example. However, such an exception clause does not nullify the coach's responsibility to maintain confidentiality.

The coach needs confirmation that the wording of the contract does not go against any laws or create an unfair business practice. In this way, legal eagles swoop in and help us define what is allowed and not allowed as per local ordinance and general law. Your local lawyer might not be adequate for all questions, however. When the legal question becomes quite specific, it could be time to consult a legal specialist. For example, a coach could sit in Tennessee while the client sits in California. What then? Here a coach might need an expert in interstate commerce. In order to avoid such jurisdictional issues, many contracts explicitly state the place of legal venue, i.e., the municipal court that would oversee the coach's business.

Chapter Summary

There are five phases in the contract-setting process. One should pay careful attention to each phase so the client understands the coaching process as well as the coaching relationship. A good practice is to demonstrate to the client the non-directive coaching approach. Only then can coach and client hammer out the true details of the contract. Boundaries and expectations occur on both sides. This chapter also points out the benefits of legal counsel.

In conflict-resolution management, a squeaky wheel is often looking for public recognition and sympathy for his or her position. This means that not treating a concerned complainant with respect could result in an undue escalation of the problem. More often than not, the problem is not one of loss or damage, but a matter of hurt pride and injured feelings. Instead of reacting quickly and casting off a concern as unwarranted, the ethical Christian coach would do well to slow down and consider whether some fault or oversight might actually belong to the coach. One should take time to reflect on the ethical principles involved and consult mature guides, such as a mentor coach, to avoid a rash reaction. If no time is available to reflect, then the coach should follow the convictions that are compatible with her ethical principles. Either way, when all is said and done, a coach should make time for additional reflection to ascertain how she could avoid the predicament in the future. One of my operative axioms is: The first time I do something wrong, I have had a learning experience. The second time I do the same thing wrong, I have actually made a mistake. Choose to learn from experience and avoid future mistakes.

Fred knows that coaching is a dynamic profession and that the way the coaching profession conducts business next year might be very different from this year. The numerous platforms for coaching and the various types of coaching keep him on his toes. However, it becomes apparent to him that the success of building quality coaching contracts hinges on building quality coaching relationships. He resolves to spend at least one hour per day building relationships with his coaches and their sponsors. The strongest contract cannot replace the foundation of a strong relationship.

What Do You Do?

Scenario A: Your client has asked you to set up the payment process in such a way that you bill her directly, and she in turn resubmits the invoice to her company for reimbursement at a higher rate. In other words, the client is actually collecting money from her company on top of your invoice. How do you respond to this request?

Scenario B: In addition to coaching, you are also a dietician. How do you distinguish between the two roles in your contracts with a client who may be interested in both coaching and dietary advice?

Scenario C: The prospective client wants to discuss price before discussing the content and the nature of the coaching relationship. How do you respond?

Scenario D: You get an e-mail from the sponsor of one of your clients. The e-mail asks you to send an evaluation of the client's performance during the coaching. Furthermore, they explicitly want facts and figures. How do you respond?

End of Chapter Questions

- What is your escape plan if something goes wrong in your home office?

- What can you put into place to ensure that you manage your cash flow well?

- Who is on your short list to call when you need advice and help?

- What are your essential boundaries? Where do you not allow clients to intrude?

CHAPTER 7
BUSINESS PRACTICES FOR COACHES: SYSTEMS AND SOLUTIONS

"There is no such thing as business ethics. There is only one kind—you have to adhere to the highest standards."

—Marvin Bower, former managing partner of McKinsey & Company,
called the father of modern management consulting by the Harvard Business School

No one begins a business with the intention of failing. To the contrary, the typical goal is to create something that serves both the business owner and the clients well for a long time. This chapter focuses on the systems and solutions that make a business—particularly a small business—sustainable, scalable, and sellable. Establishing models for sustainable growth and profit are essential. As such, we will address the many challenges to maintaining healthy profit in this chapter. One of the most significant challenges is the ability to carry one's tax burden. Furthermore, there are several other responsibilities to running an ethical business, including truthful advertising, solvency, and insurance. Having a business continuity plan is also vital to running a healthy business.

After reading this chapter, you will be able to do the following:

- create a business plan;
- understand obligations such as taxes;
- distinguish between a sole proprietorship and an LLC;
- evaluate ways to protect your business and yourself;
- discover the best way to plan for your business's future.

Elizabeth's Story

Elizabeth has been working as a life coach for about seven years. She values her ICF and CCNI credentials and feels she is well recognized and respected in the coaching community. Before she became a coach, she worked on staff at a large church as a lay counselor. She came to coaching with strong people skills and a notable lack of business skills. Recently, she read an article about business continuity, which made her think about the importance of setting up systems that ensure sustainable cash flow. She has noticed that getting clients is one thing—keeping them and getting referrals is another. She has even considered teaming up with a partner who might bring more business savvy to the mix.

Common Challenges

Elizabeth feels that she usually makes good decisions with her money. She does not spend lavishly and is happy with a simple life. Due to her concern for the future, she takes it upon herself to become a self-taught expert in small business operations. She really needs her new coaching career to propel her into the next, long-awaited phase of life: retirement. She realizes that she will need to build a substantial nest egg in order to continue living comfortably in her own house after retirement. Even then, she wonders about the funding for a retirement home if that were to become necessary. What is the best way for her to save this money? There seems to be no end to the number of possibilities for investing.

Non-Risky Living

The fortunate few are born into families where business is a typical dinner table topic. Most people, however, come from an experience base that is far from the rigors of running a business. Most people begin their careers with little sense as to how to handle the business side of the coaching.

If you are like most coaches, you enjoy helping people. One day coaching appears on your radar and things begin to change. Maybe you relate to Elizabeth who, as a lay counselor, found that the coaching approach fit well with her ministry. After learning a little about coaching, she became interested in earning money by serving people via coaching. She then experienced what start-up expert Michael Gerber calls an "entrepreneurial seizure" (Gerber 2004, 12). As a prospective coach, she was enamored with the idea of going into business for herself.

However, Elizabeth is relatively risk averse. Contrary to popular belief, most entrepreneurs do not like taking risks (Reiss 2000, 3). A business cannot move forward without some risks, but the prudent self-employed coach will do what is necessary to anticipate, reduce, circumvent, and avoid unnecessary risk. There is no such thing as running a business that is free of risk. There are, however, many ways to minimize risk, and there are many systems and tools available for risk management.

Trust Your Intuition When It Comes to Risk

The greater part of valor, in terms of risk management, is to know when to take a risk and when to avoid a risk. People tend to be risk loving when it comes to certain things and relatively risk averse with others. Allegedly, the illustrious banker Baron Rothschild once had a friend ask for help deciding between an investment with a very large rate of interest and an investment with a much smaller one. The Baron replied, "If you want to dine well, go in for the first. If you want to sleep well, invest in the second" (Selected extracts 1896, 1). Hence, a favored expression on Wall Street is "eat well or sleep well." I prefer to say, "More risk, more fun; no risk, no fun."

Many decisions in coaching warrant careful consideration. It is nearly impossible to know 100 percent about a risk in advance. We base some decisions like buying a house, getting married, or starting a business on an intuitive feeling that it is the right thing to do. Gut feelings aside, doing due diligence to thoroughly investigate the implications and ramifications of a decision can help you make well-informed choice. When it comes to partnering with other people, we should certainly vet them. The term *vetting* originally comes from horseracing and means that a veterinarian should check out a racehorse before allowing it to race. In Christian circles, we should also pray about decisions and have a peace about them. That sense of intuition might just be the nudge of the Holy Spirit. Author and entrepreneurism expert Bob Reiss comments, "Trust your gut. Do your homework first; test it against your gut; and then trust your gut. If at this point you still have a passion to forge ahead, then forge ahead. Don't let naysayers discourage you" (Reiss 2000, 85). This is good advice: When the Holy Spirit says go, don't stop.

At the Heart of the Matter

It seems to Elizabeth that business experts spend most of their time planning. Each of them seems to have a business model that they feel is the only good one. These business leaders passionately describe their plans and methods. With great vigor, they tout their results. Talking to coaches is no different. Each one has his or her own way of running a business. Elizabeth notices, however, that those coaches who have a full slate of clients every week also have a complete business operating plan. Those who are less busy with clients only have, at best, a partial plan. What are the pieces to a good plan and how can they fit into her business model?

Are You in Business?

Most readers of this book are small business owners who are offering coaching services. This means you have very little overhead and virtually no production costs. Perhaps you started a coaching business because you expect to be able to make good money at coaching. Normally, a new business should show signs that a breakeven is possible within a year. Breakeven simply means that your revenue equals or exceeds your expenses. If this does not happen, the IRS and other vested parties might get the idea

that you are engaging in an expensive hobby and not in a real business.

To be considered as a business, your coaching activities should show verifiable evidence that you tried to make a profit. How many years can you be in business before the tax authorities become skeptical of your intentions? The answer lies in your ability to demonstrate a profit motive. One simple test of the profit motive is the "three-of-five" test. When your coaching practice can make a real profit in three out of five consecutive years, then the IRS and other entities will view it as having a legitimate profit motive (Pakroo 2012, 145). For some, coaching is an experiment that, while a great experience, never becomes a lucrative business. There is no shame in closing the doors after a year and saying, "Hey, this is just not something I want to do for a living." However, if coaching is more of a ministry for you, and you get income from other sources, you might want to continue meeting with and helping people.

Profit Is the Bottom Line

Most coaches earn money from a number of different sources. In addition to the actual coaching, a coach can make use of several different revenue streams. Teaching classes, giving workshops, speaking engagements, and publishing are just a few examples.

One may deem a business profitable when the cost of running it is less than the money it brings in. In other words, the equation in its most basic form is as follows:

Revenue – Expenses = Profit

Increasing revenue and decreasing expenses is the key to long-term growth. In the short term, business owners can rely, in part, on keeping costs low. For the long term, however, the focus should be on creating sustainable growth. Your business is at risk of tottering until your structure for steady growth becomes stable.

For example, how you make and receive payments is part of the process. Getting your money (revenue) quickly and efficiently from clients is essential. At the same time, paying bills sooner rather than later saves money in charges and gives you a good reputation with vendors. The conscientious small business owner is aware of the methods of payment that will save money as well as time. Some vendors will request a business check or business charge card, while others may request a cashier's check or even cash. Keep in mind, however, that many vendors (even the IRS) will accept payment in installments.

The responsible business owner does not delegate the oversight of her fiscal viability. She knows what's going on even if an accountant or bookkeeper is the one crunching the numbers and transferring the funds.

Even if you think you are "not good at math," don't let the talk of fiscal reports scare you. At the small-business level, the majority of the required math is simple addition and subtraction. No one else should be more motivated to get the numbers working on your behalf than you are (Reiss 2000, 45). Don't abdicate your responsibility to understand your business's bottom line.

Fair Compensation

We discussed in the last chapter that prices should be fair and equitable. However, new coaches often wonder how much they should actually charge a client. The answer is relative to the coach's situation and is really a matter of supply and demand.

Let's take a simple example. You feel that your style of coaching has a market value of at least $36,000 on an annual basis. For your situation, you know that ten client meetings per week are about what you can expect to start.

$36,000 \div 12 \text{ months} = \$3,000$
per month anticipated gross
(before tax) revenue

$\$3,000 \div 40 \ (4 \times 10) = \$75$
per client meeting

Subsequently, if you feel that your services were worth $72,000 per year, you could double your hourly rate to $150 (at ten hours per week). At a market value of $108,000 per year, you would charge $225 per coaching meeting. Of course, these calculations would double again if you averaged twenty coaching meetings per week. You can and should do the math for your business projections. Besides *pro bono* coaching (charging nothing), the lowest rate I've heard is $5 per meeting and the highest is $1,500 per meeting.

If your services are in demand at your current prices, then you could increase your rate. If the price you are offering scares away potential clients who are in your target group, then the price might be too high. In this case, having a mentor coach or a group of peers to seek advice from is one of the best ways to research your market potential. What you agree to in your coaching contract becomes the basis for your compensation.

Ethical flags begin to fly when you start charging for things not in the contract. If you need to add something

to your offering, the remedy for any ethical concerns is relatively simple: re-contract. One can introduce a new contract—verbally or, preferably, in writing—that nullifies the old one at any time. I know one coach who sends updated paper contracts to her clients every couple of months. She is constantly adding and subtracting things that change the value of the service she is offering to the client.

Have a Business Plan

Those who want to borrow money for their business should expect to formulate a business plan. Even if you don't intend to borrow money, it is a good idea to create a business plan. The writing of the plan puts your commitment to coaching success into black and white. No one benefits more from the plan than the coach who writes it. Winston Churchill once said, "He who fails to plan is planning to fail." Large businesses always have a strategic plan in operation somewhere in the background. For a small business to thrive, it should follow the same practice of establishing a plan for both day-to-day operation and for long-term growth.

Several risks germane to the coaching profession require continued analysis. Besides the financial risks, a coach must make decisions about promotion, procedure, personnel, and posterity. Furthermore, the ethical coach establishes (preferably in writing) operative guidelines and frameworks that enable her to apply her operating principles to the job.

At a minimum, your business plan should include the following components: a statement of purpose, a plan to get customers, a plan to keep customers, a plan to make money, and a plan to fulfill your financial obligations. Read, study, compare, analyze, crunch numbers, project, and then make an informed statement (educated guess) as to how your business will operate. How much of your business plan will be subjective? Well, a lot of it. Ultimately, however, each situation becomes an exercise in interpretation.

Here is a typical business plan outline for a small coaching business:

- The Executive Summary describes the whole plan in less than one page. (Write this last.)
- The Purpose Statement describes why you are in business (a.k.a. mission statement).
- The Organizational Structure describes your framework for decision making and implementation.
- The Service Offering describes the way you offer your coaching and other services.
- The Marketing Plan describes your method to acquire and retain clients.
- The Management Team describes you and your key support people.
- The Capitalization Plan describes how and from where the money comes.
- The Financial Plan describes your budget and financial projections.
- The Appendix

Factors That Muddle the Issue

Until now, Elizabeth has been operating as a sole proprietor. It seemed the simplest model to use when she was getting started. However, as her business has grown, she feels increasingly uncomfortable with the thought of losing her lovely home if there were to be a catastrophe. Either a natural or court-induced disaster could take away her little nesting place. This idea scares her. She understands that she could restructure the business to become an entity unto itself. This entity is a corporation and would not include her personal assets per se. She is unsure, however, as to the best type of corporation to have. At the same time, one of her coaching friends has formed a small coaching firm and is looking for partners. This looks like a good way to rub elbows with professionals who understand the business side of things better than she does.

Sole Proprietorship or Corporation

One aspect that often befuddles the mind of the new coach is legally establishing the business. At the get-go, a new coach has to decide on a business structure. While there are many to choose from (S-Corp., C-Corp., LLC, LLP, and several variations of sole proprietorships), I want to focus on the two most prevalent small business structures in the USA, namely the sole proprietorship and the limited liability corporation (LLC). These two forms exist in every country, albeit with different names and slightly different characteristics. The key distinction is the liability factor: Who pays when things go wrong? Who gets the goodies when things go well? In the sole proprietorship, the owner's personal assets are held liable. If, for example, bankruptcy were to become necessary, the IRS could seize the personal assets of the sole proprietor to pay debtors. In the worst case, this could mean losing one's house or personal savings. In the LLC, only the assets belonging directly to the corporation are subject to seizure. This is a compelling argument for the LLC. However, an LLC is more expensive to run and taxes are generally higher. A heart-to-heart conversation about this with a qualified tax advisor

Did You Know?

As a sole proprietor or an LLC partner, you will pay self-employment tax in addition to your regular income tax. Self-employment tax is comparable to the tax paid by an employer for his employees' Social Security and Medicare taxes.

is a good idea. In the United States, the Small Business Administration is also a good source of tips and recommendations (sba.gov.).

In most places in the United States, you can start a small business by submitting the forms for a business license and paying a nominal fee to the state government of the state in which you live. I strongly recommended that you have a separate bank account in the name of your business. To start an LLC, you also need to file the articles of organization with the state. A formal approval process follows. A dedicated bank account is required, and often there are special municipal requirements. You may also need to get a federal tax ID number (FEIN or EIN) from the IRS after the state has approved you to operate. Like it or not, you must pay taxes. Again, your lawyer and CPA are good resources to call on should you need help. For most states, however, the process is fairly straightforward.

Partnerships

When the stress of doing business is such that one person does not feel adequate, a second or third partner might be the solution. Such stress factors could be positive as well as negative; stress can push you to excel or it can cause mental and physical exhaustion. Usually, however, the objective of forming a partnership is to spread the benefits among more people and to share the risk liability. Generally, this means that the partner also shares the revenue and the expenses. However, the most common complaint about business partners is that they often don't equitably share the work and risk. Here, too, a thorough agreement (preferably in writing) is essential at the beginning of any business relationship. Remember that you can renegotiate contracts. Before getting angry or threatening court action against a business brother, try re-contracting. Entering into a partnership or joint venture is obviously a risky venture; however, the rewards can be tremendous. At the same time, the potential damage can be devastating. Caution is advised.

Working with like-minded colleagues is often the most rewarding—and most challenging—aspect of running any business. One should bring on staff and contract help with thoughtful consideration of their ethical propensities. Loyalty and integrity are vital. Sometimes the best strategy is to bring on fully trained and fully competent professionals. Other times the best strategy is to initiate a newbie into your system. Most of my business partnerships have been set up with non-Christians. However, there is something to be said for a partnership where all parties actively invite the Holy Spirit to participate. Communications expert and coach Kathy Carlton Willis says that as long as a passion for Christian faith exists, the rest can be learned (Willis 2013, 249).

Data Storage

Last summer, Elizabeth experienced a hard drive crash. Fortunately, she found a local computer shop that was able to retrieve about 80 percent of the files she kept on it. She still is thanking God that she didn't lose any of her client files. Since then, she transfers her important files to a separate external hard drive about once a week. She wonders if that is enough.

A potentially confusing aspect of running a business is the keeping of client records. In chapter four, we looked at the question of note-taking. This is an operative question that each coach should answer. At a minimum, you must maintain client records to prove that you are running a legitimate business. The storage of data should be secure. Fire, theft, and disaster are all possibilities against which you need to guard. Unauthorized people should not be able to get into client files, and you probably do not want a thief to be looking into your personal financial files either. Nowadays, you can easily and cheaply store digital data in the cloud. The providers of these services

assure security and also multiple back up sites. They claim that the physical security of their servers is likely to be better than anything you can set up in your home office. In addition, having redundant offsite systems is essential in the event of catastrophe. Imagine that most of your relevant business data is stored on the hard drive of only one computer and that computer crashes. Not only do you risk negligence in the care of your client data, you also have a serious handicap for your business continuity. The cloud and other forms of back-up systems can give you added protection and peace of mind.

> Keep all paper receipts. Put them into a shoebox if you want, but do keep them for about five years.
>
> **Tip**

Take Taxes Seriously

Elizabeth knew the day would come eventually. She just got a letter from the IRS stating that an audit of her business would take place in the next three months. She is to have all relevant files available to the auditing agent who will stop by and do a site inspection as well. At least Elizabeth knows that her accountant will be able to advise her as to the best way to make this as easy as possible. Nevertheless, she worries that

> "Our new Constitution is now established, and has an appearance that promises permanency; but in this world nothing can be said to be certain, except death and taxes."
>
> —Ben Franklin

her books might not be totally understandable to an outsider.

Like it or not, you will need to pay taxes. Tax collectors the world over are like snapping turtles. They slowly and persistently pursue you for back taxes. When they catch up to you, they snap—with interest. Yes, you must pay taxes. Sometimes it feels like *the Lord giveth, and the IRS taketh away.*

As a business instructor, I find that many students do not have a fundamental understanding of what a tax does. Basically, all taxes are a form of the value-added tax. This means that in some shape, form, or fashion your gross value (a.k.a. capital value) has increased and therefore a tax is due. For instance, if you earned $10,000 on a project, you have thus added $10,000 to your equity base. Alternatively, if someone were to give you a yacht as a birthday present, you would have added that value to your personal capital structure. To figure your taxable amount, you subtract the monies spent to earn the gains you got from your total income. The total is your profit or *net gain.* On this net gain, you will pay taxes.

There is nothing wrong with making the most of deductions to avoid overpaying taxes. Ethically, there is something very wrong with evading taxes. The deductions you make on a tax return reduce the profit you made. In this way, you avoid paying a tax on the profit because you can prove that you incurred the expenses in the pursuit of acquiring the revenue. Rule of thumb: If the expense relates to making money, it is usually tax deductible. The key here is the proof. Your record keeping should clearly show that your declared deductions are fair and verifiable costs of doing business. Good record keeping is essential; bad record keeping is bad—very bad. Ideally, you should have records that the IRS can easily and quickly review should they decide to audit you. Not having well-organized records is an invitation for penalties.

Many of coaches operate their businesses from home. Below are a few tips from tax lawyer Peri H. Pakroo on how to make home-business usage more legitimate to the IRS:

1. Take pictures of your home office that show its business character.

2. Draw a diagram showing the floor plan of the house with the home office clearly defined. Include room dimensions if possible.

3. Keep a log of the times you work in the office.

4. Keep a record of all the meetings in your office, including clients you met, when you met, and the subject of the meeting. Recording client visits to your home office is especially important even if you also have an outside office.

5. Have your business mail sent to your home.

6. Get a separate phone line for the business. (Pakroo 2012, 169)

Knowing what monies you must collect from your clients is again a matter for consultation with your local tax advisor. In Europe, there are fiscal distinctions that can even vary from village to village. Because coaching is a professional service, it usually does not charge a tax per se. In general, coaching services do not charge value-added tax (a.k.a. sales tax) unless one sells tangible products to customers such as books, videos, or training materials.

Exercise

- What would it be like to hire your sister to do the accounting?

- Who is responsible for your business's profit?

- Do you hate bookkeeping? If so, what is your plan to get over it?

- What did you do yesterday to improve your business?

Which of My Values Is Relevant Here?

Elizabeth has three grown children. Much to her surprise, one day they stopped asking her for money. Recently, the youngest one even bought his own washing machine. Like her children, Elizabeth feels that her business is also slowly coming of age. She reads about key indicators and business health checks. She wonders if there is the possibility of selling the business to someone in the future. Not only would that help her retirement fund, it would also offer continuity for the client base she has built. She gets many of her clients from local businesses that she feels have become dependent on her for coaching services. It feels good to be needed and wanted.

My Business Is My Baby

When you start a business, you birth a child. In a very true sense, an entity is born that has most of the rights and privileges of a living, breathing human being. A business can get married (a.k.a. merger), get divorced (a.k.a. spin-off), or die (a.k.a. going out of business). The business being analogous to a child is easy to imagine. We often regard our businesses as our babies. All of us hope to bring up our children to the point where they become independent and strong. At first, your baby needs Mom and Dad to protect and nurture it. As it grows, the business becomes more able to make choices independent of the parent. Then one day, it becomes an adult. A coaching business will move from the growth phase to the mature phase when it starts generating more revenue than it can handle. Sounds almost too good to be true, doesn't it?

A full-grown coaching business will need additional help to handle the load. Reiss contends, "There are some problems with the company/child analogy. For example, your child doesn't usually increase your net worth. And more seriously, as a parent, you rarely sit down and reassess your relationship with your child" (Reiss 2000, 252). Can you imagine sitting down with your fifteen-year-old and telling him, "Scott, you've been a good son all these years and I really have enjoyed most of the time we've had together. However, after careful analysis, I have determined that you are producing negative cash flow, which is endangering the long-term financial well-being of this household. Therefore, you are going up for sale to the highest bidder."

All joking aside, reassessment of the financial viability of a business is a necessary and ongoing process. This is a good practice every year. Ultimately, you might grow your business by turning it into a corporation and giving it an independent life of its own. On the other hand, you might want to sell its brand name to the highest bidder and start a new one.

My Word Is My Bond

A promise is a promise. It should go without saying that the Christian coach is a promise keeper. Sadly, there are those who behave differently when it comes to business. To such people, it seems as if business life exists in a separate ethical reality from their personal life. Nowadays, most coaches will have an Internet presence. Therefore, consider stating your strong biblically based operative business values on your website. Additionally, your website should explain how you do business, as well as the terms and conditions for entering into a coaching contract. The potential client should be able to easily identify your code of conduct and your basis for ethical practice. At a minimum, you can do this in two ways. You can be a member of ICF, CCNI, or the like and advertise your membership as a badge of professional distinction. Implicit in this advertising is the connection to the organization's code of ethics and your pledge—as a member—to follow it. Secondly, you can publish your personal code of ethics and your pledge of moral conduct on your website. Many Christian coaches include a statement of faith as well as their personal mission statement, which defines their calling and professional purpose.

What Are the Dangers?

You might argue that the label you carry does not truly represent who you are. Therefore, it doesn't really matter what you call yourself. I disagree. I think the labels you choose say a great deal about the person you think you are. However, that can also be misleading. I once met a coach who advertised that she had the credential of a "Life Experience Master's Degree." When I asked her about it, she explained that all she had been through personally and professionally should be at least worth a master's degree. While there was little doubt that she was a consummate professional and an excellent coach, the fact that she had a self-proclaimed a master's degree made her professional image ring a bit hollow.

The leader of the Christian Coaches Institute, Janice Lavore-Fletcher, points out that one should designate a master's degree with its area of specialization. For example, one would clearly state the earning of a master's in communication as such. Otherwise, if a coach only stated "master's degree" without its area specialty, it might mislead the reader into thinking that it is a master's in coaching (Lavore-Fletcher 2013). You should not imply that you are more than you are.

Furthermore, the term coaching should not be misrepresented either.

Former co-chair of the ICF Ethics and Standards Committee David Matthew Prior suggests that one should never refer to coaching as a helping profession. As an alternative, he suggests descriptions such as a *personal-development profession* or a *personal-growth profession* (Weiner 2007, 21). He also advises coaches to refrain from referring to their client base as a practice, similar to that of a medical doctor or a psychologist. (Weiner 2007, 23). For the same reasons, he avoids "Intake Packet" and prefers "Welcome Packet."

QUESTION

How many executives do you need to have coached before you can make the legitimate claim that you are an experienced executive coach?

Truth in Advertising

Elizabeth receives a request to sign a petition criticizing the practices of the local municipal hospital. It seems that the staff at that facility has not been as diligent in monitoring their patient's health care as they should. What bothers Elizabeth is the hospital's advertisement, which claims that patient care is its highest priority. While she is interested in having a quality health care facility in her neighborhood, she is hesitant to put her name on the petition.

Marketing is about name recognition. A professional coach spends a lot of time on marketing. Most (if not all) ethical codes for coaching specifically forbid false advertising by a member coach. This means that all publicly displayed information must be true and substantiated. An ethical coach cannot make false or deceptive claims or make promises that guarantee a certain result ("ICF Code of Ethics" n.d.). The serious coach knows that good marketing creates awareness among prospective clients about what distinguishes her from the competition. In this sense, the ethical coach must not compare herself with any other coach directly nor criticize another coach openly. Publicly putting down another coach not only breaks the Golden Rule, it might make you liable for libel—i.e., defamation of character. God's commandment to us goes beyond not telling the truth. He commands us not to bear false witness against our neighbor (Exodus 20:16). At the same time, you should not over-inflate your image. In summary, stay positive when advertising and only promise what you can deliver. Make sure that you show who you are, what you can do, and who recommends you—and no more. "A good name is more desirable than great riches; to be esteemed is better than silver or gold" (Proverbs 22:1, NIV).

Stay Solvent

Most small businesses that fail do so because they do not have the right amount of money (capital) available at the right time. You can have a good product and good marketing. However, if you do not have enough money at the right time, consider yourself sunk. Profit is one thing; cash flow is everything. To make profit, the revenue must exceed the expenses at the reporting date. To have functional cash flow, there needs to be enough money to pay obligations at the expenses' due date. Landlords are generally unsympathetic to late rent payments. They want their money by the fifth of the month regardless of the promise that the renter will have more money later. In the short term, small business owners sometimes borrow money from family or friends, use credit cards, or

> **Tip**
>
> When strictly following a rule or a code of conduct actually produces negative consequences, one needs to revisit and possibly revise procedure. One should not continue to make demands from those who owe money in such a stringent manner that it leads to losing clients and, more importantly, referrals.

seek a line of credit from their bank. This is not unusual, yet these are only stopgap measures. In the long term you cannot keep a business afloat without having enough liquid funds.

Collecting from those who owe you money is an important part of running a business. Several merchant services are available to help you with your accounts receivable. It should be easy for clients to send you the fees due for the coaching service you offer. Most coaches I know expect the money to arrive in advance of the coaching meeting. If, for whatever reason, a client is behind in his payments, an extra charge might be appropriate. Usually, however, the coaching meetings simply go on pause until the client pays the balance due.

Some coaches will even engage the services of a *factor*. This is a service that pays the coach in full immediately and then collects the funds post facto from the clients at a marked-up price. I do not recommend this procedure, however. It tells the client that you do not trust them to keep their word to pay on time. Such a displayed lack of trust undermines the success of the coaching relationship. Usually, a reminder or two is enough. Still, we are called to be merciful, just as our Father is merciful (Luke 6:36). Being efficient and proficient at business practices should not override the need to show empathy and compassion.

What Are the Opportunities?

Some people seem to be naturally business savvy. They know how to stretch a penny and how to make a penny. Because I am not one of those people, I have invested time and money attending classes to learn how the business clock really ticks. The biggest business problem most coaches have is simply that they lack the exposure to the effective models of successful business. This is all learnable through study and/or experience. It is also attainable through revelation.

It is very easy to have a strong prayer life. Just do it. Prayer is the Christian's ace in the hole. Philippians 4:6 admonishes us to bring our concerns before the throne of God. We can receive wisdom from Him to make the right choices. We do not, however, get a secret formula delivered to us that allows us to circumvent the school of hard knocks. Marketing expert and coach Kim Avery writes, "It's natural to want shortcuts through the difficulties of building a coaching business. Like all of life, however, God has left challenges in our path so that in our areas of greatest weakness His strength will shine brilliantly" (Avery 2013, 63). The ethical Christian coach should know which business aspects are within her skill set and which are not. Particularly at the beginning of setting up a coaching business, it is wise to learn about each business function first hand. Things like accounting or website design are often aspects foreign to most coaches. Do these things yourself as long as it is practical so that you can at least learn the lingo of the trade. If you want to have a meaningful discussion with an accountant, for example, you need to understand the difference between debits and credits.

QUESTION

What are some aspects of
business that are not in
your skill set?

Play to Win

I used to coach a football team. I always got a bit tickled by the typical question reporters would ask before the game. "Coach, what is your strategy for today's game?" My standard response: "To win." A pastor friend of mine used to say, "If you play, you could win the game. If you don't play, you have already lost." You cannot win by playing only defense. Sometimes you must play offense, or you will not get any points. Spending most of your time defending your business does not bring in clients. The prudent coach does not spend all of her office time just reacting to e-mails and invoices. There should be time spent every working day on refining the business systems and improving the marketing. There is no substitute for hard work. Thomas Edison once said, "Opportunity is missed by most people because it is dressed in overalls and looks like work" (Edison n.d.).

A note of caution here: You can actually overdo the paperwork. As discussed in chapter three, one can have analysis paralysis regarding decision making. This happens when you are so concerned with doing due diligence that you are not able to make a quick decision. In every business, you must also be able to react with agile efficiency. Without the ability to both see and seize opportunity, a small business is destined to remain just that—small. Ingenuity and innovation are cousins to risk and uncertainty.

Sometimes You Don't Win

Business owners need to be aware that the possibility of going bust exists—and what to do if they find themselves in that circumstance. Under the United States tax code, bankruptcy protects the insolvent business owner from continued lawsuits from credit holders who want their money. When a person files bankruptcy, her assets are liquidated or a repayment plan is worked out. The intention is that hopefully the person can continue doing business and become solvent again. Both the court and the credit holders must approve such a repayment plan.

It seems that, nowadays, bankruptcy is an intentional, strategic initiative used by many an unscrupulous business operator (Reiss 2000, 266). Unfortunately, it has become a necessary reality for many a Christian business owner as well. However, it should be the last resort and not a way to just close shop and open up a new one down the street. It is the duty of the Christian business owner to pay her debts. Being insolvent does not alleviate the responsibility to pay her debts later on. Romans 13:8 (NIV) says, "Let no debt remain outstanding, except the continuing debt to love one another, for whoever loves others has fulfilled the law."

Who Is Going to Know?

Intellectual Property

Elizabeth is in tears. She just got a cease and desist letter demanding that she stop using a phrase that the lawyer's client had coined and got a copyright for five years ago. Indeed, Elizabeth has developed a workshop which she entitled, "Live right, sit tight; don't let the lazy bug bite." She took the title from someone's website without really thinking about it. It just sounded like a catchy phrase. She immediately writes a letter of apology and promises to remove all references to that phrase from her materials. Yet she still fears that there might be other implications to the matter.

When someone creates something, they own it. A product, picture, or painting created for professional purposes is the property of the creator. A song, text, or graph is regarded as intellectual property in that it does not have a tangible form. One can transfer (sell) property rights to someone else. Nevertheless, ownership exists and taking it without permission is theft. Professional misconduct occurs when the use of someone else's property exceeds the limits of the fair use doctrine. As coaches, we can use other material if we publicly give credit to the owner.

When one publishes a work in any form (print or electronic), it falls under the copyright protection of that publisher. If I publish an article in *XYZ Magazine* that owns all rights to the text and I want to reuse a sentence from the article in a new publication, I need to get permission from *XYZ Magazine* to quote myself.

In the past, it was legally required to include the copyright symbol (©) on materials you created, so that people would know your product was protected (Reiss 2000, 239). Nowadays, the assumption is that everything is owned and thereby protected. Still, having a copyright statement on your website is a good idea. People should be reminded that they just can't take anything they can access.

> Your logo or other graphics could be protected by having a registered trademark (®). In the United States, you can apply for this through the US Patent Office (uspto.gov), and it is not very expensive. Furthermore, it gives your logo a professional flair and makes you look more legitimate.

Tip

Unfortunately, there are coaches who steal material from other sources. Having locked down a copyright on your published material will help you win in court. If you find your material has been unofficially "borrowed" by someone, go after them. It is not in your interest or in the interest of the coaching industry to let such misconduct slide. As discussed in an earlier chapter, it is usually better to seek settlement out of court. However, if you must go to court, don't go alone. Hire a lawyer to represent you. By the way, a young lawyer might be cheaper than an old one. Reiss says, "Copyright infringements are usually very simple to document and to take to trial, so a recent law school grad can probably handle your case. If they suspect they can't, they'll probably tell you so" (Reiss 2000, 242).

Plagiarism

As a university professor, I see copyright infringement often in the papers of my students. Despite the fact that I teach only adults in Christian schools, there is still a considerable amount of plagiarism. Most of the time, it is technical plagiarism that is unintentional. The students don't always know the rules for proper citations and references and often make mistakes. On the other hand, sometimes there are cases of blatant theft of intellectual property.

This is easy for a professor to find these days because we run the student's content through a university-driven search engine that finds matches from online sources and other universities.

What really disturbs me is the type of students who tend to plagiarize. Over dozens of years and thousands of students, I have found that the most flagrant plagiarizers (male and female) are police officers, soldiers, and pastors. One day at lunch, I confirmed this supposition with the dean of my business school. He said that the head of financial accounting had told him pretty much the same thing, except that the financial cheaters he recognized were mostly the soldiers and pastors. It seems that the enforcers of the law (legally and biblically) feel that they are above the law. Since they interpret the law for others, they might feel free to interpret the law in a way that is convenient for them. On numerous occasions, I have seen papers written about the topic of ethics that contained plagiarism. Ironic, isn't it?

In Leviticus 19:14, we read that we should not put a stumbling block in front of the blind. This means that we should not be doing anything that would take advantage of someone who cannot see it coming. Borrowing material from others and reworking it so that no one can see the footprint of the original work is still dishonest gain. By doing so, you make yourself look better. This is cheating your clients. Even though they will most likely never see the deception behind such action, deception is there nonetheless. Sooner or later, this practice will catch up with you.

QUESTION

Who do you think would never plagiarize?

How Do I Do It Right?

Insurance

The following are typical questions I often get from coaches regarding insurance:

- Do I really need insurance?
- What type(s) of insurance do I need?
- Who do I get this insurance from and what does it cost?

The answer to these questions is the quintessential response: it depends. How you do your coaching and the type of risk you assume are the keys to determining your risk liability. This means that there must be a risk that is worthy of coverage before an insurance carrier will consider underwriting you. For insurance purposes, this risk must be qualifiable and quantifiable. In other words, the risk must be real and possible. Furthermore, it must be financially significant and measurable. Stated simply, if there is money involved, you can insure most anything. For example, you can insure

Tip

If you give advice, you carry a responsibility that your advice is sound and viable. If that advice leads to a financial loss for the client, you might need an insurance policy to cover you in the event a client sues you for those losses. For example, if you recommend that your client divorce his wife (not an ICF- or CCNI--condoned thing to do, by the way) and that ex-wife can prove your part in her divorce, you may be subject to litigation and, subsequently, financial retribution for having "caused" the divorce. Sounds like sticky, tricky stuff.

An E&O (errors and omissions) type of insurance policy can serve as a malpractice coverage for non-medical professionals. For example, architects and accountants often have E&O coverage called *professional liability insurance*.

your daughter's wedding. Say you are planning a big bash outside, and you fear the party might get rained out. You could purchase a type of event cancelation insurance that would cover the expenses of the vendors who may demand payment regardless of whether the event actually takes place.

In Europe, the professional can acquire just legal protection insurance that potentially covers legal expenses if a court proceeding were to be litigated against the professional. In the United States, such insurance is much more precarious. With the unlimited permutations possible due to exclusions and riders, the coach would do well to have any worrisome risk coverage defined in writing. For example, if you are worried that one day a client or former client might sue you for slander, you should have your insurance carrier issue you a written statement as to the extent they will or will not cover you. The only way to be really sure that your professional liability insurance covers a certain risk is to get a statement of coverage in writing from the insurance carrier.

If your coaching business is at a physical location other than your home, you should consider getting a commercial general liability (CGL) policy. This would protect you from liability risks resulting from bodily injury or property damage. For a home office, your homeowner's insurance policy usually covers these risks. If the proverbial client slips and falls on your proverbial stairway and injures his proverbial patella, you should have liability coverage. If a falling tree branch in your driveway hits your client's car, this needs coverage. If you have employees or in-house consultants, you might also want special insurance for employee risks. Peri H. Pakroo notes, "Most CGL policies do not cover certain employment claims such as harassment, discrimination, and wrongful termination. And all insurance companies refuse to insure you against bad business decisions, criminal acts, or intentional acts of harm" (Pakroo 2012, 133). To repeat, the only sure way to know the extent of your coverage is to obtain written statements from your insurance carrier. The alternative is to find out the hard way that you have no coverage once you file a claim. Your homeowner's or renter's policy might not have the same scope of coverage as a commercial policy. Furthermore, the possibility exists that running a business from your home might actually void your homeowner's policy.

These are obviously things worth checking out before the storm hits. Another noteworthy point is that losses due to criminal activity, as well as punitive damages, rarely qualify for insurance coverage.

Reserving Funds without Reservation

An alternative to having insurance is not to have insurance. If you elect to forego insurance, it is prudent to put the amount of money you would have spent on premiums into an interest-bearing savings account. Regrettably, most small businesses do not have the funds to self-insure. Since insurance expenses are usually tax deductible, this advantage is lost if you are not spending the money on the premiums. Of course, you might have enough money in savings to cover your assets in the event of catastrophic risk exposure. If so, may God continue to bless you.

Monies for future expenses should be set aside in the same way your tithe should be set aside. Just because the bill is not due until the end of the year does not mean that expensing (i.e., reserving) the funds in advance is not necessary. One, it shows up as a capital reserve and makes your banker happy (a good strategy); and two, it forms a discipline which will enable you to weather most fiscal storms (also a good strategy). When you form good fiscal habits at the beginning of your business practice, they tend to last indefinitely.

Monitor the Results

In this day and age, several relatively inexpensive software solutions for managing cash flow are available. Your CPA can also advise you on software solutions that could interact with his. Working with an accountant is usually a good way to spend money to save money. If you both use compatible software, you save time converting the numbers from one system to another. Time is money. There are numerous ways to track your money, and your accountant can tell you which measures are the key for your type of business, such as a cash flow forecast. Furthermore, you should monitor and review the time you spend on marketing and business improvement. In terms of time, your marketing hours plus your business improvement hours should be at least one-fifth of the total hours you spend on doing business in

> Not planning for retirement would be about the biggest long-term risk you could take. *No funds, no future.* Rule to live by: Save 10 percent of your earnings (e.g., retirement fund), give away 10 percent (e.g., tithe), live from the 80 percent (not forgetting to reserve some for taxes and other obligations).

Tip

a month. You should spend the other four-fifths on the service to your clients, either directly or administratively. "Don't scrimp on the analysis, but don't overdo the reporting" (Reiss 2000, 63). Producing monthly progress reports is a good idea as long as you use them. A report that nobody reads is useless. Your goal should be to sell what you do, do what you sold, and manage the money during the time in between.

Chapter Summary

This chapter has focused on establishing systems that ensure the sustainability of your coaching practice. Writing a business plan is one of the most beneficial ways to map out the future for a small business. Ultimately, the type of business model utilized has a significant effect on the business's continuity. Many key elements go into assuring positive cash flow and sustainability. At the same time, certain obligations, such as taxes, require appropriate planning and allocation. Of course, another significant obligation is the promise to operate openly, honestly, and fairly.

After reading several books about operating a small business, Elizabeth decides to take an accounting class at the local community college. She feels this is one area of business that she cannot master without additional knowledge and training. She also has started writing a business plan that encompasses all the aspects of her coaching business in its present form. She wants to show this plan to a friend who asked her to join their partnership. She feels a peace about teaming up with other like-minded professionals. What intrigues her most about the partnership is the potential to mentor both new and aspiring coaches. In this way, she feels that she is helping to establish a long-term vision for coaching to thrive in her local area.

What Do You Do?

Scenario A: Someone steals your laptop from your vehicle. In it are many files that relate to the business you do with your clients. What steps should you have taken to ensure that the sensitive information doesn't get into the hands of the wrong people?

Scenario B: A law firm contacts you with a sample list of areas where your website could be in violation with a number of statutory laws and copyright infringement. For a nominal fee, they will give you their complete list of accusations against you as well as their recommendations for how to fix such problems and avoid them in the future. If you are unwilling to take their advice, they threaten to sue you for unfair business practices. How do you respond?

Scenario C: There is an opportunity for you to join a coaching team that will service a large corporation for the next three years. Part of the requirement of being on this team is that you have a business continuity plan that ensures your sustainability as a coach for at least that long. What can you do to show that you are up to the task?

End of Chapter Questions

- How much of your income goes into a form of savings?

- What is your personal mission statement?

- Do you really want to give advice in a coaching meeting? Are you ready to carry the liability?

- Would you take disability insurance in case you became permanently unable to work?

- What key elements of your business need close tracking?

- Another coach has an excellent graphic/illustration on her website; there is no copyright symbol ©. Can you use it?

CHAPTER 8
LIABILITY AND RISK READINESS

*"Every right implies a responsibility;
every opportunity, an obligation; every possession, a duty."*

—John D. Rockefeller, Jr. (1874-1960)

Few clients come to the coaching relationship looking for ways to become the Six Million Dollar Man—better, faster, stronger. Most of the time, the client is stuck and looking for a way to make forward progress. If they were able to forge ahead on their own, they would not need a coach. For this reason, many counselors and therapists are adding the coaching approach to their skill set or are switching entirely to coaching.

In this chapter, we will explore the distinctions between therapy and coaching. The difference is mainly a question of control and contextualization. The therapist looks to healing the past, while the coach looks to creating the future. The coach manages the process but does not assume responsibility for the results. This minimizes, but does not eliminate, the potential of risk liability. Being risk-ready is part of being professional.

After reading this chapter, you will be able to do the following:

- distinguish between therapy and coaching;
- explain the purpose of giving advice;
- determine when a client would benefit from therapy rather than coaching;
- evaluate your liability and risk-readiness;
- find ways to the path of discovery in coaching.

Milton's Story

Milton was a practicing, licensed psychotherapist. He enjoyed the time he spent with clients and never felt burdened by their problems. About three years ago, however, he discovered that non-directive coaching was more fun and got better results for the type of client he wanted to work with. He earned a certification in life coaching from a reputable school and set up shop in his home in the suburbs. Although he has not renewed his therapy license, he continually has clients coming to him with needs that speak more to therapy than coaching. He wonders how he should position himself.

Common Challenges

Milton wonders what he might be doing to trigger the question, "What should I do?" He seems to be getting this question in almost every coaching meeting. When he first started coaching, he had no problem giving advice. That seemed right. Now he wonders if there is not a better way to set up the coaching conversations so that requests for advice don't come as regularly.

The Quick Fix

Part of the ethical dilemma behind the non-directive coaching approach is that people are often looking for an easy solution. Clients can be so tired of not moving forward that they look to the coach to alleviate the pain of paralysis so they can get themselves in gear. The quick fix is to go ahead and give the client your advice. This is a normal thing to do when two people are talking. One person might ask, "So what do you think I should do?" The other person naturally responds with his opinion. Some people might consider it impolite to evade such a direct question. As we've seen several times, giving advice is not part of the coaching approach. All coaches have experienced how stubborn clients can be on this point. They will literally bait the coach into giving them advice.

My Professional Christian Coaching Institute teaching colleague Mike Pfau is fond of saying, "Don't get hooked." The coach should not let the client's frustration with the problem become the basis for cheap coaching. Stay the course. The client needs to own the solution for it to really work for her.

When You Are an Expert on the Topic

Most of you have an area or two in which you could be considered a subject matter expert. As mentioned in chapter six, the client often initiates a contract with a specific coach for the very reason that the coach has an area of expertise from which the client hopes to glean. A typical client will feel they have hired the coach to give them counsel when they need advice. Here too, however, the coach should check that the client is not averting the responsibility of discovery.

For the record, there is nothing wrong with consulting, counseling, or advising when that is the service that has been contracted. A problem here, though, is that the client does not always know the difference between directive and non-directive coaching. When the client has hired you to be a non-directive coach, then that is what they should get. Irrespective of your knowledge of the topic, the client seeks to gain discovery that comes from inside her. Later in this chapter, we will look at the coach's ability to contextualize a question when he is familiar with the topic. At the same time, the coaching process might involve exploring whether another professional might help the client make the best decision.

At the Heart of the Matter

It is interesting to Milton that the more he reads the Bible and the more he seeks God's perfect will for his life, the more his clients want to do the same. Milton does not talk about his ever-closer walk with God. Yet his clients seem to intuitively know that they are on safe ground discussing this with him. Milton feels blessed, enriched, and encouraged when his clients talk about their walk with God.

The Coach Is Part of the Process

It would be easy to posit that the coach carries no liability if he never gives the client advice. Such an oversimplification, however, skirts the core responsibilities germane to coaching. Due to the coach's past experience, training, and education, he brings a rich skill set to the table. All the coach has to offer becomes part of the process. At the Professional Christian Coaching Institute, we are fond of saying that *the coach manages the process, and the client manages the progress.* However, the coach who only keeps himself at a safe and protected distance without being fully engaged in the process takes the low road. Conversely, the coach takes the high road when he is self-aware and reflective during a coaching meeting, allowing the process to transform him while learning from it as well. We refer to this interactive exchange between the coach and the client as *coaching presence.* Hence, it is not possible to fully coach without the obligation to participate fully in the process.

The coach and the client are partners. By focusing on the client's agenda, the coach relinquishes responsibility for the client's successful results. However, if the coach maintains no liability in the process, it is highly unlikely that the client will gain sufficient value from the process. While a client orientation keeps the focus on the client's agenda, the coach is still responsible for seeing that the process evolves and furthers the client's best interests. The coach is an integral part of the process.

Shame

Tamara, Milton's newest client, tells him that she often feels a profound sense of guilt when she does not perform to her high level of expectation. She sets rigorous standards for herself and feels badly when she falls short. Milton wonders what he can do to best encourage her.

As previously mentioned, we first process all decisions emotionally before we can process them rationally. The amygdala will process the fear factor before the neocortex can process the logic. Research in neuroscience has shown that the intermingling of emotion and cognition is greater than what researchers previously held in philosophical and psychological circles (Phelps 2006, 46).

One of the strongest emotional inhibitors to learning is shame. People are embarrassed to not know an answer. This sense of shame is one of the reasons why confidentiality is paramount in the coaching relationship. Humiliation and embarrassment are feelings people will fight to avoid. A client looks to the coach for help, and the job of the coach should take place on a platform of trust and encouragement. The coach should encourage the client to move from a place where she feels that she messed up to a place where she feels that she is "struggling well."

Imagine the sense of betrayal a client might feel if the coaching relationship results in a sense of shame. Most adults would probably not lash out at the coach. Rather, they would beat themselves up with feelings of failure and hopelessness. In such situations, the coach should focus on encouraging the client. We might quote verses like Joshua 1:9, 2 Timothy 1:7, or Psalms 37:4. Here again, the coach stands at the line between counseling and non-directive coaching. On the counseling side of the line, an exploration of the sense of shame is called for so that the client can get healing and gain peace. On the coaching side of the line, an exploration in self-forgiveness is called for so that the client can move on and gain progress.

QUESTION

What is your coaching response to "I'm a failure"?

Control

When coaching is your work, you might succumb to the feeling that you have to perform. To truly trust the process, the coach must have confidence that the results will help the client without the coach controlling the results. Having control means having power. Having power means influencing things to go in a certain way. Exercising power means working.

Sometimes coaches feel they are not working if they are not controlling the process. Since the client is responsible for the change, the client is actually doing most of the work (Bacon 2003, 75). The coach guides the process by listening, asking powerful questions, and making insightful observations. Having the client discover their own path usually takes more time and more mental energy than simply giving advice and being done with it (Rock 2009, 211). Despite its inefficiencies, non-directive coaching is usually preferred over advice-giving by most clients. Author and coaching expert Terry R. Bacon states, "I found that over 60 percent of coachees said they preferred non-directive coaching" (Bacon 2003, 74).

QUESTION

What is your coaching response to a client asking what you think she should do?

Factors That Muddle the Issue

Milton notices that his normally calm and collected client is particularly restless today. When he makes an observation to this effect the client responds with, "Yeah, well I guess it is because it is the thirteenth of the month. I'm always afraid something weird will happen to me on the thirteenth." Milton wonders if the client suffers from triskaidekaphobia, the fear of the number thirteen. Milton asks, "How important would it be for you to get over this fear?" After a long pause, the client responds, "Very." For the next five minutes or so, they work on a plan that will help the client get professional support from a psychotherapist the client has worked with before.

When Therapy Is Needed

Since the coach has entered a significant and meaningful relationship with the client, the coach has certain responsibilities like any significant other would have. There are certain red flags that the coach should be able to identify as symptomatic of the need for therapy. These include persistent anger or aggression, suicidal ideation, self-destructive impulses or behaviors, and extreme dependency (Hart, Blattner, and Leipsic 2001, 233). Anyone can be having a bad hair day. In the short term, such symptoms belong to many coaching conversations. In the long term, a professional referral might be in order. This might mean that you refer the client to someone else and lose that client's revenue. It might also mean that the client can get the right help from the right person.

Professional Life Coach Mary Sorrentino says, "It may almost seem that I'm *trying* to lose clients, but unless they know the difference between coaching and counseling and seek help from the right professional at the right time, their lives won't change and work will fail" (Sorrentino 2013, 211). Referring a client away does not necessarily mean losing the client, either. Often they will come back to you after the relevant issue has been resolved.

How Coaching and Therapy Differ

In general, a therapist looks for problems, conflicts, insecurities, and emotional issues (like anger and depression). They diagnose and prescribe. Coaches look for opportunities and new perspectives. They facilitate and encourage. A therapist's training is in counseling. A coach's training is in listening and asking questions.

In therapy, the therapist is in charge and directs the activity. In coaching, the client is in charge, and both the coach and client alike share the direction of the activity.

Therapy looks to the cause of a problem. *Coaching looks to the solution for a situation.*

Therapy focuses on what is wrong.

Coaching focuses on what is possible.

Therapy tries to bring healing for the past. *Coaching tries to create energy for the future.*

Therapy is an exercise. *Coaching is a dance.*

In coaching, the coach focuses on increasing the client's capacity and reaching goals. The coach is there to facilitate action that helps the client achieve results. Coaching is about listening for possibilities, goals, dreams, and aspirations. It is the task of the coach to harness and expand the client's strengths. Coaching is not listening for problems, pathologies, history, pain, and mental blockages. It is not the task of the coach to root out problems and tackle them. The coach assumes that the client already has the ability to move forward. The therapist assumes that the client needs to gain the ability to move forward.

Pathology Belongs to the Mental Health Profession

Most coaches are not qualified to recognize pathology. However, most therapists should be able to do this, according to psychologists Hart, Blattner, and Leipsic. When in doubt, consult an expert. "The exploration of depth issues is perceived as outside the boundaries of coaching for nonclinically trained coaches" (Hart, Blattner, and Leipsic 2001, 230).

Is there something the coach *can* do when the coaching is out of his league? Ethics professor Richard Rowson recommends asking the following questions:

- Is the client drawing on the professional expertise available to her?
- Has she made the effort to become well informed?
- Has she thought through the issues as much as she can in the time available?
- Has the client made the arrangements necessary to carry out the tasks properly?
- Has she used the resources available to her? (Rowson 2006, 90)

It would not be morally correct to abandon someone in need (Luke10: 25-37). Most of the time, a referral to another professional is a temporary situation, and the client comes back later with renewed capacity to move forward and increased loyalty to his coach, who sought the best care for him. By the way, God likes this, too (Psalms 18:20).

Dealing with the Past

"Am I crazy?" April asks. "I really wonder sometimes if I'm not crazy."

Milton responds, "What makes you think that you might be crazy?"

In Milton's eyes, April is certainly not symptomatic of any mental health issues. Although there are many things from April's past that continue to negatively impact her life, that reality doesn't necessarily exclude her from coaching. She might, however, need more than coaching to figure out what issues in her past need healing.

In coaching, the past is a reference point. For example, when clients say they are unsure how to solve a particular problem, the coach might ask them to recall a similar situation in the past and remember how they dealt with the problem then. However, for the most part, coaching is a forward view. It focuses on passion and purpose. It assumes the person is relatively healthy and prepared to find his or her solutions. Counseling, on the other hand, helps people deal with inner turmoil, anxiety, and interpersonal conflict (Collins 2002, 15). In coaching, the focus goes from the present to the future. In counseling, the focus goes from the past to the present. A survey of mental health professionals who also practice coaching noted that this lack of emphasis on the past was the most notable difference between coaching and therapy (Hart, Blattner, and Leipsic 2001, 231).

Very often, the client simply needs to know that their feelings and perspectives are not crazy, flipped out, or abnormal. For the coach to reassure the client that everything is copacetic, the coach needs to have a qualitative understanding about the context of the client's situation. This can happen because (a) the coach has been there himself, or (b) he has gained a perspective on the topic through study, knowledge or expertise. People often feel very bad about the past and are frustrated because the events of the past are not changeable. The *person*, however, *is* changeable. The coach can help the client engage actively in changing the meaning of the past. In this way, the past becomes an operative springboard for the future during the coaching meeting.

Relational Dynamics

As the medical professional vows to *do no harm*, the coach pledges *to do what is best for the client*. In view of both principles, an ethical dilemma for the coach surfaces when what is best for the client is not good for society. If the client were to feel the most self-actualized by sitting naked on a statue in Central Park, the coach would be hard-pressed to affirm such an action. Generally, coaches help clients move up the ladder of Maslow's hierarchy of needs. However, a coach should not permit this at any expense. Damage could result when a coach encourages the client to perform acts that are harmful to society in general.

The coach should be aware that pathological issues might underlie the client's drive to perform, or even over-perform. By developing a profound understanding of the client's objectives, the coach can assist the client in reaching new levels of performance. We should be mindful that a coaching style that ignores the relational dynamics behind a client's motives could be contributing to an effort that hurts someone. In other words, the best for the client might be doing what is best for society at large.

Let's consider an example. Your client comes to the coaching session with the goal of figuring out how to get her son a treehouse. That is what he said he wanted for his birthday. During the coaching meeting, the client envisions hiring a carpenter, roofer, electrician, and safety inspector. All of the elements of a good coaching conversation are there. The client has a plan in mind and numerous ways to get the job done. You, however, have the nagging feeling that the son doesn't want a high-tech superstructure in the backyard. He might want to actually build his own treehouse. Your coaching would be amiss if you didn't ask something like, "What does your son want?" Part of your task as a coach is to check that the client has considered alternatives and options. We call this *creating awareness*. In the ethics of relational dynamics, the coach should not be afraid to step on the client's toes.

Self-Sufficiency

Sports coaches create dependencies. The coach tells the athlete what to do, and the results show improvement. A team-sport coach can also be the source of strategies that will win games. In non-directive coaching, the difficulty in getting the client to change an existing process is easy to underestimate. If the coach were to resort to the "tell and do" approach, the client might become dependent on the coach for the advice or reject the advice as without merit. I know from my high school sports day that when I listened to the coach, things went well; when I did not listen, things went badly. Many of your clients will approach the coaching conversation with this type of past experience. They expect you to tell them what to do. They expect to become dependent. You can hear this in the client's words when you find they are *explaining* rather than *exploring*. After a lengthy explanation, the client will often expect advice from you.

Your task as a coach is to build the client's ability to self-sufficiently reach her own conclusions. As time goes on, however, the coaching relationship should mature, and the client should become able to independently process and decide for herself. When the coaching relationship is mature and the client is self-sufficient, direct communication and observation become more prevalent. The client knows what works yet still employs the coach to keep her sharp and at the top of her game. I find it interesting when someone hires me for performance coaching that we usually slide very quickly into life coaching. After a period when values, goals, and awareness increase to a point of synergy, we then slide back into performance coaching. Very soon after that, the client is self-sufficient and ready to move on.

Exercise

- How/when does the coach speak the truth in love (Ephesians 4:15)?

- True or false? "He who does not learn from the past is doomed to repeat it."

- What is your coaching response to "My goal is to stop the production of coffee"?

- How do you feel when someone says, "That's good advice. Thank you"?

Which of My Values Is Relevant Here?

Illumination Lights the Path to Discovery

The illustration below shows the road to discovery. When the road is dark, we can add illumination by ourselves, as with the flashlight. We can also wait for the sun to rise and receive the illumination that God has provided for us. To safely stay on the road, we need to see where we are going. Along the way, there are signs to advise us. The illumination—provided by us or provided by God—shows the curves and the potential hazards.

I include this simple illustration to make one point: For all her potential and promise, the client can illuminate only a portion of the road by her own means. She will only see what she shines the light on. Her ability to see what is really going on pales in comparison to what God reveals with His all-pervading light (Ephesians 5:13, 1 Corinthians 4:5, Job 12:22). Whether counseling or coaching, our task as Christians is to help the client see the light.

Biblical Worldview

This book departs from a secular book on ethics at the point of biblical worldview. The majority of the literature on ethics condemns the myopic perspective of a professional who believes that a book written 2,000 years ago can address the complete code of conduct necessary for a coach to practice professionally in the twenty-first century. Indeed, there are many religious gurus who claim to have discovered the truth and brand their version of the interpretation as the new gospel. This is not Christianity.

Do we, as Christians, believe that we have a correct view of human nature? No, most of us do not. Do we believe that our God has a correct view of human nature? Yes, most of us believe He does. We believe in a God who knows and understands all things. This is not only a comfort for today; it is also a hope for tomorrow. Our sense of hope subsequently undergirds our coaching questions. In the non-directive approach to coaching, we expect the Holy Spirit to speak to the client. We hope the client will be willing to hear His voice and act accordingly. We coaches are not the voice of God. We coaches are process managers who enable the client to hear the voice of God.

The operative mantra in secular coaching is that the client is fully creative, resourceful, and whole. In Christian coaching, however, we identify God as the source of that creativity. God is the source of our resources. Jesus Christ is the source of our wholeness. The source of all good things is God. It is hubris for man to think that his goodness can rise above the righteousness of Christ. We have all have sinned and fallen short of the glory of God (Romans 3:23). We do work with generally healthy individuals, but apart from God, we on our own are not enough. While God's wisdom may seem foolish to mankind, it should be noted that mankind's wisdom may seem foolish to God (see 1 Corinthians 3:19).

Hopefully, the Christian coach reading this book is inspired to act professionally and righteously. If one must be brought before the governors and kings of this world, let it be for the sake of the Gospel (Matthew 10:18). I do not ignore the possibility that the Christian nature of this text on ethics will be poorly received by those who maintain that man is the center of all things. However, this book on Christian coaching ethics stands on the biblical foundation: "For I am not ashamed of the gospel, because it is the power of God that brings salvation to everyone who believes" (Romans 1:16, NIV).

What Are the Dangers?

Milton reads an article that explains how true coaching occurs when all questions asked are discovery questions. He realizes that his questions have been probing into reasons, not solutions. Certainly, this is a habit he developed when he was a practicing psychotherapist. This explains why his clients also seem to get locked onto problem solving and not goal setting. He realizes that creating awareness is a two-way street. It can lead to the past or to the future. He resolves to focus on more forward-looking questions and avoid backward-looking ones.

Not Giving Advice When Coaching

Many new coaches find it counter-intuitive to withhold advice or guidance when clients specifically ask for it. Before they started coaching, it was common for them to share their thoughts with friends and family, thoughts generally well received. I find that this is the impetus for some to toy with the idea of becoming a life coach. However, as they become more experienced coaches, they see that giving advice actually takes away from the client's ability to choose the right solution. Without the client internalizing the ultimate decision, they have little chance of owning the decision and, consequently, the result. When a coach gives advice, it takes away the client's power of choice. Their ability to make autonomous decisions becomes limited.

One of the dangers of giving advice is that the listener's decision-making parts of the brain go into "off mode" when this happens. When financial risk is involved, for example, studies show that the brain effectively goes into neutral when given advice. In other words, the decision-making process becomes offloaded, and the advice does not embed in the listener's brain at that time (Engelmann, Capra, Noussair, and Berns 2009). Consequently, the client moves into "intake" mode while listening to the advice. Since most people are not able to make a decision while listening to advice, the best-case scenario occurs only when they can remember the advice well enough to process and reach a decision at a later point. Forgetfulness, apathy, and disagreement will affect the receiver's ability to act positively on such advice. Furthermore, if a client is under extreme stress, the probability of processing the advice correctly is miniscule (see chapter three).

The coaching approach listens for the client's agenda, not the coach's agenda for the client. The coach integrates and builds on the client's ideas. The coach uses the client's vocabulary. The questions the coach asks are ones that evoke discovery, insight, and commitment. The coach challenges the client's assumptions. "When you and I coach, we frequently find ourselves at the crossroads of choosing between giving knowledge through advice or giving the gift of self-discovery through questions. I am sure you know this crossroads well," says Professional Christian Coaching Institute faculty member Anne Denmark. "Be wise. Help your client hear his or her own heart by *staying with the questions*" (Denmark 2013, 101; italics added).

The Banner of Coaching Is No Protection from Risk Liability

Milton's client Sam is a recovering alcoholic. They have discussed this at length and determined that their coaching meetings will focus only on topics that help Sam move forward. Sam recognizes that he alone is responsible for his future actions, yet Milton feels a certain amount of responsibility to help Sam stay away from alcohol.

Another danger for counselors, as well as coaches, is the line that they may cross when a dual relationship is present. For the most part, therapists are not allowed to have a dual relationship with a client (as discussed in chapter

five). However, due to the nature of coaching, the client and coach often best build rapport when they share a common interest that allows the client to feel they are on the same page. Looser boundaries exist for the coach than for the therapist (Hart, Blattner, and Leipsic 2001, 235). Dual relationships are not uncommon among coaches and clients. When it comes to liability, however, the banner under which the coach performs the service (counseling, therapy, coaching, etc.) will not play a significant role before a board of inquiry. The substance of the relationship and the power to do harm will be the points of liability that a review board will want to investigate. In other words, if the coach abuses the dual relationship, the same amount of accountability will apply as if he were a therapist. The banner of coaching in and of itself does not protect the coach from risk liability.

Risk Readiness

One of Milton's friends from the psychotherapy community is being sued for malpractice. His friend is being accused of deliberately misdiagnosing a patient. While Milton seriously doubts his friend will be found guilty, he begins to wonder if anything in his coaching business might lead to a lawsuit. For example, he is considering advertising himself as a wellness coach. He is concerned that some might misinterpret his intentions.

Outside of going to court, there is no surefire way to determine in advance whether you can be held responsible for a particular risk. If you really want to know, going to court is an expensive way to find out. Knowing why, how, and when someone might sue you is part of protecting yourself from attack. Having a game plan for such scenarios is the better part of valor. You need not be an expert in jurisprudence to adequately defend yourself. However, I recommend that there be someone on your team (like a lawyer) who knows about the order of legal proceedings. Justice can only be served when the systems in place are scrupulous and proper. The ethical coach must comply with these systems and offer as much assistance as is reasonable to his own defense.

That being said, there are not many documented cases of a coach actually being sued for negligence. British ethics professor Jonathan Passmore reports that coaching is a low-risk activity in England. In Australia, the legal environment is a bit tense since coaches occasionally find themselves working with clients who have needs that are more challenging than the coach is prepared to handle (Passmore 2009, 7). In some places, coaches are encouraged to have clients sign a statement clarifying that they have no mental health issues upon entering the coaching relationship. In the eyes of the court, however, a judge might not see this as material evidence. The health care industry is careful to prevent imposters from practicing in their jurisdictions. In Norway, there is a great deal of scrutiny directed toward professions like coaching since many officials view it as offering "alternative treatment" to public health care (Svaleng and Grant 2010, 10).

QUESTION

How would you define "wellness coaching"?

Who Is Going to Know?

Milton often gets calls from coaches who are concerned that a client might have a mental disorder. The first thing Milton does when he gets an inquiry is to ask the coach to disguise anything that might identify the client. These conversations are strictly confidential. The second thing he does is ask, "What makes you think that there might be a mental disorder?" The answer is almost always, "Well, something just doesn't feel right."

Sometimes, the client is so stuck that she cannot find a way forward. The coach has already checked for pathologies that indicate mental instability where the client initially seemed healthy. The client, however, might mask her pathology, and unhealthy emotions may only surface after several sessions. The coach could find himself in the honorable position of being the first one to suggest to the client that she seek the help of a mental health professional (Hart, Blattner, and Leipsic 2001, 232). Here, the coach's intuition is an important tool.

If the coach has a tight feeling in the pit of his stomach about a client, it might be the Holy Spirit is prompting. In a podcast conversation with Jory Fisher, Professional Christian Coaching Institute founder Chris McCluskey said that early in his coaching career, he sometimes found himself saying, "God help this person," after hanging up the phone with a client or potential client. He subsequently recognized this as the prompting of the Holy Spirit to explore whether the client needed professional help from someone else (Fisher 2013). Therapy is a way for the client to discover past hurts and fears that limit the potential to move forward. In some cases, a chemical imbalance requires correction with medication. The ethical coach should work with his clients to see that their full potential is reachable. Sometimes that means correcting the darkness of the past so that the future can be brighter. Therapy is not a road to shame; it is a road to healing.

How Do I Do It Right?

Contextualization lies in the tension between giving and withholding advice. The coach's ability to put the question or observation into the right context is a key to unlocking hidden potential. By using the client's vocabulary and identifying the client's situation correctly, the coach can help the client release ideas that hinder or derail her success. The coach and the client are in familiar territory when they both understand the context of the situation.

Let's look at an example. The client says, "The ROI on this project is terrible. Our current capital commitment to the R&D is beyond anything anyone envisioned a year ago. Our debt-to-equity ratio is upside down. There is no way the board will approve next year's budget if the NPV and IRR don't improve. Perhaps we can find an angel investor or drum up some VC. I don't know what to do."

The coach says, "Well, it sounds like you have a problem. What do you think you should do about it?"

In this example, the coach has responded correctly. The coach is not leading the client, nor second-guessing the client. The client is still in charge of her progress, and the coach is managing the process. The question begging an answer is whether the coach has understood what the client said and whether the coach needs to be *able* to understand such things. If the coach has a background in financial management, the above statement is not difficult to understand. If the client is confident in the coach's knowledge of capital investments, the conversation will move forward as normal. The client and the coach are on the same page. If the client is confident in the coach's ability to manage the process, the conversation can also move forward. Solid knowledge of the client's situation helps the coach to properly contextualize the next step. This helps the coach ask good questions. At the same time, solid knowledge of the coaching process helps the coach dance in the moment. You don't have to know the lyrics of the song to be a good dancer.

Along these lines, it is entirely possible that the coach has no idea about the context the client is experiencing. For example, once a client of mine wanted coaching around what to wear to a professional event. Insofar as I know nothing about women's fashion, this scenario was obviously outside of my wheelhouse. Nevertheless, the client was pleased with the action plan she formulated and happy with the coaching she got. The coaching approach will, in and of itself, generate discovery. When the client can increase awareness at any level, there is a notable gain resulting from the coaching conversation.

Effective coaches know enough about the context to ask a powerful question yet maintain a deep and constructive childlike curiosity. The ethical coach should recognize when the context of the client's situation requires a level of service that the coach cannot accommodate. A referral is in order when this happens.

QUESTION

Given that neither of your thumbs is green, what is your coaching response to "My garden is dying"?

Chapter Summary

There are significant differences between therapy and coaching. These differences should be clear to the Christian coach so he knows when to refer a client. Clients will often feel ashamed of their lack of progress. It is the task of the coach to help the client move forward with encouragement and empowerment. Doing so involves a certain amount of risk for which the coach must be prepared. Specifically, not giving advice is an essential aspect of keeping the coach's risk to a minimum. It is better for the client to *own* her own plan for moving forward. If and when that plan includes gaining knowledge possessed by the coach, there is nothing ethically wrong with the coach sharing that knowledge in the spirit of discovery. As long as the client fully accepts the responsibility for making a decision based on that knowledge and accepts the consequences that result from that decision, sharing one's knowledge is ethically sound.

Milton has determined that rather than giving the advice his clients ask for, he will risk losing clients in order to be a truly non-directive coach. He became convinced of this after a recent meeting with a client who had again asked him, "What do you think I should do?" To this Milton responded, "Well, what do *you* think you should do?" He then sat there, relaxed, and waited for her to respond. From his vantage point, Milton could see from the clock on the wall that over three minutes had elapsed before the client suddenly exclaimed, "I know exactly what I should do!" Sure enough, the solution she came up with was perfect. Milton is now thoroughly convinced that non-directive coaching is extremely beneficial for the client.

What Do You Do?

Scenario A: Your client has come to the last four or five coaching meetings feeling overwhelmed. You have pointed this out as an observation a couple of times, yet the client is not able to articulate why she feels overwhelmed. How might you help her explore this?

Scenario B: Your client is preoccupied with introducing hydroponics into developing countries. Your noted lack of vocabulary of botany keeps you guessing about what the client is really telling you. What are your alternatives?

Scenario C: Your client seems to have leveled out. She no longer brings goals and aspirations to the coaching conversations. Subsequently she seems more content to tell you about her daily life and unresolved issues. She has not followed through on her action plans in months. What would you need to do in this situation?

Scenario D: Your client decides to change her diet to lose weight and improve her health. Although her plan was completely self-driven, she often refers to it as the advice you gave her. Do you defend yourself as not having actually given her that advice? How would you do this?

End of Chapter Questions

- Are you willing to become vulnerable as a coach?

- The client says, "I think you are the only person who really cares about me." What do you do next?

- Which of these trumps the others: the ICF code of ethics, the CCNI code of ethics, or the Bible?

- What role does shame play in coaching?

CHAPTER 9
ETHICAL TRAINING AND ESTABLISHING AN ETHICS PLAN OF ACTION

"We can't solve problems by using the same kind of thinking we used when we created them."

—Albert Einstein, (1879–1955)

Professional organizations provide codes and guidelines for ethical behavior. However, an organization's big-picture view of things does not address all of the day-to-day dilemmas and contingencies. Credentials and certificates show a certain level of proficiency. However, the ethical coach might need to go beyond professional codes and guidelines to find ways to get the training, skills, and accountability needed to run an ethical business. We will examine mentoring, supervision, peer groups, and other activities in this chapter. The subject matter of ethical discussions is dynamic and requires constant attention from the conscientious coach. Furthermore, the ethical coach will need to look inside herself to find areas that might require additional help.

After reading this chapter, you will be able to do the following:

- determine your need for an industry-recognized credential;

- examine your need for introspection;

- ascertain your need for additional tools and trainings;

- find ways to be held accountable;

- discover what you need to do to stay current.

Karen's Story

Karen never really intended to become a coach. But one day, she realized that she was more a coach than a consultant. She prefers asking questions to giving answers. To her, this was enough justification to call herself a coach. She is less concerned about the semantics of the label and more concerned with delivering to the client what he needs and wants. To her, it's all about results. If the client gets the results he wants, who cares which methodology is used? Her motto is "I can be all things to all people."

Karen views the client relationship as a facilitated information exchange. When a client contacts her, either in person or by phone, she asks lots of questions. This continues until she is able to formulate the client's need. Karen then makes a projection on the amount of time it will take her to evaluate the needs and make suggestions. Typically, in about two or three weeks, she has compiled a list of three or four alternatives. She meets again with the client to select or modify the alternatives and establish a plan of action. She has heard of non-directive coaching, but does not think it would fit her target market.

Common Challenges

Karen attained a bachelor's degree in international business when she was in her early twenties. Since then she has had very little to do with international business. Yet somehow that has not seemed to matter. She finds a way to ask good questions and get good results. When a potential client asks if she has a credential or any training certificates in coaching, she responds, "My success record with clients speaks for itself." She does not believe that any tools or assessments are specific enough to help her clients. She feels that the important thing is that the client is content with what she can deliver. If the client is dissatisfied, well, that's too bad.

Do You Need a Coaching Credential?

A coaching credential is a designation of a recognized level of professional training, proficiency, experience, and adherence to ethics and standards. It is a measure of professional quality. There are numerous credentialing bodies from which to choose. The two delineated in this book are those of ICF and CCNI. These two organizations offer well-respected credentials for non-directive coaching. One should keep in mind that the strength of the credential is only as good as the standards established by the credentialing

program. "Make sure you associate yourself with the right program" cautions Luoma (2014). There are various levels of credentials offered, and one need not have the highest-level credential to be considered professional.

Credentialing in the coaching industry is a voluntary process. Your skills, abilities, and knowledge are measured against requirements deemed standard for the industry. This helps ensure that you are a coach with a recognized level of proficiency. Since a credentialing organization is not a training school, their unbiased assessment of your performance level is validation of your professionalism. Part of the credentialing process is to also ensure that you know and understand their code of ethics.

QUESTION

What level of credentialing fulfills your professional aspirations?

Do You Need a Lot of Acronyms After Your Name?

Here is an example of too much alphabet soup after one's name:

M. J. Marx, BA (GS), MBA (IB), EdD (AE), PCC (ICF), CPCC (CCNI), CPLC (PCCI) and 360 assessor.

Too much.

Did You Know?

Credential Types - ICF

- ACC - Associate Certified Coach (60 training hours, 100 client hours)

- PCC - Professional Certified Coach (125 training hours, 500 client hours)

- MCC - Master Certified Coach (200 training hours, 2,500 client hours)

Credential Types - CCNI

- CCC - Certified Christian Coach (60 training hours, 100 client hours)

- CPCC - Certified Professional Christian Coach (120 training hours, 500 client hours)

- CMCC - Certified Master Christian Coach (200 training hours, 1,000 client hours)

certain level of competency within the industry as a whole. Certificates show that you have completed coursework from a particular school. Who needs them? Well, you do. You are the one who needs to know that you are professional and can hold your own with the competition. You need to know a body of believers attests to your ability to perform at the level you advertise. You need to know that you are good at what you do.

Do You Need a College Degree to Coach?

To date, neither ICF nor CCNI require that a member have a degree from a school of higher education. It seems that most coaches do, indeed, hold some kind of university degree, though. A degree shows that you have received an above-average education. In my opinion, a bachelor's degree proves that you know how to perform at a relatively high level over an extended period.

In the past, students regarded a bachelor's degree as an entry ticket to a job interview. Nowadays this is not always the case. Many people regard a BA or BS as an essential educational requirement for becoming a professional *anything*. Mostly I find that your *major* gets less attention in the marketplace than the school attended. This shifts once you receive an advanced degree. A

My example does not look impressive. It looks cluttered and overdone. Admittedly, there are cultures that admire numerous acronyms after a person's name. However, most people look at a long string of credentials and certifications as overbearing and egotistical. Coaches will often find their reputation in the marketplace is enough to get service and keep clients. Very, very rarely does someone ask if I hold a certain credential or certificate. Credentials mean that you can prove a master's degree denotes a high degree of specialization and an ability to operate independently and proficiently. For most coaching endeavors, a master's is more than enough.

Do You Need to Use Assessment Tools?

Numerous assessments are available to coaches to aid in the evaluation of the client's awareness of self. Some of the most popular are the Myers-Briggs Type Inventory (MBTI), the 360 degree assessments, the RightPath, the DiSC® Personality Types assessment, and the EQ Test (emotional intelligence quotient test). With a little time and money, the coach can get a certification for a smorgasbord of assessment tools. One should take care that any assessment offered is for the benefit of the client, not just the financial gain of the coach.

As a qualified assessor, coaches can use their tools to help the clients uncover and/or discover traits and talents previously unknown. The ethical coach should be trained, knowledgeable, and experienced in the tool's usage. If a client were to want an assessment not offered by the coach, a referral is in order. An untrained coach should not try to interpret a set of assessment results. It is a good idea to partner with another coach who has the needed certification for the assessment tool (Nash, Christian, and Anderson 2011, 315–316).

Do You Need Continuing Education?

Professional organizations such as ICF or CCNI require that credential holders stay sharp by continuing to learn. A professional must not stagnate. There are several ways to accumulate the training hours needed to renew a credential. One of the most fun ways is to attend a convention or seminar where governing bodies have approved the workshops and sessions for the requisite continuing education units (CEUs). One can also submit writing, research, and self-study as proof of continuing education.

There are many reasons a professional coach might want to continue taking classes from a coaching training school even if she already possesses a credential. It is important for the coach to keep up with the continuing

---

?

Did You Know?

A credential in coaching means that you have proven your ability to meet the standards of the industry. A certificate usually means that you have met the requirements set forth by a certain school or training program. Most credentials include the word "certified," e.g., Professional Certified Coach.

---

education requirements needed for her level of license or credential. Most training schools offer some type of certificate for the coursework taken. When approved, one can use these certificates to fulfill the requirements of a larger certification or a credential. Furthermore, human resources representatives looking for coaches often require that all contracted service providers have training only from certified or accredited schools. Many organizations require that at least one training certificate in ethics be attained every three years. Recently, ICF has introduced a requirement for ethics training in order to renew one's credential. Another advantage is that training certificates look good on a résumé.

At the Heart of the Matter

To Whom Are You Accountable?

Jason, Karen's client, is perturbed. He just hung up the phone with Karen, who told him that she was giving his preferred appointment time slot—Thursdays at 10:00 a.m.—to another client that she deemed more important. This is the third time she has pulled something like this, and Jason is getting tired of it. Talking to Karen about it doesn't seem to do any good. However, is her action wrong? Who can Jason turn to in order to find out whether such actions are acceptable business practices for coaches?

Some people prefer to be a sole proprietor because it means no one is looking over their shoulders. In the above example, the client questions the integrity of the coach's actions. Jason could call the Better Business Bureau, the Chamber of Commerce, or even his pastor. They are all likely to have an opinion. If Karen is a member of a professional or civic organization, Jason may consult with that organization.

A professional should belong to organizations that hold their members accountable. Some examples: one of the operative goals of the Rotarians is to encourage its members to practice high ethical standards at work (Rotary International n.d.). The International Coach Federation (ICF) and the Christian Coaches Network International (CCNI) also have accountability as part of their charters. One could even argue that it is unethical *not* to belong to a professional organization, as the clients have no independent body to turn to when they have a complaint. Ultimately, as members of the body of Christ,

Christian coaches are obliged to honor the pledges made to man as well as God (Numbers 30:2).

---------- QUESTION ----------

How do you treat a client who is not "convenient"?

With Whom Do You Fellowship?

Karen likes to go to lunch with her friends. Like her, most of them are single, professional, and dedicated to their jobs. One of her friends is always talking about how much she gets from some of the professional groups she belongs to. This sounds to Karen like a very time-consuming effort. If belonging to such a group were to bring her more clients, she might be interested. Otherwise, she is too involved with her work to give up what little free time she has for "professional development."

It is not necessary to participate in major organization events to glean from the knowledge and experience of others. Accountability can be brought down to a local level. Throughout the world, small groups of coaches meet to discuss the hows and whys of coaching. ICF calls these groups chapters. Topics that are intended to provoke discussion of ethical dilemmas are often brought up at these chapter meetings. ICF also sponsors topic-oriented discussion groups called Communities of Practice (CP). Like-minded coaches meet regularly to discuss ethical issues that coaches and training schools face. In a similar manner, CCNI regularly hosts mastermind groups and accountability groups. Either online or face-to-face, coaches get together regularly for fellowship and conversation.

With Whom Can You Experiment?

On a less formal basis, coaches often meet with peer group members who form a fellowship of like-minded coaches. Often these peer groups become a platform for the coach to practice coaching with the other group members. This is a good opportunity for new coaches to hone their coaching skills in a low-risk environment (Parker, Kram, and Hall 2012). New coaches often find that peer coaching helps them experiment with various coaching methods without the concerns of having all their coaching ducks in a row.

Among other things, peer coaching fosters self-disclosure, empathy, respectful engagement, and mutual learning (Parker, Kram, and Hall 2012, 375). Typically, peer groups consist of students enrolled in a course offered by a training school. These groups might dissolve when the course is over, or they may continue.

ICF also offers a system for coaches to engage in reciprocal peer coaching.

This is a type of barter coaching among coaches with similar qualifications. It can also be a good way to get experience coaching someone from a different culture and receive coaching by someone from a different country.

QUESTION

Who do you count on
to guard your back?

From Whom Do You Get Professional Training?

Karen often gets emails from training schools offering the latest, greatest way to become a perfect this or a highly-qualified that. Since none of the schools can guarantee that their training will increase her profit, she holds them at arm's length. She did once attend a locally held workshop on how to gain more customers, but the information shared was not new to her. She often wonders whether the instructors of such workshops have ever actually been in business for themselves.

There are many successful coaches who just *do* coaching without formal training. Similarly, there are many successful electricians who just *do* electrical work without formal training. However, if one were to discover that a non-certified electrician did electrical work, then the fire insurance might not pay for a claim resulting from an electrically triggered fire.

Since coaching is not a regulated industry, there is no insurance that will actually underwrite the quality of the coaching work. Consequently, the coach cannot and should not offer any guaranteed results. What the coach can offer a certified training experience as validation of coaching skill. In terms of quality, getting training from a school of high standards is your best insurance policy. I believe that, along with skills acquisition, training in ethics is a must. A coach should never feel blindsided by an ethical dilemma. There should be at least a theoretical basis laid for the aspiring coach to stand on. Proper training and analysis of case studies are an integral part of the coach's growth curve.

In their book, *Ethical Maturity in the Helping Professions,* Dr. Michael Carroll and Elisabeth Shaw admonish that one should not experience ethics training as a "tick in the box" (Carroll and Shaw 2013, 293) exercise. They claim that too much of professional development emphasizes the regulations and *shall nots*. Many professionals will just scan over such a list of rules because they believe that they already know them. The larger task at hand is for coaches to internalize ethical behavior and truly learn ethics—not only as knowledge, but also as lifestyle. We can learn proper ethical behavior by studying it. We can also learn proper ethical behavior by practicing it. Either way, it is a learned behavior. As described in the passage below, learning ethics should be a lifetime project.

The process of having made ethical decisions is itself fertile ground for learning from that experience. It influences the process in terms of how to make future ethical decisions and how to learn from those experiences in order to continue to build moral character. We revisit the ethical experience itself to set it up as a learning project.

Learning from experience means that:
- data becomes information
- information becomes knowledge
- knowledge becomes wisdom
- wisdom becomes practical action
- practical knowledge becomes embedded in who we are (Carroll and Shaw 2013, 261)

─────── **QUESTION** ───────

In terms of ethical growth
and behavior, what have
you become?

──────── **Factors That Muddle the Issue** ────────

Karen wonders if training in ethics is not just another form of control. After all, you either get paid or you don't. Why should she learn how to behave when no one really cares how she behaves? As long as none of her clients lose money as a result of her coaching, what's the harm? One thing she learned in college is that you can never really learn anything useful under the guise of theory. What you learn is practical or it is useless.

Training in Ethics Might Not Be Enough

Learning, for many of us, becomes a lifestyle, a ritual, a permanent practice. Most of what we learn happens informally. We learn by listening, watching, and doing. Formal education, however, becomes a game for some—a seasonal attempt at conquering the system on the academic battlefield. Another degree or another certificate does not make you a better coach. Becoming better at coaching makes you a better coach. You can get a doctorate in coaching and not be proficient at coaching. Some trust in chariots, and some trust in university degrees, but we Christian coaches trust in the Lord [Psalms 20:7, somewhat paraphrased].

Knowledge gained can be a useful tool. Knowledge can show you where you might be vulnerable and where you might be subject to manipulation (Carroll and Shaw 2013, 279). The ethical Christian coach knows

Exercise

- Who can a coach call when she has a question regarding ethics?

- How does your lifestyle help or hinder coaching?

- What information is on your business card? Why?

- What do you think of the saying: "If it's going to be, it's up to me"?

that protection from harm entails more than getting a training certificate. It means depending on God for direction. Professor and coach Renee Oscarson talks about the confidence in her ethics and supervision coursework having actually been misplaced: "I should have placed my confidence in God" (Oscarson 2013, 46). To be truly looking after what is best for the client, assistance from above is key. She writes further, "Pray for wisdom, and pray regularly for your clients. Wisdom requires that we be prepared. Seeking adequate training is good as long as that training is not our ultimate source of confidence. Be familiar with ethical standards for coaches" (Oscarson 2013, 46–47).

The coach who has a lifestyle of learning good ethics regularly reviews ethical issues. There are numerous ways to deep-dive into a topic. You can even write a dissertation on a topic only to discover that your knowledge of the topic is superficial. We refer to a doctorate as a *terminal* degree. It is called terminal because it becomes the last level of deep knowledge you can reach in formal education (either that or it kills you).

Having a big goal is a good way to ensure that the energy you expend on moving forward is on track toward a worthwhile destination. Don't be afraid of making big plans. You would be surprised how small your plans are compared to the ones God has for you.

Checklists Might Not Be Enough

We task-oriented folk like making lists. We get satisfaction out of seeing each item checked off or crossed out. Checklists help us remember important things. These days, we do checklists on paper, on computers, on cellphones, or on whatever medium works for us. I know a gardener who writes his daily checklist on the dashboard of his truck with chalk—whatever works. There is no right or wrong way to do a checklist. "Checklists can help people avoid blind spots in a complex environment," write authors Heath and Heath in their book *Switch: When Change is Hard* (Heath and Heath 2011, 221). They also write the following:

People fear checklists because they see them as dehumanizing—maybe because they associate them with the exhaustive checklists that allow inexperienced teenagers to operate fast-food chains successfully. They think if something is simple enough to put it in a checklist, a monkey can do it. Well, if that's right, grab a pilot's checklist and try your luck with a 747. (Heath and Heath 2011, 222)

Having a good, well-executed plan is better than having powerful chaos unleashed on your business. There are a couple of things coaches should regularly work into their planning. Having a checklist is a good way to make sure that each needed item gets some attention. Having a goal-oriented action plan, however, is a better way to ensure that the important things actually get done. A checklist without a purpose is like coffee without caffeine.

Which of My Values Is Relevant Here?

Karen believes that the entirety of the world's economy is in the hands of a few individuals. She feels that the best she can do on a daily basis is to scratch out an existence for herself and hopefully harm no one in the process. She has heard that having a written personal code of conduct will make a person more responsible, but she does not believe it. She feels that anything you write about your operations today will have to change tomorrow when the super-rich start pulling the strings that keep people like her at a disadvantage.

Responsibility for Decisions

In ethical terms, one considers a professional to be an agent of morality who takes full responsibility for their conduct and actions. This being so,

they must therefore be responsible for their own decisions. The public expects (demands) that professionals seek the best results for the individuals they serve. Ethical professionals should be able to articulate why they made the decisions they did given the particular circumstances (Rowson 2006, 175). If, for example, the coach were to reveal client information, the coach would then be obliged to explain why he felt that this breach of confidentiality was justified. A coach should follow the professional code of conduct as much as possible, and any deviation from the code should be justifiable and explainable under the circumstances (Rowson 2006, 167).

The ethical Christian coach not only follows the letter of the law but the *Spirit of the law* (Romans 2:28-29). Some professionals find it useful to keep a journal (or notes) detailing significant decisions they make. Recording the dates, facts, and figures relating to the decision will help you remember the essential elements later on. Impressions and suspicions might also be good things to record. Most of us feel that an important decision permanently burns into our active memory only to find that even a couple of weeks later the details become fuzzy. Also, keep in mind that your coaching notes may be requested as evidence in a dispute. Don't record statements that you might later be embarrassed to show to others.

Locus of Control

Research shows that those with a stronger internal locus of control are more likely to correctly answer questions about proper ethical behavior. They are also less susceptible to pressure from bullies and more able to resist coercion (Collins 2009, 116; Trevino and Youngblood 1990, 382). Many make decisions under pressure from external sources.

Some people feel that outside circumstances dictate the outcomes of their lives. We refer to this as an external locus of control. In other words, the force that controls a person's destiny is located outside (versus inside)

of themselves. The person who exhibits an internal locus of control believes that they alone are responsible for their outcomes. The ability to be introspective is a good quality to have. While having an internal locus of control helps you own your situation and take direct responsibility for it, it can also have some disadvantages. When perfectionism leads to anxiety that something might not be 100 percent, a sense of guilt might develop. This could hamstring the over-conscientious coach.

Forces within are not the cause of all bad things. Sometimes bad things happen to good people. We cannot expect that all of our efforts will get the results we expect. Sometimes we need to shake the dust off our feet and move on. Part of the responsibility of the coach is to allow the client to get to the point where he can make good decisions. The coach should consequently not internalize the client's decision to the point that the coach also owns the client's decision.

Reflection

In German, we say someone is "learnable" (*lernfähig*) when she can notice what she did wrong the first time and not repeat it a second time. Learning from your own experience is wisdom. Learning from someone else's experience is efficient. Either way, the goal is to reflect on what worked and what did not work in order to establish a plan for doing it right in the future. As noted by psychologists Mark Duffy and Jonathan Passmore, "Ethical decision making is a cognitive process. It is important that the coach find time to reflect on the situation" (Duffy and Passmore 2010, 147). Many good top executives take time to reflect in a similar manner after a meeting. In the same way, many good coaches take a few moments after every call to reflect on what went well and what they could have done better. This is one way capable people learn to maximize the moment.

When we feel good about an encounter with another person, it is worthwhile to think about the reasons for the happy interaction. Learning multiplies when we can successfully reflect on our limitations and discover our capacity to solve problems within our skill set. Good coaches do this often with their clients. They help the client see what is going well and what needs work. You can do the same assessment for yourself, a.k.a. self-coaching. Learning without reflection is like baking without yeast. Reflection is the yeast that raises the dough.

QUESTION

When was the last time you reflected about a coaching call?

The ethical coach is concerned with getting it right. The professional coach is concerned about not making the same mistakes. When we reflect, we look at what we have done from an observer's point of view. This takes practice. Some coaches will ask that the meetings be recorded so that the coach (and possibly also their mentor coach) can listen to the session later. Listening to a recording made yesterday can be a humbling experience. We can hear that we made choices that we would have rather not made. By the same token and on a larger scale, we might also reflect back on the entirety of a coaching relationship that lasted eighteen months.

Our brains are learning machines that are always looking for meaning and sense in our lives. "We sit at the feet of our experience and ask that experience to teach us" (Carroll and Shaw 2013, 254). We ask the Holy Spirit to take the events of our lives and shape us and define us into the person He would have us become. He can also help us become the coach He would have us become.

A note of caution: When one takes reflection to the extreme, it can become worry. Being afraid about what might or might not happen in the future rarely does any good. If reflecting to the point of worry keeps you awake at night or drives you out of bed in the morning, you might be overdoing it. You may be creating unnecessary anxiety for yourself. A professional should not be so worried about tomorrow he misses today's opportunities. Remember, being fully present is an expectation of the good coach.

Having a Personal Code of Conduct Might Not Be Enough

Formal training is a good way to get going on what you should learn. Being aware of ethics, however, is a question of paying attention to the hazards and pitfalls so that you don't get trapped. Actually practicing ethical behavior is a question of living righteously (Hebrews 13:18).

Indeed, one can have an ethical lifestyle without a formal code. While some people proudly display the Ten Commandments as a plaque on the wall, other people have an ingrained disdain for any list of 'ought-tos' and rules. It is not the code that has value; it is the practice of the code that is important. One should incorporate the values of practicing a code of conduct into daily habits.

Since the most recent global financial crisis, a large number of companies have worked very hard to establish ethical guidelines and standards for their employees. This was a necessary and urgent development in a world where corporate self-governance had been lacking. The results of these efforts have shown little actual change in the workplace (Pink 2012, 138). There is no evidence that putting a code of conduct out there for employees actually leads to increased ethically correct behavior. It is clear that *having* a theoretical guideline and *practicing* it are not the same. People are motivated to practice a principle when the benefits are immediate and apparent to them. When a code becomes a person's conduct, it's usually because there are tangible or perceived rewards. Few people follow rules because they like following rules. We usually follow rules because we don't like what will happen if we don't follow the rules.

QUESTION

True/false? "Sometimes you just gotta break the rules."

The obligations to act fairly, to act with integrity, and to respect autonomy are good premises by which to operate a coaching business. In the day-to-day grind of making a living, such principles may conflict with getting the best economic results. Written guidelines and operating standards are good things to refer to when information is sparse and a coach needs to make a decision quickly. In the long run, however, embedded personal goals form the basis for innately correct decision making.

A code of conduct should become a plan for moral living. If you, as an ethical Christian coach, were to focus on one conduct goal at a time, your lifestyle would show steady improvement.

What Are the Dangers?

Karen knows that many professionals in her city have been sued for malpractice and have lost their licenses to practice. She wonders if these individuals would have been better off operating independently, as she does. If there is no one to look over your shoulder, there is no one to call you out when things go wrong. Since things inevitably will go wrong, a businessperson should simply cut his losses and move on. "You can't win 'em all," she repeats to herself.

Regulation

To practice as a lawyer, psychiatrist, or physician, one must obtain an advanced degree and a license to practice. These professions, and many others, operate within regulated industries. Coaching is a very young industry and is still finding its place in the labor market. Around the world, coaches struggle to make the title of "coach" meaningful. In Europe, for example, professional coaches have difficulty with their tax filings because

the authorities don't have a category designated for coaching.

Some believe that it is only a matter of time before some type of licensure will be required of the coach. To date, no national or local government has officially regulated coaching. In Norway, an initiative to establish a national standard for coaching was cancelled in 2007, after a seventeen-month review process (Svaleng and Grant 2010, 5). In the United States, there has been some commotion regarding the need for licensure in the states of Washington, Colorado, and Tennessee. In each case, the major point of contention has been that a coach should not (i.e., cannot) practice therapy unless they are qualified to do so. Let the reader beware: Any unqualified coach who coaches a client with a pathological mental disorder does so at his or her own risk. Neither the ICF nor the CCNI look favorably on a coach who tries to play doctor with a client.

In my opinion, coaching will thrive and grow as a respected profession as long as those who bear the title of coach do so with integrity and honesty. I like the suggestion of the title *Life Coach* since all coaching seems eventually to lead to life coaching. Therefore, the Executive Coach could be called an "Executive Life Coach ," a wellness coach a "Wellness Life Coach," and so on.

Formal Review Proceedings

There are occasions when the client does not feel that the coach is behaving ethically and any attempt to talk to the coach about this directly seems to fall on deaf ears. In a Christian environment, the client has the ability to turn to the pastor of the coach or even the denominational leadership of the coach's church. Alternatively, the injured person might seek the aid of a lawyer, mediator, or ombudsman. If criminal activity is evident, the victim could seek assistance from the law enforcement community and/or a patent and copyright oversight body. More practically, the injured party might get the best results from contacting the Internal Review Board (IRB) of any professional organization to which the coach belongs. Most cases that go

before a coaching IRB are complaints from a coach about another member coach of that organization. That said, clients can voice concerns directly to the organization as well.

In the case where a credentialed coach faces an IRB for misconduct, the board could revoke both her credential and membership if it confirms misconduct. Usually, a plan is set in motion involving mentor coaching to bring the coach back on track professionally and ethically.

However, if there is criminal activity suspected, the complainant would first sue the coach in court before filing with the IRB. Even if the complainant wins the case against the coach, there remains the possibility that the coach might continue to operate unethically. There is still the option of filing a complaint with the IRB of a professional organization the coach belongs to, such as the ICF. "Go to court, then IRB. A client can file a complaint against you for at least a year," says IRB expert Tina Elliot (2014). If a court convicts a coach of criminal activity, it is possible that the organization's IRB will enact a sanction against the member coach as well.

What Are the Opportunities?

Karen operates by the principle that you can only trust yourself. No one else is as interested in her business as she is. No one else really cares what she does or why she does it. Since she is a sole proprietor, she alone is responsible. She believes that holding herself accountable to other people takes effort and ultimately just wastes time.

Accountability with a Mentor Coach

Most people benefit from talking through issues with someone who understands where they are coming from. This is one of the foundational aspects of coaching. It should not be surprising, then, that coaches need trusted mentors with whom they can discuss issues related to life *and* business. Talking to a friend is a normal way to get one's feelings out in the open, but not all friendly listeners will understand the dynamics of coaching.

A mentor coach is someone who has been there and done that. By definition, a mentor coach takes the role of the personal advisor and guide. For most credentialing processes, a certain amount of mentor coaching is required. When taken to its fullest extent, mentor coaching provides performance-based correction of the coach protégé and monitors her ethical behavior (Johnson and Ridley 2004, 28). A good mentor will provide clear communication about the protégé's ability to coach with proficiency. The mentor coach is in the best position to help the aspiring coach learn about their professional role, set boundaries, and get honest feedback—even if it might be unpleasant at times (Johnson and Ridley 2004, 97). While a coach might not want to spend money for expensive consultants, lawyers, and advisors, getting a mentor coach is an excellent investment. Having a mentor coach is among the easiest of ways to minimize and mitigate risks.

QUESTION

Who can you call when you are unsure about ethics?

Accountability with a Supervisor

In many healthcare professions, it is common during staff meetings to review and regularly discuss the caseload of the practitioner. Supervisors consider a patient *staffed* when both the peers and the supervisor of the practicing professional review his progress and prescriptions. In many countries, this practice manifests in the coaching profession. In England, for example, coaches and mental health professionals often have a supervisor. The professional coach will regularly meet with his supervisor to review clients and monitor coaching process. The supervisor can also function as a contact for emergency situations in case a dilemma has the coach stumped. In addition, having a peer practice group that includes formal supervision is a good way to brainstorm through scenarios and discuss possible outcomes. Note: Here we are talking about the coach's dilemmas and outcomes, not the client's.

Who Is Going to Know?

When Is It Time to Move Forward?

No one will know when you have made a decision unless you broadcast it. Reflecting, learning, and planning, are all passive (introspective) activities that are the recipe for future action. Sometimes stopping and regrouping is an important part of the growth phase. You might find it a bit embarrassing to realize that you have been practicing an unethical behavior for years. Generally, no one will criticize you for coming to such a conclusion. On the contrary, friends and associates are happy to see your desire and commitment to positive change.

A good steward knows when to call for help. This is what the client does in the coaching process. We help clients determine whether they need forward progress now or in the near future.

Indeed, it is sometimes prudent to wait and see what happens or to see how things develop.

What we do for our clients is something we can do for ourselves. We should be able to distinguish between procrastination and inaction. Indecision is when you are not yet convinced that forward motion is the best idea. Inaction happens when the person is not yet convinced that using one's energy for this is the best idea. The forward moving coach, however, knows when it is time to get in gear. The forward moving coach knows when she has reached the critical point where enough is enough. Now it's time to get going. A friend of mine likes to say, "Look up and look forward." Look to God for direction and keep moving in the way He shows you. Then, even if you fall, you will at least fall forward.

How Do I Do It Right?

Karen operates under the premise that if there is something significantly new in the industry, her customers will tell her about it. She is too pragmatic to believe she can know everything she needs to know. Things seem to naturally gravitate towards those who are ready to receive them. She will find out what is important if she asks the right questions. That should be enough, she hopes. She also believes that help only comes to those who help themselves. At the end of the day, she will have more than she had the day before due to hard work and clear thinking. That there are winners and losers in life is just one of those unfortunate realities people must face.

Plan to Stay Up-to-date

You might be old enough to remember when a telephone was first installed in your house. You might also remember your first computer, fax machine, and cell phone. Today, we carry devices in our pockets that were only imaginable in comic books a few years ago. Times change and so do the requirements for keeping up with the changes. Like most professions, coaching is part of a dynamic industry. There will always be new situations and challenges to deal with. The ethical issues coaches need to pay attention to are also constantly changing. Staying informed of these dynamics is essential.

The integration of ethical practices into your coaching business should be a regular exercise. Coaches should consistently evaluate their ethical code and review case scenarios. All professional organizations call for continuing education units (CEUs) that relate to the latest findings and interpretations of ethical practice. Furthermore, coaches who work for corporations should especially have a system in place that assures they are up-to-date regarding the ethics of that corporation's industry. The saying, "Change is the only constant," goes back to Ancient Greece. To say that the current pace of change makes keeping up-to-date difficult does not give us permission to circumvent our responsibility to learn and to grow.

Plan to Improve

A coach should plan for business, professional, and personal development. The art of running a business is a science of practice. Often, one will need additional resources and abilities in order to move forward. Learning is a lifetime endeavor. A professional coach will never finish the process of becoming a professional coach. Becoming a good coach is a work in progress. An oft-overlooked part of the process is taking care of oneself and planning for self-care. Our bodies are temples that require upkeep and maintenance (1 Corinthians 6:19).

Plan to keep your priorities. Stay connected to God. *The main thing is to keep the main thing the main thing.* You should never place your highest values—God, family, country—second to your business. In order to know your priority perspective, practice regular reflection. Plan time for that reflection. Plan time for planning.

Chapter Summary

In the coaching industry, skill is often emphasized over knowledge. A lot of time and effort goes into becoming a professional. A certificate from a reputable training school and a credential from an organization with integrity go a long way in providing evidence that the coach is as good as she claims to be. To behave ethically correctly, a coach should keep up with new developments in the industry.

An ethical coach has accountability partners such as a mentor coach or a peer group to help her see situations with a fresh set of eyes and diverse perspectives. The coach with integrity will often reflect on her coaching to see if there are some areas that need improvement.

Karen knows that she has disappointed a few people along the way.

However, she feels that it's okay because she has been disappointed, too. Coaching, to her, is a good profession because it carries few preconceptions. She can twist and mold it to be anything she wants it to be. If someone were to prove to her that she could not use the coach label on her banner, she would change the word back to consultant and keep on going. Who really cares what it's called? Karen will not pursue any training or credentials for coaching because it will probably all change in the near future. Ten years from now, there could be another label that is more beneficial for her, and she will adapt. After all, being flexible is what will keep her in business the longest.

What Do You Do?

Scenario A: You need forty continuing education units every three years to renew your coaching credential. You often talk to people about coaching, yet you have not attended formal seminars or workshops in a while. Now your renewal is due in three months. What can you do?

Scenario B: A highly visible coach in your community advertises that she fixes problems and guarantees results. You are aware of a long list of former clients of hers who would neither endorse her nor feel that her advertisement is justified. To your knowledge, this coach does not belong to any professional organizations. What, if anything, should you do about her?

Scenario C: Your organization sends out a newly revised code of conduct to which all employees must adhere. As a team leader, what can you do to ensure that employees put the code into practice?

Scenario D: You missed the deadline for an opportunity to bid on a large coaching contract with a major corporation. You realize that you were simply not paying attention to the market. How can you correct this in the future?

End of Chapter Questions

- How can you establish ethics accountability for yourself?

- What does your professional organization (e.g., ICF, CCNI) provide in terms of ethics guidance?

- What are ways you can get CEUs and learn more about ethics at the same time?

- How often do you sit back and reflect on your coaching skills?

- What is coaching for you? Is it a ministry, a profession, or a hobby?

- What do you need to add or eliminate to support your mission?

- Who needs to know what you know about ethics?

CHAPTER 10
VISION FOR THE FUTURE AND UPHOLDING THE INTEGRITY OF THE PROFESSION

*"As the circle of knowledge increases,
so does the circumference of darkness around it."*

—Albert Einstein, (1879–1955)

This chapter concludes our review of ethics and risk management for Christian coaches. We will revisit several important concepts that have the potential to significantly impact the coaching industry in the future. For the Christian coach, staying informed and building on the foundation laid throughout this book is paramount to acquiring and keeping satisfied clients. Relationships based on respect and care will allow the coach to help the client move forward boldly. In addition, we will examine how the coach processes the clients' statements. Finally, this chapter concludes with an exhortation to add grace to your coaching.

After reading this chapter, you will be able to do the following:

- assess your need for additional knowledge about ethics;
- explain coaching as an industry;
- distinguish between qualifications;
- evaluate coaching in terms of respect;
- understand how grace affects your coaching.

Your Story

This is *your* story. You have been reading and studying the implications of ethics and risk management for many days and potentially months. You know by now that there are many dangers and pitfalls. You are competent in ethical procedures but not experienced with ethical conflict. Don't worry—your day will come.

You wish everything was easy and that risk would pass you by, but you know that risks are inevitable. If you were able to predict the future, you would be able to plan better. On the other hand, knowing the events of the future might send you ducking for cover.

Common Challenges

Underqualified, underworked, and underpaid were never the aspirations you had when you considered entering coaching as a profession. You also know that failure is a possibility and that there is a lot you still don't know. You also realize that knowing everything is not really important, or even possible, but you wonder, how much should you know to be effective?

Knowledge

To say that the proportion of darkness increases around the circumference of a growing circle implies that there is always more darkness than light. This is not so. A small candle drives out a lot of darkness. Light is the more powerful force. Indeed, no matter how many books you read, there is always plenty more that you still don't know. Yet if you have read this book to this point, you probably have more knowledge of ethics and risk management than the average coach. Now that you know something about ethics and risk management for Christian coaches, you might be inspired to pray for guidance and discernment. Ignorance and complacency are not qualities of the professional coach. *Ignorance* exists when you do not know what you should know. *Complacency* happens when

gaining appropriate knowledge does not matter to you.

One of the truisms about ethics—and law for that matter—is that there are many gray areas. Not everything is black and white. This is why courts use juries of a group of peers to determine whether a defendant's actions are justified as measured by the reasonable and prudent person. This does not mean that you must always be right. Nor are you always wrong. The problem with being wrong is that it gives us the feeling that our status decreases if we admit fault. This is also known as pride. None of us likes the feeling of being wrong. It feels dangerous and unnerving.

You are not required to be the same person tomorrow that you are today. In fact, you should expect to improve with time. Ethical maturity means that you have to own up to your vulnerabilities with regard to ethical behavior and conscious awareness. There is probably room for improvement. There is a place where you can go to find consolation from confusion, a place where knowledge and practice join together. This is where a sense of justice that transcends culture and education unfolds. You awaken each day to new possibilities and wonders. This challenge awaits us all.

"Out beyond ideas of wrongdoing and rightdoing, there is a field. I'll meet you there."

—Jalal al-Din Muhammed Rumi,
Persian philosopher (1207–1273)

Getting Clients

A common challenge is finding clients who want coaching *and* have the means to pay for it. A 2014 ICF survey of more than 18,000 people worldwide showed that 58 percent of the respondents recognized that coaching could be helpful to them ("ICF Global Consumer Awareness Study" 2014). This percentage was significantly lower for those survey participants who were over fifty-five years old. Apparently, people between the ages of twenty-five and fifty-five more strongly feel the need fulfilled by coaching. In fact, the perceived need for coaching was proportionately higher among younger respondents. Here, however, the biggest obstacle is the cost of coaching. Spending $1,000 per month or even $1,000 per year is simply a lot of money for an individual. This is one reason corporate coaching presently shows a higher growth potential than private coaching. In the near future, millennials will occupy the seats of management. This generation of managers will want the coaching approach at every turn—not only in receiving coaching themselves but also in using the coaching approach with their subordinates.

The challenge to the professional who regards coaching as a ministry is to find ways to reach those consumers who do not have the means to pay for coaching directly. To attract coaching clients, many coaches supplement their services with products such as videos, webinars, and training materials. Additionally, coaches will often give speeches, workshops, seminars, and training courses related to their area of expertise. Aside from the tax ramifications, there are ethical considerations at play here. These offerings should be of high quality and substantiated with validated research. Just because some people will buy it does not mean that you should sell it. Greed for financial gain should not drive the agenda of the ethical Christian coach. There is a challenge on the supply side, as well as the demand side, of coaching to have high-quality coaching that lives up to industry standards.

At the Heart of the Matter

Your best friend is a soccer coach. Your Sunday school teacher is a wellness coach. Your dentist is a coach for oral hygiene mastery. You are a nondirective life coach. How can all of you use the same label and still respect one another?

"Coaching"

The term *coach* comes from the French word *coche*. It referred to a carriage of Hungarian design from the village of Kocs used during the reign of King Matthias Corvinus who lived from 1458 to 1490 (Merlevede, Bridoux, and Wilkinson-Carr 2003). Such a carriage was used to transport the king and his most trusted advisors.

The word *coach* has a long history. To this day, we still sometimes call a wagon or bus a coach. We call a trainer of athletes and a trainer of hunting dogs a coach. Numerous jobs and services exist under the name of coaching. There is no limit to the use of the word *coaching* by people who want to help others.

In this book, we have been exploring the field of formalized coaching. It is becoming a fully recognized profession and even a budding industry unto itself. A 2004 *Harvard Business Review report* showed coaching to be a $1 billion industry (Sherman and Freas 2004). A 2014 report from the AnythingResearch website ("market research report" n.d.) showed coaching to be a $4 billion industry. The growth rate in the last ten years has been phenomenal. Behind information technology (IT), coaching is the second-fastest-growing profession in the world (Williams 2007).

A 2014 study commissioned by the ICF revealed an increase in coaching awareness of 1 percent in developed countries and 9 percent in developing countries since 2010 ("ICF Global" 2014, 13). Consumers of coaching are increasingly demanding that those who claim the title of coach show credentials and certifications from accredited professional coaching organizations ("Coaching Services Assessment" 2014, 8). It is a fair assumption that coaching will face some form of state-sponsored regulation in the future. This is the nature of all industries that reach such a point, particularly in the United States (Williams 2006, 17). The rapid growth of coaching makes ethical supervision precarious at best. The ethical coach has good potential to survive the impending regulation storm if her integrity is intact and her qualifications are impeccable.

Factors That Muddle the Issue

You know that qualifications are important. You also know that you cannot really afford expensive training without some form of income to offset the costs. You also know that the credentialing process takes time. A couple thousand dollars and one to three years' time commitment seems like more than you can handle. Is it worth it to you?

Qualifications

Having a professional license is a relatively new concept in the grand scheme of things. The oldest government-endorsed licensure in the United States is the MD, the doctor of medicine. The first formalized medical licensing authority established itself in Texas in 1873. Most states followed suit by the turn of the century (Derbyshire 1969).

By the same token, coaching as a business practice began in the 1970s and has only been organized into professional associations since the 1990s. Relatively speaking, coaching as an industry is in its young adult phase. Like all valid industries, the profession of coaching has begun to create barriers to entry, such as credentialing. As time goes on, there are likely to be more requirements levied onto the professional who bears the title of coach.

Numerous schools offer coaching at a variety of levels. Some training programs only ask their participants to watch videos, fill in worksheets, and take tests to fulfill the requirements. Other programs require a full academic commitment with certifiable hours of practice with the addition of mentor coaching. There is room in the industry for coaches at various levels of skill and experience, and an aspiring coach can find a program that meets his or her expectations. Ironically, the light versions and the heavy versions are remarkably similar in price. The difference, of course, is the amount of study and work involved. The former executive director of CCNI, Marcie Thomas, notes the following:

The unsuspecting coach-training consumer is sometimes unaware of the credentialing distinctions in the industry and thereby makes unwise training choices. Later, much to their dismay, they discover that their coaching skills do not meet the expectations of the general public nor express the rigor expected in the industry. The consumer of coaching training needs a fair representation of the industry to make informed choices between the various coach-training providers so they don't waste time or money. (Thomas, personal communication, September 8, 2014)

All coach-training programs use vocabulary such as accredited, certified, professional, and credentialed. But the definitions of these words vary depending on the program. When we talk about the rigor of the credential, we are referring to how well the program stands up to external evaluation. To date, the ICF stands out as the foremost organization for the credentialing of coaches who ascribe to the non-directive coaching approach. CCNI does the same for the Christian coach who adheres to the non-directive coaching approach. Note: We are talking here about credentialing and not membership. The criterion for becoming a member (in either ICF or CCNI) does not distinguish between directive and non-directive coaching.

A primary ethical consideration regarding credentialing is that of fair disclosure. One must be ready to explain to the purchaser of your services the extent of the *rigor* of your qualifications. There is an obvious difference between a coach who has watched videos to get his credential and a coach who has practiced coaching under the watchful supervision of qualified trainers. To say that you ride horses well because you watched a series of instructional videos is ludicrous. It takes time in the saddle before you can make such a claim.

In the same way, studying coaching academically does not prove that one knows how to coach human beings. I can personally attest that writing a dissertation on coaching will not help you get an ICF or CCNI coaching credential. Like every other PCC-credentialed coach with ICF, I had to prove that I had taken at least 125 hours of coach-specific training, coached more than 500 hours, had at least ten hours of mentor coaching, and passed a written and oral test. This package of training, coaching, mentored coaching, and testing is what we refer to as "rigorous."

Among corporate and governmental consumers of coaching, there has been a notable preference for coaches with rigorously gained credentials. Decision-makers increasingly regard an ICF credential (or its equivalent) as an important criterion for selecting a coach ("Coaching Services Assessment" 2014, 37). A study done in 2014 by PricewaterhouseCoopers for ICF showed that 83 percent of 3,277 people who had already had some coaching said that it was important or very important that their coach hold appropriate credentials. Of those who were aware of coaching, but had not yet been in a coaching relationship, 81 percent said credentials were important ("ICF Global" 2014, 25). Furthermore, the same study showed that credentialed coaches were likely to be recommended by clients 34 percent of the time versus 19 percent for non-credentialed coaches ("ICF Global" 2014, 23). In sum, the study revealed that credentialed coaches have a higher satisfaction level among clients than those who lack a credential.

Exercise

- Does your target market expect you to be a credentialed coach?

- How rigorous has your coaching training been so far?

- How do the non-coaching services you offer hold up to high ethical standards?

- Do you treat your clients with the same dignity as you do your friends?

Which of My Values Is Relevant Here?

One thing you really like about coaching is the friendly atmosphere and congeniality you have with your clients. It hardly seems like working to you because it is so much fun. Your clients seem to genuinely respect you, and that feels pretty good, too.

Friendship-Type Relationships

The coach with a credential holds a key that could open the client's door. Gaining access to clients is often the hardest part of setting up a contract negotiation. However, the ability to *stay* in the client's office will depend on a lot more than a piece of paper. Coaches who are genuine, authentic, open, honest, and are congruent with what they believe and how they behave, will have the best chance of maintaining long-term relationships with their clients. The business relationship a good coach forms with a client is similar to the relationship one forms with a friend (Marx 2009). The ethical coach does not treat her clients by a different set of standards than her friends. Ethics expert Michael Josephson says, "There's no such thing as 'business ethics'—there's only ethics. Such fundamental standards of right and wrong as trustworthiness, respect, responsibility, fairness, caring, and good citizenship do not become irrelevant when we enter the workplace" (Josephson 2012). In other words, the ethical coach treats all people with the same amount of consideration and respect. This means that the coach has the ability to build a sustainable relationship with the client; the client then relies on the coach to do things that provide benefit to her. Consequently, the coach will refrain from doing things that cause harm to the client. The coach who endeavors to understand human nature and to continuously improve her professional conduct will eventually surpass the expectations of the most skeptical client.

Respect

One word drives ethical Christian coaching: *respect*. Viewing people as valuable, important, and worthy of fairness exemplifies respect. Every human is worthy of high esteem simply because he is created in the image of God (Genesis 1:27). Because of this truth, we can treat each person with kindness, gentleness, and love. John Maxwell says, "Try to *be kind* instead of treating people *in kind*. You'll find that it's very freeing" (Maxwell 2003, 114). The ethical Christian coach does not try to seek gain at the expense of someone else's accomplishments, status, or privilege. Creating dependency, shame, or fear are not activities of the Christian coach.

In 1 Corinthians 13:4-10 (The Message), the Apostle Paul defines *respect* with the word *love:*

If I give everything I own to the poor and even go to the stake to be burned as a martyr, but I don't love, I've gotten nowhere. So no matter what I say, what I believe, and what I do, I'm bankrupt without love.

Love never gives up.

Love cares more for others than for self.

Love doesn't want what it doesn't have. Love doesn't strut,

Doesn't have a swelled head,

Doesn't force itself on others,

Isn't always "me first,"

Doesn't fly off the handle,

Doesn't keep score of the sins of others,

Doesn't revel when others grovel,

Takes pleasure in the flowering of truth,

Puts up with anything,

Trusts God always,

Always looks for the best,

Never looks back,

But keeps going to the end.

Love never dies. Inspired speech will be over some day; praying in tongues will end; understanding will reach its limit. We know only a portion of the truth, and what we say about God is always incomplete. But when the Complete arrives, our incompletes will be canceled.

Amen.

What Are the Dangers?

Your coaching business sees its fair share of conflicts. Although you know that peace does not always come without conflict, you are resolved to live at peace with everyone (Romans 12:18).

Conflict Resolution

The future of coaching will, in part, depend on coaches being able to monetize skills such as conflict management across a wider playing field. In the same manner, coaches will increasingly be called upon to exercise conflict resolution in all of their business dealings. This is risk management in practice. In order for the coach to perform as an expert in conflict resolution, she should be able to accept views that are not her own, understand dilemmas she has no personal experience with, and overcome the fear of being wrong. Morally speaking, the coach must be able to live with the results, her own as well as those of the client. This requires both humility and confidence on the part of the coach. There is no outcome that can require her to behave unethically, no matter the discomfort she might experience. None of the obligations that she puts on herself or that the client puts on her can require her to make an unethical choice.

For example, an external coach working for a corporation has the well-being of the client as her highest priority while the internal coach working for the same company has prioritized obligations to the company. Despite the fact that corporate decision-makers perceive external and internal coaching as two services which complement each other ("Coaching Services Assessment" 2014, 6), these two coaches might experience some conflict when asked to work together. When both coaches can assess the situation for what it is, including the restrictions involved, empowered action should be the result. All coaches share a common interest in the advancement and empowerment of their clients. Even if the individual coach comes from a different approach to coaching, the obligations are the same. Strong ethical values should bind together rather than separate coaches with different objectives.

Part of the effectiveness of coaching centers on the coaching process being one of conflict resolution. At the basic level, the coach helps create a system that gets "good" results for the situation at hand, i.e., consequentialism.

> **Tip**
>
> Try using the coaching approach with your teenagers. It beats arguing with them.

The problem with "good" is that what is good for one person in one situation might not be good for another person in a similar situation. The ethical coach will develop a reputation for being both impartial and consequential in her coaching. In other words, the ethical coach is consistently fair in her own business's actions, and the client can depend on the coach to help her become consistently fair as well. The processes used in the coaching approach are, therefore, similar to those used in conflict management. The coach listens, points out common ground amongst seemingly divergent points, and fosters a process for developing a common goal. The coaching approach is a skill that can keep a person out of a lot of trouble. (It can reduce a lot of family conflict as well.)

What Are the Opportunities?

You have learned to trust the Holy Spirit in your coaching. You pray before each meeting that the Holy Spirit will use you as an instrument.

Processing Client Information

A coach might feel discomfort with what a client says during the coaching conversation due to a disconnect in the coach's cognitive reasoning. Something feels off. A subtle alarm rings in the back of the coach's mind. Misunderstanding, distraction, disagreement, and incongruity might all be reasons for this disconnect. The coach might say, "Something doesn't sound right with what you are saying." Rather than discounting the emotion she is feeling, the coach speaks it out. She is able to describe and articulate her intuitive response to what the client is saying. This, too, is value-added direct communication.

An ethical coach is able to process client information fully in four ways:

- Reflecting and examining the depth of the issue
- Rationalizing and sorting through the possible conclusions
- Being in touch with one's own feelings and emotions about what is happening
- Knowing the difference between intention and action (Carroll and Shaw 2013, 137–138)

All four ways are part of the value-added process and can occur in any order. On the spot and in the moment, there is little opportunity for the coach to process one before the other.

Joining Together with Other Coaches

You know that you can't go it alone. One way or the other, you have a need to stay connected with other professionals of like mind and spirit. At the very least, praying together gives you a sense of belonging and protection. You are also open to business opportunities that will enhance your position in the industry.

Indeed, there are many obstacles that coaching, as a relatively young profession, needs to overcome. The amount of empirical evidence on the validity of non-directive coaching is ever increasing, as is respect for coaching in the marketplace. Professional training, mentoring, and continuing education will become more prevalent among the rank and file coaches as the industry expands and grows. It is predictable, consequently, that professional coaches will increasingly group together into organizations that offer only qualified and experienced coaches to their clientele. Such contracting organizations (a.k.a. custom houses) will consider adherence to ethical standards as a paramount requirement for their coaches. Many of these contracting organizations will cater to the business coaching market because, frankly, that is where the big money is. Independent coaches and church-sponsored coaching programs will also be in high demand.

Generally, in the United States, the Christian coach stands under a respected banner when she labels herself a follower of Jesus. In European countries, on the other hand, potential clients are likely to perceive the Christian banner as lacking impartiality and objectivity. Around the world, believers struggle with maintaining their Christian witness without compromising their ethics and morals. This creates both opportunity and challenge for the Christian coach. We have the opportunity and the challenge to be a witness—either a good one or a bad one.

Who Is Going to Know?

You pray for your clients and other coaches. You are willing to help them in any way you can, even if it means doing work that brings little, if any, financial reward. That's okay—God knows about it and that's enough (Colossians 3:23–24).

The Extra Mile

The caring coach usually puts more time and effort into the coaching relationship than is required. Although the client may not notice the extra work, there is little danger of the client feeling poorly treated when the coach does more than is expected. The concept of going the extra mile is not only good business, it is also a proactive defense against complaints. Noted keynote speaker and author John Maxwell explains it this way:

A person with an extra-mile attitude is someone who:

Cares more than others think is wise,

Risks more than others think is safe,

Dreams more than others think is practical,

Expects more than others think is possible,

Works more than others think is necessary. (Maxwell 2003, 116–117)

How will you go the extra mile for your client? Will you pray for them, visit them in the hospital, or send birthday and Christmas cards? What will you do to ensure that the coach–client relationship results in genuine value-added service?

How Do I Do It Right?

Stay Informed

Lack of information is the downfall of good decision making. It is incumbent on the ethical coach to stay informed about industry standards. While an online resource list for coaching in general would be rather extensive, the list of resources for Christian coaching of the non-directive model is manageable. Here are a few places where you can find up-to-date information regarding this profession:

- christiancoachingresources.com
- christianlifecoaching.com
- christiancoachingmag.com
- christiancoaches.com
- christiannewswire.com

Be Bold

You sometimes have an unexpected thought while coaching and wonder if it is the Holy Spirit wanting to enter the conversation. At other times, you get nervous when the client does not seem to be on the track to forward progress. You feel he needs to be interrupted and reminded of the agenda for the conversation. When these thoughts and concerns come to mind, you remind yourself that you do not want to *lead* the client. How do you deal with such feelings?

A trusting client appreciates when his coach can bring clarity to his situation. A coach brings value to the conversation not by being timid, quiet, or passive but by being bold, truthful, and active. The excellent coach is not afraid of saying something that will shake up the client's way thinking. "Fear is the enemy of ethical excellence" (Carroll and Shaw 2013, 84). Being ethical in coaching does not mean that one indifferently adheres to the law with blind impartiality. Good coaching should be a friendly and interpersonal exchange of ideas among partners.

The coach adds value to the client's life by facilitating client discovery and implementation of his vision, goals, priorities, and life direction (Collins 2002, 39). The Christian coach adds supernatural value to the proposition by allowing the Holy Spirit to be a part of the decision-making process. Active listening includes summarizing, paraphrasing, and reiterating the client's expression of his perceptions. Active listening is more than hearing and never interrupting the client. It is a dynamic process of listening and inviting discovery. The coach must manage the process, which may require interrupting the client every now and then in order to get him back on task. Helping the client move forward with focused process management is one of the added values a good coach brings to the table.

QUESTION

Is your coaching disagreeable at times?

Search for Spirituality

Many adults accept the tenet of God as the Creator of the universe. Jesus, however, is the hard sell. Most people regard God as real, yet Jesus as Lord and Savior is a different consideration. I find that agreeing with the client on their concept of God is a good way to start the discussions related to spirituality. The definition of a coach according to the Christian Coaches Network International ("CCNI Definition of Christian Coaching" n.d.) does not include evangelizing or proselytizing. That said, there is a notable increase in the number of executives seeking coaches who can handle spiritual issues experienced by business leaders (Migge 2010, 47). To the extent that a client believes or does not believe in the power of God, faith plays a role in everyone's lives. Ultimately, faith trumps rationality in the minds of most clients (Migge 2010, 44).

The search for spirituality is on the increase. Due to the dicey history of Christianity, many would-be believers are, unfortunately, looking for spiritual answers outside the church. Regardless of the coach's stance on God or the Bible, there are often questions coaches will need to process in their coaching conversations. Here we are talking about values. The professional coach needs to be ready to help the clients bridge the gap between disconnected principles and values. The Christian coach need not, and most often should not, teach biblical principles during the coaching conversation. Let the client learn the biblical principles on his own. A suggestion I often give to clients is to put their question into an online search engine and add the word *Bible* at the end of the search string. In seconds, the client will have a million possible references in front of him.

Put God's Grace into Your Ethical Coaching

As Christians, we have the tendency to seek safety in our religious communities in the hope that the walls we build around us will protect us from the wiles of secular humanism lurking outside our doors. Our noble Christian ideals are not the result of thousands of years of tradition or a long history of success compared to other major religions. Our ideals come from the Bible, and the Bible comes from God. Our ideals matter because God said they matter. We need not join together to defend or fight for God's integrity. He can do that quite well all by Himself.

We mortals can go down two basic paths according to John Maxwell: "You can go for the gold, or you can go for the Golden Rule" (Maxwell 2003, 129). As Christian coaches, we are called to be examples of empathy and compassion. Our need to make a living at professional coaching should never supersede God's requirement for us to regard others as better than ourselves (Philippians 2:3).

The good news is that you can do this. Really. You can be the Christian coach that exhibits the values and principles God expects from you. God believes in you, Jesus believes in you, and the Holy Spirit believes in you. That's three. A Trinity of powerful forces, capable of enacting the type of change you want, works in and through you. You can be ethical, moral, and righteous. God and Jesus will empower you. If you are feeling weak, know that He is strong. God says to us, "My grace is enough; it's all you need. My strength comes into its own in your weakness" (2 Corinthians 12:9, The Message).

Chapter Summary

This chapter has examined the gaining of knowledge and qualifications needed to serve an increasingly demanding clientele in a growing industry. A good coach is able to fill a dynamic role in helping the client process conflict and ambiguous goals. Coaches form relationships with clients that carry the same level of respect as a friendship would. Good coaches go the extra mile. Coaches who add grace and love into their conversations can serve their clientele with boldness.

The ethical coach is able to sustain long, beneficial working relationships with clients when the benefit to the client far outweighs the cost of coaching. *You* are an ethical coach who can think through the issues and make ethically correct business decisions based on *your* values and principles. You have no problem with others holding you accountable for all of your decisions. You are able to adapt to changes and adopt new best practices. You are at peace with yourself.

I am at peace with myself.

4/27/17

What Do You Do?

Scenario A: You're vying for a large corporate coaching contract. Some of the competitors bidding for the same contract are not qualified coaches, in your opinion. What can you do/say to assure that the company understands the value of your qualifications?

Scenario B: You are asked to consider joining a coaching organization. What will you do to vet the agency in terms of integrity and quality?

Scenario C: You, as an external coach for the company, have often worked with clients who are also getting coaching from an internal coach with the same company. How will you go about assuring that potential conflicts are resolved?

Scenario D: You realize that you made a decision that was ethically (and potentially morally) wrong. You also lost the client in the process. What will you do to move forward?

End of Chapter Questions

- What are all the possible applications of the coaching approach in your life?

- How do you integrate the Bible into your coaching practice?

- Should a coach be disagreeable at times in her coaching?

- What is the best thing you can do at this point to ensure that you become a highly ethical coach?

- How can you go the extra mile?

REFERENCES

Allen, A. L. (2006). Moralizing in public. *Hofstra Law Review, 24,* 1325–1330.

Aoun, S., Osseiran-Moisson, R., Shahid, S., Howat, P., & O' Connor, M. (2011). Telephone lifestyle coaching: Is it feasible as a behavioural change intervention for men? *Journal of Health Psychology, 17*(2) 227–236. Retrieved from http://hpq.sagepub.com/content/17/2/227

Avery, K. (2013). Marketing: A path to trusting God. In G. Shaffer (Ed.), *Coaching the coach: Life coaching stories and tips for transforming lives* (pp. 61–63). Friendswood, TX: Bold Vision Books.

Bacon, R. (2003). Helping people change. *Industrial and Commercial Training, 35*(2), 73–77. doi: 10.1108/00197850310463797

Brennan, D. (2008). Leadership coaching: The impact on the organization. In D. B. Drake, D. Brennan, & K. Gørtz (Eds.), *The philosophy and practice of coaching: Insights and issues for a new era* (pp. 239–258). San Francisco, CA: Jossey-Bass.

Bond, T. (2007). Ethics and psychotherapy: An issue of trust. In R. Ashcroft, A. Dawson, H. Draper, and J. McMillan (Eds.), *Principles of Health Care Ethics*, (2nd ed.). London, UK: John Wiley & Sons.

Bond, T. (2013). The ethics of research: Enhancing knowledge and being ethically mature. In M. Carroll & E. Shaw (Eds.) *Ethical maturity in the helping professions*, (pp. 238–328). London, England: Jessica Kingsley Publishers.

Boss, J. A. (2008). *Ethics for life: A text with readings* (4th ed.). NY, NY: McGraw-Hill.

Brinkman & Kirschner. (2002). *Dealing with people you can't stand: How to bring out the best in people at their worst.* NY, NY: McGraw-Hill.

Carroll, M. & Shaw, E. (2013). *Ethical maturity in the helping professions.* London, England: Jessica Kingsley Publishers.

CCNI definition of Christian coaching (n.d.). In Christian Coaches network. Retrieved from http://www.christiancoaches.com/about/christian-coaching-definition.htm

Coaching Services Assessment: Research Report (2014, February) *Ipsos: Social Research Institute.* Retrieved from http://www.coachfederation.org/files/FileDownloads/188-CoachingServicesAssessment.pdf?_ga=1.980 19423.178469809.1410156086

Collins, D. (2009). *Essentials of business ethics: Creating an organization of high performance integrity and superior performance.* Hoboken, NJ: Wiles & Sons, Inc.

Collins, G. R. (2002). *Christian coaching: Helping others turn potential in reality* (2nd ed.). Colorado Springs, Colorado: Navpress.

Covey, S. (2006). Living the 7 habits: The courage to change. London: Simon & Schuster.

Denmark, A. (2013). Staying with the questions. In G. Shaffer (Ed.), *Coaching the coach: Life coaching stories and tips for transforming lives* (pp. 99–101). Friendswood, TX: Bold Vision Books.

Drucker, P. F. (2005, January). Managing oneself. *Harvard Business Review, 83*(1) 100–109.

Duffy, M. & Passmore, J. (2010). Ethics in coaching: An ethical decision making framework for coaching psychologists. *International Coaching Psychology Review 5*(2) 140–151.

Engelmann J. B., Capra, C. M., Noussair, C., & Berns, G. S. (2009). Expert financial advice neurobiologically "offloads" financial decision-making under risk. *PLoS ONE 4*(3): e4957. doi:10.1371/journal.pone.0004957

Fisher, J. (2013, March 13). *Ethics and liability risk management* [Audio podcast]. Retrieved from http://christianlifecoaching.com/jory-fisher-ethics-and-liability-risk-management/

Garrett, J. T. & Garrett, M. T. (2002). *The Cherokee full circle: A practical guide to ceremonies and traditions.* Rochester, Vermont: Bear & Company.

Gerber, M. (2004). *The e-myth revisited: Why most small businesses don't work and what to do about it.* NY, NY: HarperCollins.

Grayling, A. C. (2010). *Ideas that matter: The concepts that shape the 21st century.* NY, NY: Basic Books.

Haidt, J. (2001). The emotional dog and its rational tail: A social intuitionist approach to moral judgment. *Psychological Review, 108*(4), 814–834.

Hart, V., Blattner, J., & Leipsic, S. (2001). Coaching versus therapy: A perspective. *Consulting Psychology Journal: Practice and Research 53*(4) 229–237. doi: 10.1037//1061-4087.53.4.229

Heath, C. & Heath, D. (2011). *Switch: When change is hard.* NY, NY: rh Business Books.

Howard, R. A. & Korver, C. D. (2008). *Ethics for the real world: Creating a personal code to guide decisions in work and life.* Boston, MA: Harvard Business Press.

ICF code of ethics. (n.d.) *International Coach Federation.* Retrieved from http://www.coachfederation.org/ethics/

ICF code of ethics FAQs. (2009, October 21). *Coaching World: Special Issue.* Retrieved from: http://coachfederation.org/files/includes/docs/Ethics-Issue-Oct-09Revised.pdf

ICF eleven core competencies. (n.d.) *International Coach Federation.* Retrieved from: http://coachfederation.org/credential/landing.cfm?ItemNumber=2206

ICF global consumer awareness study. (2014). *International Coach Federation.* Retrieved from: http://coachfederation.org/consumerstudy2014

Josephson, M. (2012, February 8). There is no such thing as business ethics; There's just ethics. *Josephson Institute* (blog). Retrieved from http://josephsoninstitute.org/business/blog/2012/02/there-is-no-such-thing-as-business-ethics-theres-just-ethics-by-michael-josephson/

Johnson, W. B. & Ridley, C. R. (2004). *The elements of mentoring.* NY, NY: Palgrave Macmilan.

Kidder, R. M. (1995). *How good people make tough choices.* NY, NY: William Morrow.

Lavore-Fletcher, J. (2013, February 18). *Professional coaching and ethics.* Retrieved from http://www.christiancoachinstitute.com/professional-coaching-ethics/

Lennick, D. & Keil, F. (2011). *Moral intelligence 2.0: Enhancing business performance and leadership success in turbulent times.* Boston, MA: Prentice Hall.

Luoma, R. (2014, August 28). A tale of two certifications: Not all credentialing programs are created equally (blog). Retrieved from http://partnerspreceptors.com/2014/08/28/ a-tale-of-two-certifications-not-all-credentialing-programs-are-created-equally/

Maestripieri, D. (2012, March 8). Games primates play. *Psychology Today.* Retrieved from http://www.psychologytoday.com/ blog/games-primates-play/201203/the-truth-about-why-beautiful-people-are-more-successful

Mann, H. (1867). Duty a happiness. In M. Mann (Ed.) *Thoughts: Selected from the writings of Horace Mann.* Boston, MA: H.B. Fuller and Company.

Maxwell, J. (2003). *There is no such thing as "Business Ethics": There's only one rule for making decisions.* NY, NY: Warner Business Books.

McCluskey, C. (2013). Growing your business by doing less. In G. Shaffer (Ed.), *Coaching the coach: Life coaching stories and tips for transforming lives* (pp. 234–237). Friendswood, TX: Bold Vision Books.

Marx, M. J. (2009). *The processes which promote learning in adult mentoring and coaching dyadic settings.* (Doctoral dissertation, Regent University, 2009). ProQuest Digital Dissertations. (UMI No. 3367156)

Merritt, J. (2002, December 8). Talk show. *Bloomberg Business Week Magazine.*

Migge, B. (2010). Spiritualität im coaching: Psychologische zugänge zur religiosität und spiritualität im beratungsformat coaching [Spirituality in coaching: Psychological access to religiosity and spirituality in directive coaching]. *Organisationsberat Superv Coach 17,* 37–50. doi: 10.1007/s11613-010-0171-3

Moberg, D. J. (2006). Ethics blind spots in organizations: How systematic errors in person perception undermine moral agency. *Organization Studies, 27*(3), 413–428. doi: 10.1177/0170840606062429

Morris, K. (n.d.). A father's heart (blog). Retrieved from https://soundfaith.com/ sermons/93341-a-fathers-heart

Nash, M. M., Christian, D. & Anderson, J. B. (2011). Use of assessments in coaching. In L. Wildflower and D. Brennen (Eds.), *The handbook of knowledge-based coaching: From theory to practice* (pp. 315–338). San Francisco, CA: Jossey-Bass.

Oscarson, R. (2013). Confidence…after one more class? In G. Shaffer (Ed.), *Coaching the coach: Life coaching stories and tips for transforming lives* (pp. 43–47). Friendswood, TX: Bold Vision Books.

Paine, L. S. (2000, January). Does Ethics Pay? *Business Ethics Quarterly 10*(1) 319–330. Retrieved from http://www.jstor.org/ stable/3857716

Pakroo, P. H. (2012). *The small business start-up kit: A step-by-step legal guide* (7th ed.). Berkeley, CA: NOLO Law for all.

Parker, P., Kram, K. E., & Hall, D. T. (2012, December). Exploring risk factors in peer coaching: A multilevel approach. *Journal of Applied Behavioral Science 49*(3) 361–387. doi: 10.1177/0021886312468484

Passmore, J. (2009). Coaching ethics: Making ethical decisions - novices and experts. *Coaching Psychologist, 5*(1), 6–10.

Patterson, K., Grenny, J., McMillan, R., & Switzler, A. (2002). *Crucial conversations: Tools for talking when the stakes are high*. NY, NY: McGraw-Hill Books.

Phelps, E. A. (2006). Emotion and cognition: Insights from studies of the human amygdala. *Annual Review of Psychology 57*(1), 27 - 53. ISSN 0066-4308, 2006

Pink, D. H. (2012). *Drive: The surprising truth about what motivates us*. NY, NY: Riverhead Books.

Piper, W. (1930). *The little engine that could*. NY, NY: Platt & Munk, Publishers.

Reiss, B. (2000). *Low risk, high reward: Practical prescriptions for starting and growing your business*. NY, NY: The Free Press.

Rock, D. (2009). *Your brain at work: Strategies for overcoming distraction, regaining focus, and working smarter all day long*. NY, NY: HarperCollins books.

Rock, D. & Page, L. J. (2009). *Coaching with the brain in mind: Foundations for practice*. Hoboken, NJ: John Wiley & Sons, Inc.

Rotary International (n.d.). *The rotary club code of ethics*. Retrieved from http://altongodfreyrotary.org/page2.htm

Rowson, R. (2006). *Working ethics: How to be fair in a culturally complex world*. London, UK: Jessica Kingsley Publishers.

Scanlan, C. (2013). Bye for now. In G. Shaffer (Ed.), *Coaching the coach: Life coaching stories and tips for transforming lives* (pp. 195–198). Friendswood, TX: Bold Vision Books.

Schulte, T. (2010). *Coaching als weg: Was moechten sie ihren enkeln einmal erzaelen?* [The path of coaching: What do you want to tell you grandchildren one day?] Acht, Germany: Achter Verlag.

Selected Extracts. (1896, February 27). *Bathurst Free Press and Mining Journal* (NSW : 1851–1904), p. 1. Retrieved from http://nla.gov.au/nla.news-article63934644

Shabbir, S. (2010, July 24). Trust! *Business Recorder*. Emmayzed Publications (PIT) Ltd. GALE: A232535020

Sherman, S. & Freas, A. (2004). The wild west of executive coaching. *Harvard Business Review*. Retrieved from http://hbr.org/2004/11/the-wild-west-of-executive-coaching/

Skinner, D., Dietz, G., & Weibel, A. (2014). The dark side of trust: When trust becomes a 'poisoned chalice.' *Organization 21*(2), 206–224. doi: 10.1177/1350508412473866

Smith, N. (2012). *How excellent companies avoid dumb things. Breaking the 8 hidden barriers that plague even the best businesses*. NY, NY: Palgrave Macmillan.

Sorrentino, M. (2013). Walking the fine line. In G. Shaffer (Ed.), *Coaching the coach: Life coaching stories and tips for transforming lives* (pp. 211–13). Friendswood, TX: Bold Vision Books.

Svaleng, I. J. & Grant, A. M. (2010). Lessons from the Norwegian coaching industry's attempt to develop joint coaching standards: An ACCESS pathway to a mature coaching industry. *Coaching Psychologist, 6*(1), 5–15.

Townsend, C. (2011). Ethical frameworks in coaching. In J. Passmore (Ed.), *Supervision in coaching: Supervision, ethics and continuous professional development* (pp. 141–159). Philadelphia, PA: Kogan Page.

Weiner, K. C. (2007). *The little book of ethics for coaches: Ethics, risk management and professional issues*, (2nd ed.). Bloomington, IN: AuthorHouse.

Williams, P. (2006). The profession of coaching: Its emergence and intersection with ethics and law. In P. Williams & S. K. Anderson (Eds.), *Law and ethics in coaching: How to solve and avoid difficult problems in your practice* (pp. 1–20). Hoboken, NJ: John Wiley and Sons.

Williams, P. & Menendez, D. S. (2007). *Becoming a professional life coach: Lessons from the institute for life coach training.* NY,NY: Norton & Company, Inc.

Willis, K. C. (2013). Every coach needs a team. In G. Shaffer (Ed.), *Coaching the coach: Life coaching stories and tips for transforming lives* (pp. 247–250). Friendswood, TX: Bold Vision Books.

Zak, P. J. (2008). The neurobiology of trust. *Scientific American, 298*(6), 88–95.

Zur, O. (2007). *Boundaries in psychotherapy: Ethical and clinical explorations.* Washington, DC: American Psychological Association.

ABOUT THE AUTHOR

Dr. Michael J. Marx, PCC, CPCC, was born and raised in the United States but has spent most his adult life in Germany. After starting as an architectural student in Berlin in the early 1980s, Marx found his calling as a teacher of business and communications. His assignments took him behind the doors of some of Germany's leading companies and gave him a foundation in the international business world.

In the late 1980s, Marx and his wife returned to the United States so he could pursue an MBA. Later, they returned to Europe, where he coached and consulted as a freelancer for many large firms in Hannover, Germany. His clients were those involved in risk management and risk mitigation. Additionally, the couple learned the rigors of running a small business as the owners of a travel agency.

Ever curious as to how the human mind thinks and learns, Marx immersed himself in the study of adult education at the postgraduate level. He completed his doctorate in education (EdD) in 2009, and shortly thereafter became a credentialed coach. He joined the International Coach Federation (ICF) and became a member of the ICF Global Ethics and Standards Committee as well as the subcommittee for ethics education.

Today, Marx is a faculty member of the Professional Christian Coaching Institute. In addition to his work at the institute, he is involved with coaching ethics on a global scale, leading the International Coach Federation (ICF) Ethics Community of Practice and serving on its Independent Review Board (IRB). He is the president of Christian Coaches Network International (CCNI), where he leads the organization ethics initiatives.

CPSIA information can be obtained
at www.ICGtesting.com
Printed in the USA
LVOW09*1041210217
524932LV00013B/132/P